The Great Depression and the New Deal:
Core Documents

The Great Depression and the New Deal: Core Documents

Selected and Introduced by

John E. Moser

Ashbrook Press

© 2017 Ashbrook Center, Ashland University

Library of Congress Cataloging-in-Publication Data

The Great Depression and the New Deal: Core Documents;
Selected and Introduced by John E. Moser

p. cm.
Includes Index
1. United States – Politics and government.

ISBN 978-1-878802-34-7
(pbk.)

Cover photos:
Herbert Hoover, photograph by Underwood and Underwood, 1928. Courtesy of Library of Congress. http://www.loc.gov/pictures/item/96522651/

Associate Justice Owen J. Roberts, Harris and Ewing Collection, 1936. Courtesy Library of Congress. https://commons.wikimedia.org/wiki/File:Owen_J._Roberts_cph.3b11988.jpg

FDR, photographed by Elias Goldensky, 1933. Courtesy Library of Congress.
https://commons.wikimedia.org/wiki/Franklin_Delano_Roosevelt#/media/File:FDR_in_1933.jpg

Senator Huey P. Long, 1933 – 1935, Courtesy Library of Congress.
https://commons.wikimedia.org/wiki/File:HueyPLongGesture.jpg

Senator Robert Wagner, Harris and Ewing Collection, between 1905 and 1945. Courtesy Library of Congress. http://www.loc.gov/pictures/item/hec2009008291/

Bonus Army sits in demonstration on Capitol steps, Harris and Ewing Collection, 1932. Courtesy Library of Congress. http://www.loc.gov/pictures/resource/hec.36872/

Ashbrook Center at Ashland University
401 College Avenue
Ashland, Ohio 44805
www.ashbrook.org

About the Ashbrook Center

The Ashbrook Center restores and strengthens the capacities of the American people for constitutional self-government. Ashbrook teaches students and teachers across our country what America is and what she represents in the long history of the world. Offering a variety of resources and programs, Ashbrook is the largest university-based educator in the enduring principles and practice of free government. Dedicated in 1983 by President Ronald Reagan, the Ashbrook Center is governed by its own board and responsible for raising all of the funds necessary for its many programs.

Visit us online at Ashbrook.org, TeachingAmericanHistory.org, and 50coredocs.org.

Contents

General Editor's Introduction i

Introduction iii

1. Herbert Hoover, Speech on the "Principles and Ideals of the United States Government" (October 22, 1928) 1

2. President Herbert Hoover, Statement announcing a Series of Conferences with Representatives of Business, Industry, Agriculture, and Labor (November 15, 1929) 9

3. President Herbert Hoover, Statement on the Signing of the Smoot-Hawley Tariff (June 16, 1930) 11

4. Representative Jacob Milligan, Speech on the Smoot-Hawley Tariff (July 3, 1930) 15

5. President Herbert Hoover, Press Statement on the Use of Federal Funds for Relief (February 3, 1931) 17

6. President Herbert Hoover, Veto of the Muscle Shoals Resolution (March 3, 1931) 21

7. President Herbert Hoover, Special Message to Congress on Economic Recovery Program (January 4, 1932) 24

8. The Norris-La Guardia Act (March 23, 1932) 28

9. Franklin D. Roosevelt, Radio Address on "The Forgotten Man" (April 7, 1932) 32

10. Franklin D. Roosevelt, Acceptance Speech at the Democratic National Convention (July 2, 1932) 36

11. President Herbert Hoover, Veto of the Emergency Relief and Construction Bill (July 11, 1932) 43

12. President Herbert Hoover, Statement on the Dispersal of the Bonus Army (July 29, 1932) 48

13. Philo D. Burke, Letter from Bonus Army leader to President Hoover (July 29, 1932) 51

14. Franklin D. Roosevelt, Commonwealth Club Address (September 23, 1932) 54

15. President Herbert Hoover, Consequences of the Proposed New Deal (October 31, 1932) 66

16. President Herbert Hoover, Letter to Senator Simeon Fess (February 21, 1933) 77

17. President Franklin D. Roosevelt, First Inaugural Address (March 4, 1933) 82

18. President Franklin D. Roosevelt, Call for Legislation to Create the Tennessee Valley Authority (April 10, 1933) 87

19. President Franklin D. Roosevelt, "Fireside Chat" on the Purposes and Foundations of the Recovery Program (July 24, 1933) 89

20. "Black Labor and the Codes," Editorial, *Opportunity* (August 1933) 97

21. Mauritz Hallgren, "The Right to Strike" (November 8, 1933) 99

22. President Franklin D. Roosevelt, Speech to Congress on Foreign Trade (March 2, 1934) 106

23. President Franklin D. Roosevelt, Speech to Congress on Social Security (January 17, 1935) 110

24. Senator Robert F. Wagner, Speech on the National Labor Relations Act (February 21, 1935) 114

25. E.E. Lewis, "Black Cotton Farmers and the AAA" (March 1935) 119

26. Representative James W. Wadsworth, Speech on Social Security (April 19, 1935) 125

27. Senator Huey P. Long, Statement on the Share Our Wealth Society (May 23, 1935) 128

28. Chief Justice Charles Evans Hughes, *Schechter Poultry Corp. v. United States* (May 27, 1935) 134

29. Paul Taylor, "Again the Covered Wagon" (July 1935) 139

30. President Franklin D. Roosevelt, Annual Message to Congress (January 3, 1936) 147

31. Associate Justice Owen J. Roberts, *United States v. Butler* (January 6, 1936) 153

32. Al Smith, "Betrayal of the Democratic Party" (January 25, 1936) 163

33. President Franklin D. Roosevelt, Acceptance Speech at the Democratic National Convention (June 27, 1936) 174

34. Father Charles Coughlin, "A Third Party" (July 1, 1936)...179

35. Herbert Hoover, "This Challenge to Liberty" (October 30, 1936) 184

36. Edward Levinson, "Detroit Digs In" (January 16, 1937) 193

37. President Franklin D. Roosevelt, Second Inaugural Address (January 20, 1937) 199

38. President Franklin D. Roosevelt, "Fireside Chat" on the Plan for Reorganization of the Judiciary (March 9, 1937) 205

39. Senator Carter Glass, Radio Address on Judicial Reorganization (March 29, 1937) 211

40. President Franklin D. Roosevelt, Message to Congress on Establishing Minimum Wages and Maximum Hours (May 24, 1937) 216

41. President Franklin D. Roosevelt, "Fireside Chat" on the Recession (April 14, 1938) 220

42. Representative Wade Kitchens, Speech on the Fair Labor Standards Act (May 16, 1938) 228

43. President Franklin D. Roosevelt, "Fireside Chat" on "Purging" the Democratic Party (June 24, 1938) 231

Appendices 241

Appendix A: Thematic Table of Contents 243

Appendix B: Study Questions 246

Appendix C: Suggestions For Further Reading 259

General Editor's Introduction

This collection of documents on the Depression and New Deal is the second volume in an extended series of document collections from the Ashbrook Center that will cover major periods, themes, and institutions in American history and government. The series began with a collection on the Founding. This volume follows appropriately, because it makes clear the reasons why and the degree to which Franklin Roosevelt intended the New Deal to be a re-founding of the American republic. In presenting the words that Roosevelt spoke, the collection shows us not only his arguments but his masterful rhetoric, which presented the New Deal as only an updating of the Founding. The collection presents as well the arguments of those who opposed the New Deal – Democrats as well as Republicans – and those who thought it did not go far enough. Taken together, the documents in the collection are an enlightening guide to one of the most consequential periods in American history.

When the series of Ashbrook document collections is complete, it will be comprehensive, and also authoritative, because it will present America's story in the words of those who wrote it—America's presidents, labor leaders, farmers, philosophers, industrialists, politicians, workers, explorers, religious leaders, judges, soldiers; its slaveholders and abolitionists; its expansionists and isolationists; its reformers and stand-patters; its strict and broad constructionists; its hard-eyed realists and visionary utopians—all united in their commitment to equality and liberty, yet all also divided often by their different understandings of these most fundamental American ideas. The documents are about all this—the still unfinished American experiment with self-government.

As this volume does, each of the volumes in the series will contain key documents on its period, theme, or institution, selected by an expert and reviewed by an editorial board. Each volume will have an introduction highlighting key documents and themes. In an appendix to each volume, there will also be a thematic table of contents, showing the connections between various documents. Another appendix will provide study questions for each document, as well questions that refer to other documents in the collection, tying them together as the thematic table of contents does. Each document will be checked against an authoritative original source and have an introduction outlining its significance. We will provide notes to each document to identify people, events, movements, or ideas that may be unfamiliar to non-specialist readers and to improve understanding of the document's historical context.

In sum, our intent is that the documents and their supporting material provide reliable and unique access to tjust he richness of the American story.

John E. Moser, Professor of History, Ashland University, selected the documents and wrote the introductions. Ellen Tucker and Josh Distel edited the collection. Lisa Ormiston of the Ashbrook Center oversaw production.

David Tucker
Senior Fellow
Ashbrook Center

Introduction

The late 1920s were a time of great optimism in the United States, and few in public life expressed this optimism more clearly than Herbert Hoover. Even before becoming president in 1928, Hoover was one of the most respected men in the country, if not the world. Born in a rural village in Iowa and orphaned at the age of nine, he earned an engineering degree from Stanford University. After graduation he began a career in mining, becoming a millionaire by launching successful operations in Australia, Asia, Africa, and Latin America. During and after World War I he organized a massive relief effort to feed starving people in war-torn Europe, and became an international celebrity in the process. Later, as secretary of commerce under Presidents Harding and Coolidge, he inaugurated the policy – which continues to this day – of collecting statistical data on unemployment. He sincerely believed that American individualism, supported by a dynamic federal government, could end the nation's problems. As he put it in a campaign speech in 1928, the country had "come nearer to the abolition of poverty, to the abolition of fear of want, than humanity has ever reached before" (Document 1).

On October 24, 1929 – only seven months after the start of Herbert Hoover's presidency – the economic boom that had characterized so much of the 1920s came to an abrupt end. The stock market crashed, and the thousands of investors who had purchased stock on credit were asked to make good on their promise to pay. When they could not, they were forced to sell their stocks, so that securities prices continued to plummet over the next two weeks. For ten years thereafter, the country would continue to struggle through the worst economic crisis of its history – the Great Depression. Banks, threatened with insolvency, called in their loans; and businesses, cut off from their sources of capital, scaled back their operations. Over the next few years millions would be laid off from their jobs. This in turn made the situation worse, since unemployed people could not buy the sort of consumer goods – radios, washing machines, vacuum cleaners, and most importantly automobiles – that had sustained the economic growth of the 1920s. Throughout Hoover's presidency, therefore, the economy continued to deteriorate.

Hoover believed that the severity of the crisis demanded a strong response by the federal government. He held a series of conferences with business and labor leaders in which he exacted promises not to reduce wages, even as profits fell (Document 2). He authorized new federal public works projects, and urged states and localities to do likewise. He signed a new tariff bill designed to protect American agriculture and manufacturing from cheap foreign imports (Documents 3 and 4). Hoover also argued that capital had to be pumped into the economy so that business confidence would be restored and the unemployed put back to work. It was in this spirit that he established, with congressional approval, the Reconstruction Finance Corporation (RFC) (Document 7). The RFC made loans to banks and other major financial institutions in the hope that they would, in turn, extend credit to corporations, allowing them to hire more employees, place new orders with other firms, and invest in new enterprises.

There were, however, certain steps that Hoover refused to take. He opposed the idea of making direct relief payments to individuals and families, fearing that this would foster an un-American dependence on the federal government (Document 5). He therefore vetoed legislation such as the Veterans' Bonus Bill in 1931 and the Emergency Relief Bill in 1932 (Documents 12, 13 and 11). Moreover, he did not believe that the government should compete with private business, leading him to veto a congressional resolution to bring electricity to parts of the rural South (the Muscle Shoals joint resolution of 1931; see Document 6). Finally, by 1932 Hoover was concerned that large budget deficits would impede recovery, so he tried to reduce overall federal spending.

In spite of Hoover's best efforts, the economy continued to slump. By late 1932 American banks were collapsing at an alarming rate, and some writers were beginning to call for the adoption of fascist or communist forms of government, such as those already in existence in Italy and the Soviet Union. Nevertheless, Hoover stood again as the Republican presidential nominee (Document 15). Very few people expected him to win; in fact, many people had come to believe that Hoover was simply not interested in the plight of ordinary people affected by the Depression. On Election Day, therefore, the voters turned overwhelmingly to the candidate of the Democratic Party, Franklin Delano Roosevelt.

Unlike Hoover, Roosevelt had been in politics all his life. He had served in the New York state legislature, served as assistant secretary of the navy under Woodrow Wilson, and had run unsuccessfully for vice president on the Democratic ticket in 1920. In the early 1920s he was struck with polio, which left him paralyzed from the waist down, but a few years later he returned to public life and, in 1928, was elected governor of New York. During the 1932 presidential campaign he promised "a new deal for the American people," but remained vague as to what this might mean (Documents 10, 14). Ultimately his victory resulted from Hoover's extreme unpopularity and Roosevelt's own cheery, optimistic style. As one Supreme Court justice put it, he may have been a "second-class intellect," but he possessed a "first-class temperament."[1]

In his inaugural address (Document 17), Roosevelt promised quick and dramatic action, and he was as good as his word. His election had coincided with the Democratic Party picking up 101 seats in the House of Representatives, strengthening their majority, and 12 in the Senate, giving them majority control in that house as well. Within the first hundred days of Roosevelt's administration Congress passed an amazing number of bills that the president recommended or favored. In an attempt to increase the supply of money, he removed the dollar from the gold standard. An Agricultural Adjustment Act promised aid to farmers, but only on the condition that they reduce the amount of agricultural goods that they produced so that prices would rise. A public works bill authorized spending millions of dollars to put the unemployed to work. Another bill created the Tennessee Valley Authority, which brought the federal government into the provision of electricity to rural areas (Document 18); still another set up the National Recovery Administration, which oversaw the drafting of codes of conduct for various industries (Document 19). A few of the measures enacted during this period were extensions of Hoover's own program; most, however, went far beyond, involving the federal government in areas that Hoover had insisted should remain within the scope of the private sector.

But although Roosevelt's New Deal was wildly popular, it immediately drew fire from both the Right and the Left. Conservatives in both the Republican and Democratic parties claimed that the president was violating the Constitution (see Documents 32 and 35). In several instances the Supreme Court agreed, striking down the National Industrial Recovery Act in 1935 (Document 28), and the Agricultural Adjustment Act in the following year (Document 31). Radicals, meanwhile, complained that Roosevelt was not doing enough to destroy the power of large banks and major corporations. Many on the Left demanded the nationalization of certain industries, the redistribution of wealth, and the creation of a full-scale social welfare system similar to those which had already been established in some European countries (see Documents 27 and 34).

---

[1] David M. Kennedy, *Freedom from Fear: The American People in Depression and War* (New York: Oxford University Press, 1999), p. 100.

When the early legislation of the New Deal failed to bring about economic recovery, Roosevelt himself veered sharply to the left. In 1935, he unveiled a series of new, more radical measures. These included nearly $1 billion in new spending on public works projects, new taxes that would fall on the wealthiest Americans, and a system of old-age insurance called Social Security. The National Labor Relations Act gave a tremendous boost to labor unions, by guaranteeing the right of workers to organize and requiring employers to bargain with union representatives. The Fair Labor Standards Act (Document 39) abolished child labor and established a federal minimum wage. Many on the Left applauded these moves, while conservatives complained that Roosevelt was turning America into a socialist country (see Document 41).

Although the promised recovery was slow to come, most Americans believed that the New Deal had improved their lives, so they gave it their enthusiastic support. Roosevelt managed to create a new coalition of reliably Democratic voters. Union workers in the Northeast joined with farmers from the South and Midwest, while African-Americans abandoned their traditional support for the Republican Party. When the president stood for reelection in 1936 against Alf Landon, the Republican governor of Kansas, the voters returned him to office in a landslide.

Roosevelt's second term, however, would bring disappointment. His attempt to add more justices to the Supreme Court (Document 38) was interpreted as an attack on the Constitution, leading Congress to hand the president his first serious political defeat. Moreover, the economy took a sudden downturn in 1937, underscoring Roosevelt's failure to bring the country out of the Depression. The president's efforts to drive more conservative members of his own party from Congress by campaigning for their opponents in the 1938 primaries (Document 42) met with disaster. Not only did nearly all of the conservatives survive the challenge, but they returned to Washington vowing revenge against the president who had tried to unseat them. The general elections compounded the president's problems, as Republicans made major gains in Congress for the first time in ten years. Thereafter, Republicans were able to join with conservative Democrats to block further presidential initiatives.

By 1939, then, the New Deal had effectively ended, although the Great Depression went on. Gross domestic product did not exceed its 1929 level until 1941; unemployment remained above pre-Depression levels until 1943; and the stock exchange did not return to its pre-crash height until the late 1950s. The crisis – and the way the Hoover and Roosevelt administrations responded to it – would forever change the relationship between Americans and the federal government. Many of the agencies established during the 1930s, such as the National Labor Relations Board, the Securities Exchange Commission, the Federal Housing Administration, the Federal Deposit Insurance Corporation, the Tennessee Valley Authority, and, of course, Social Security, continue to affect the lives of millions of people. More broadly, the Depression and the New Deal altered Americans' expectations of the federal government. Before the 1930s few believed that Washington, DC was responsible for the nation's economic health, or for the wellbeing of its citizens. Since that time almost no one denies it.

The Great Depression and the New Deal: Core Documents

Document 1

Speech on the "Principles and Ideals of the United States Government"
Herbert Hoover
October 22, 1928

As the 1928 presidential race was nearing its conclusion, the Republican candidate, former Secretary of Commerce Herbert Hoover, outlined his governing philosophy and contrasted it with that which he attributed to his Democratic opponent, New York Governor Al Smith. At this point there was little doubt that Hoover was going to win. After eight years of Republican governance the country was at peace and enjoying unprecedented prosperity, and any rural Democrats were lukewarm on Smith due to his New York City roots and outspoken opposition to Prohibition. In fact, the 1928 election proved to be one of the most lopsided in U.S. history, with Hoover winning 40 of the 48 states and more than 58 percent of the popular vote.

The speech later became famous not only for Hoover's use of the term "rugged individualism," but also for his bold claim that the country had "come nearer to the abolition of poverty, to the abolition of fear of want, than humanity has ever reached before." These were words that would soon be used against him when the country fell into depression.

Source: Herbert Hoover: 1929: Containing the Public Messages, Speeches, and Statements of the President, March 4 to December 31, 1929. In Public Papers of the Presidents of the United States (Washington, DC: United States Government Printing Office, 1974), p. 586. Also available online from: American President: Presidential Speech Archive, Miller Center, University of Virginia, http://millercenter.org/president/speeches/speech-6000.

. . . .After the war,[1] when the Republican Party assumed administration of the country, we were faced with the problem of determination of the very nature of our national life. During 150 years we have builded up a form of self-government and a social system which is peculiarly our own. It differs

---

[1] World War I

essentially from all others in the world. It is the American system. It is just as definite and positive a political and social system as has ever been developed on earth. It is founded upon a particular conception of self-government; in which decentralized local responsibility is the very base. Further than this, it is founded upon the conception that only through ordered liberty, freedom and equal opportunity to the individual will his initiative and enterprise spur on the march of progress. And in our insistence upon equality of opportunity has our system advanced beyond all the world.

During the war we necessarily turned to the Government to solve every difficult economic problem. The Government having absorbed every energy of our people for war, there was no other solution. For the preservation of the State, the Federal Government became a centralized despotism which undertook unprecedented responsibilities, assumed autocratic powers, and took over the business of citizens. To a large degree we regimented our whole people temporarily into a socialistic state. However justified in time of war, if continued in peace time it would destroy not only our American system but with it our progress and freedom as well.

When the war closed, the most vital of all issues both in our own country and throughout the world was whether Governments should continue their wartime ownership and operation of many instrumentalities of production and distribution. We were challenged with a peace-time choice between the American system of rugged individualism and a European philosophy of diametrically opposed doctrines – doctrines of paternalism and state socialism. The acceptance of these ideas would have meant the destruction of self-government through centralization of government. It would have meant the undermining of the individual initiative and enterprise through which our people have grown to unparalleled greatness.

The Republican Party from the beginning resolutely turned its face away from these ideas and these war practices. A Republican Congress cooperated with the Democratic administration to demobilize many of our war activities. At that time the two parties were [in] accord upon that point. When the Republican Party came into full power, it went at once resolutely back to our fundamental conception of the state and the rights and responsibilities of the individual. Thereby it restored confidence and hope in the American people, it freed and stimulated enterprise, it restored the Government to its position as an umpire instead of a player in the economic game. For these reasons the American people have gone forward in progress while the rest of the world has halted, and some countries have even gone backwards. If anyone will study the causes of retarded recuperation in Europe, he will find much of it due to the stifling of private initiative on one hand, and overloading of the Government with business on the other.

There has been revived in this campaign, however, a series of proposals which, if adopted, would be a long step toward the abandonment of our American system and a surrender to the destructive operation of governmental conduct of commercial business. Because the country is faced with difficulty and doubt over certain national problems – that is, prohibition, farm relief and electrical power – our opponents propose that we must thrust government a long way into the businesses which give rise to these problems. In effect, they abandon the tenets of their own party and turn to state socialism as a solution for the difficulties presented by all three. It is proposed that we shall change from prohibition to the state purchase and sale of liquor. If their agricultural relief program means anything, it means that the Government shall directly or indirectly buy and sell and fix prices of agricultural products. And we are to go into the hydroelectric-power business. In other words, we are confronted with a huge program of government in business.

There is, therefore, submitted to the American people a question of fundamental principle. That is: shall we depart from the principles of our American political and economic system, upon which we have advanced beyond all the rest of the world, in order to adopt methods based on principles destructive of its very foundations? And I wish to emphasize the seriousness of these proposals. I wish to make my position clear; for this goes to the very roots of American life and progress.

I should like to state to you the effect that this projection of government in business would have upon our system of self-government and our economic system. That effect would reach to the daily life of every man and woman. It would impair the very basis of liberty and freedom not only for those left outside the fold of expanded bureaucracy but for those embraced within it.

Let us first see the effect upon self-government. When the Federal Government undertakes to go into commercial business, it must at once set up the organization and administration of that business, and it immediately finds itself in a labyrinth, every alley of which leads to the destruction of self-government.

Commercial business requires a concentration of responsibility. Self-government requires decentralization and many checks and balances to safeguard liberty. Our Government to succeed in business would need become in effect a despotism. There at once begins the destruction of self-government.

The first problem of the government about to adventure in commercial business is to determine a method of administration. It must secure leadership and direction. Shall this leadership be chosen by political agencies or shall we make it elective? The hard practical fact is that leadership in business must come through the sheer rise in ability and character. That rise can only take place in the free atmosphere of competition. Competition is closed by bureaucracy. Political agencies are feeble channels through which to select able leaders to conduct commercial business.

Government, in order to avoid the possible incompetence, corruption and tyranny of too great authority in individuals entrusted with commercial business, inevitably turns to boards and commissions. To make sure that there are checks and balances, each member of such boards and commissions must have equal authority. Each has his separate responsibility to the public, and at once we have the conflict of ideas and the lack of decision which would ruin any commercial business. It has contributed greatly to the demoralization of our shipping business. Moreover, these commissions must be representative of different sections and different political parties, so that at once we have an entire blight upon coordinated action within their ranks which destroys any possibility of effective administration.

Moreover, our legislative bodies cannot in fact delegate their full authority to commissions or to individuals for the conduct of matters vital to the American people; for if we would preserve government by the people we must preserve the authority of our legislators in the activities of our government.

Thus every time the Federal Government goes into a commercial business, 531 Senators and Congressmen become the actual board of directors of that business. Every time a state government goes into business, one or two hundred state senators and legislators become the actual directors of that business. Even if they were supermen and if there were no politics in the United States, no body of such numbers could competently direct commercial activities; for that requires initiative, instant decision and action. It took Congress six years of constant discussion to even decide what the method of administration of Muscle Shoals should be.

When the Federal Government undertakes to go into business, the state governments are at once deprived of control and taxation of that business; when a state government undertakes to go into business, it at once deprives the municipalities of taxation and control of that business. Municipalities, being local and close to the people, can, at times, succeed in business where Federal and State Governments must fail.

We have trouble enough with log rolling[2] in legislative bodies today. It originates naturally from desires of citizens to advance their particular section or to secure some necessary service. It would be multiplied a thousandfold were the Federal and state governments in these businesses.

The effect upon our economic progress would be even worse. Business progressiveness is dependent on competition. New methods and new ideas are the outgrowth of the spirit of adventure, of individual initiative and of individual enterprise. Without adventure there is no progress. No government administration can rightly take chances with taxpayers' money....

The Government in commercial business does not tolerate amongst its customers the freedom of competitive reprisals to which private business is subject. Bureaucracy does not tolerate the spirit of independence; it spreads the spirit of submission into our daily life and penetrates the temper of our people not with the habit of powerful resistance to wrong but with the habit of timid acceptance of irresistible might.

Bureaucracy is ever desirous of spreading its influence and its power. You cannot extend the mastery of the government over the daily working life of a people without at the same time making it the master of the people's souls and thoughts. Every expansion of government in business means that government in order to protect itself from the political consequences of its errors and wrongs is driven irresistibly without peace to greater and greater control of the nations' press and platform. Free speech does not live many hours after free industry and free commerce die.

It is a false liberalism that interprets itself into the Government operation of commercial business. Every step of bureaucratizing of the business of our country poisons the very roots of liberalism – that is, political equality, free speech, free assembly, free press, and equality of opportunity. It is the road not to more liberty, but to less liberty. Liberalism should be found not striving to spread bureaucracy but striving to set bounds to it. True liberalism seeks all legitimate freedom first in the confident belief that without such freedom the pursuit of all other blessings and benefits is vain. That belief is the foundation of all American progress, political as well as economic.

Liberalism is a force truly of the spirit, a force proceeding from the deep realization that economic freedom cannot be sacrificed if political freedom is to be preserved. Even if governmental conduct of business could give us more efficiency instead of less efficiency, the fundamental objection to it would

---

[2] Log rolling is the practice of legislators voting for legislation that they would not normally support in order to get support for their own pieces of legislation.

remain unaltered and unabated. It would destroy political equality. It would increase rather than decrease abuse and corruption. It would stifle initiative and invention. It would undermine the development of leadership. It would cramp and cripple the mental and spiritual energies of our people. It would extinguish equality and opportunity. It would dry up the spirit of liberty and progress. For these reasons primarily it must be resisted. For a hundred and fifty years liberalism has found its true spirit in the American system, not in the European systems.

I do not wish to be misunderstood in this statement. I am defining a general policy. It does not mean that our government is to part with one iota of its national resources without complete protection to the public interest. I have already stated that where the government is engaged in public works for purposes of flood control, of navigation, of irrigation, of scientific research or national defense, or in pioneering a new art, it will at times necessarily produce power or commodities as a by-product. But they must be a by-product of the major purpose, not the major purpose itself.

Nor do I wish to be misinterpreted as believing that the United States is free-for-all and devil-take-the-hind-most. The very essence of equality of opportunity and of American individualism is that there shall be no domination by any group or combination in this Republic, whether it be business or political. On the contrary, it demands economic justice as well as political and social justice. It is no system of laissez faire.

I feel deeply on this subject because during the war I had some practical experience with governmental operation and control. I have witnessed not only at home but abroad the many failures of government in business. I have seen its tyrannies, its injustices, its destructions of self-government, its undermining of the very instincts which carry our people forward to progress. I have witnessed the lack of advance, the lowered standards of living, the depressed spirits of people working under such a system. My objection is based not upon theory or upon a failure to recognize wrong or abuse, but I know the adoption of such methods would strike at the very roots of American life and would destroy the very basis of American progress.

Our people have the right to know whether we can continue to solve our great problems without abandonment of our American system. I know we can. We have demonstrated that our system is responsive enough to meet any new and intricate development in our economic and business life. We have demonstrated that we can meet any economic problem and still maintain our democracy as master in its own house and that we can at the same time preserve equality of opportunity and individual freedom.

In the last fifty years we have discovered that mass production will produce articles for us at half the cost they required previously. We have seen the resultant growth of large units of production and distribution. This is big business. Many businesses must be bigger for our tools are bigger, our country is bigger. We now build a single dynamo of a hundred thousand horsepower. Even fifteen years ago that would have been a big business all by itself. Yet today advance in production requires that we set ten of these units together in a row.

The American people from bitter experience have a rightful fear that great business units might be used to dominate our industrial life and by illegal and unethical practices destroy equality of opportunity.

Years ago the Republican Administration established the principle that such evils could be corrected by regulation. It developed methods by which abuses could be prevented while the full value of industrial progress could be retained for the public. It insisted upon the principle that when great public utilities were clothed with the security of partial monopoly, whether it be railways, power plants, telephones or what not, then there must be the fullest and most complete control of rates, services, and finances by government or local agencies. It declared that these businesses must be conducted with glass pockets.

As to our great manufacturing and distributing industries, the Republican Party insisted upon the enactment of laws that not only would maintain competition but would destroy conspiracies to destroy the smaller units or dominate and limit the equality of opportunity amongst our people.

One of the great problems of government is to determine to what extent the Government shall regulate and control commerce and industry and how much it shall leave it alone. No system is perfect. We have had many abuses in the private conduct of business. That every good citizen resents. It is just as important that business keep out of government as that government keep out of business.

Nor am I setting up the contention that our institutions are perfect. No human ideal is ever perfectly attained, since humanity itself is not perfect. The wisdom of our forefathers in their conception that progress can only be attained as the sum of the accomplishment of free individuals has been re-enforced by all of the great leaders of the country since that day. Jackson, Lincoln, Cleveland, McKinley, Roosevelt, Wilson, and Coolidge have stood unalterably for these principles.

And what have been the results of our American system? Our country has become the land of opportunity to those born without inheritance, not merely because of the wealth of its resources and industry but because of this freedom of initiative and enterprise. Russia has natural resources equal to ours. Her people are equally industrious, but she has not had the blessings of 150 years of our form of government and of our social system.

By adherence to the principles of decentralized self-government, ordered liberty, equal opportunity and freedom to the individual, our American experiment in human welfare has yielded a degree of well-being unparalleled in all the world. It has come nearer to the abolition of poverty, to the abolition of fear of want, than humanity has ever reached before. Progress of the past seven years is the proof of it. This alone furnishes the answer to our opponents who ask us to introduce destructive elements into the system by which this has been accomplished....

My conception of America is a land where men and women may walk in ordered freedom in the independent conduct of their occupations; where they may enjoy the advantages of wealth, not concentrated in the hands of the few but spread through the lives of all, where they build and safeguard their homes, and give to their children the fullest advantages and opportunities of American life; where every man shall be respected in the faith that his conscience and his heart direct him to follow; where a contented and happy people, secure in their liberties, free from poverty and fear, shall have the leisure and impulse to seek a fuller life.

Some may ask where all this may lead beyond mere material progress. It leads to a release of the energies of men and women from the dull drudgery of life to a wider vision and a higher hope. It leads to the opportunity for greater and greater service, not alone from man to man in our own land, but from our country to the whole world. It leads to an America, healthy in body, healthy in spirit, unfettered, youthful, eager – with a vision searching beyond the farthest horizons, with an open mind sympathetic and generous. It is to these higher ideals and for these purposes that I pledge myself and the Republican Party.

Document 2

Statement announcing a Series of Conferences with Representatives of Business, Industry, Agriculture, and Labor

President Herbert Hoover
November 15, 1929

There was little reason to believe, in November 1929, that the economy was in long-term trouble. The stock market crash of late October had indeed been traumatic, but many leading figures in business, politics, and academia had been saying for some time that stock prices had been overvalued. The collapse in prices therefore represented nothing more than a correction. Still, Hoover believed that some federal action was necessary, leading him to call a series of conferences aimed at using voluntary cooperation to prevent "over-pessimism" from inflicting long-term damage to the economy. Among the tangible results of these conferences was a promise by leading manufacturers not to reduce costs by cutting wages.

Source: Herbert Hoover, "Statement Announcing a Series of Conferences With Representatives of Business, Industry, Agriculture, and Labor," November 15, 1929. Online by Gerhard Peters and John T. Woolley, The American Presidency Project. http://www.presidency.ucsb.edu/ws/?pid=22006.

[handwritten annotation: all of this stuff is not direct govt. intervention by the state]

I have during the past week engaged in numerous conferences with important business leaders and public officials with a view to the coordination of business and governmental agencies in concerted action for continued business progress.

I am calling for the middle of next week a small preliminary conference of representatives of industry, agriculture, and labor to meet with the Secretaries of the Treasury, Agriculture, Commerce, and Labor, together with the Chairman of the Federal Farm Board to develop certain definite steps.

For instance, one of the results of the speculative period through which we have passed in recent months has been the diversion of capital into the security market, with consequent lagging of the construction work in the country. The postponement of construction during the past months, including not only buildings, railways, merchant marine, and public utilities, but also Federal, State, and municipal public works, provides a substantial reserve for prompt expanded action. The situation is further assured by the exceptionally strong cash position of the large manufacturing industries of the country.

The magnificent working of the Federal Reserve System and the inherently sound condition of the banks have already brought about a decrease in interest rates and an assurance of abundant capital – the first time such a result has been so speedily achieved under similar circumstances.

In market booms we develop over-optimism with a corresponding reverse into over-pessimism. They are equally unjustified but the sad thing is that many unfortunate people are drawn into the vortex of these movements with tragic loss of savings and reserves. Any lack of confidence in the economic future or the basic strength of business in the United States is foolish. Our national capacity for hard work and intelligent cooperation is ample guaranty of the future.

My own experience has been, however, that words are not of any great importance in times of economic disturbance. It is action that counts. The establishment of credit stability and ample capital through the Federal Reserve System and the demonstration of the confidence of the administration by undertaking tax reduction with the cooperation of both political parties, speak more than words.

The next practical step is the organizing and coordinating of a forward movement of business through the revival of construction activities, the stimulation of exports and of other legitimate business expansion, especially to take such action in concert with the use of our new powers to assist agriculture. Fortunately, the sound sense, the capacity and readiness for cooperation of our business leaders and governmental agencies give assurance of action.

Document 3

Statement on the Smoot-Hawley Tariff Bill
President Herbert Hoover
June 16, 1930

Even during his 1928 presidential campaign, Hoover had been calling for tariff reform, specifically for the protection of agriculture. Congressional leaders began work on a new trade bill in 1929, but it soon became clear that it would seek to protect more than just farmers. Fearing that the worsening global economic downturn would result in a flood of cheap foreign goods hitting U.S. markets, manufacturers lobbied hard for higher rates on their products. The resulting Smoot-Hawley Tariff (named for its sponsors in the Senate and House, Senator Reed Smoot [R-Utah] and Representative Willis C. Hawley [R-Oregon]) raised rates on practically everything. In spite of warnings from economists that it could worsen the global depression by making it harder for foreign countries to sell their products in the United States, Hoover announced that he would sign the bill.

Source: Herbert Hoover, "Statement on the Tariff Bill," June 16, 1930. Online by Gerhard Peters and John T. Woolley, The American Presidency Project. http://www.presidency.ucsb.edu/ws/?pid=22233.

I SHALL approve the tariff bill. . . .

This tariff law is like all other tariff legislation, whether framed primarily upon a protective or a revenue basis. It contains many compromises between sectional interests and between different industries. No tariff bill has ever been enacted or ever will be enacted under the present system that will be perfect. A large portion of the items are always adjusted with good judgment, but it is bound to contain some inequalities and inequitable compromises. There are items upon which duties will prove too high and others upon which duties will prove to be too low.

Certainly no President, with his other duties, can pretend to make that exhaustive determination of the complex facts which surround each of those 3,300 items, and which has required the attention of hundreds of men in Congress for nearly a year and a third. That responsibility must rest upon the Congress in a legislative rate revision.

On the administrative side I have insisted, however, that there should be created a new basis for the flexible tariff and it has been incorporated in this law. Thereby the means are established for objective and judicial review of these rates upon principles laid down by the Congress, free from pressures inherent in legislative action. Thus, the outstanding step of this tariff legislation has been the reorganization of the largely inoperative flexible provision of 1922[1] into a form which should render it possible to secure prompt and scientific adjustment of serious inequities and inequalities which may prove to have been incorporated in the bill.

This new provision has even a larger importance. If a perfect tariff bill were enacted today, the increased rapidity of economic change and the constant shifting of our relations to industries abroad will create a continuous stream of items which would work hardship upon some segment of the American people except for the provision of this relief. Without a workable flexible provision we would require even more frequent congressional tariff revision than during the past. With it the country should be freed from further general revision for many years to come. Congressional revisions are not only disturbing to business but with all their necessary collateral surroundings in lobbies, log rolling,[2] and the activities of group interests, are disturbing to public confidence.

Under the old flexible provisions, the task of adjustment was imposed directly upon the President, and the limitations in the law which circumscribed it were such that action was long delayed and it was largely inoperative, although important benefits were brought to the dairying, flax, glass, and other industries through it.

The new flexible provision established the responsibility for revisions upon a reorganized Tariff Commission, composed of members equal of both parties as a definite rate making body acting through semi-judicial methods of open hearings and investigation by which items can be taken up one by one upon direction or upon application of aggrieved parties. Recommendations are to be made to the President, he being given authority to promulgate or veto

---

[1] The "largely inoperative flexible provision of 1922" refers to the Fordney-McCumber Tariff, sponsored by Representative Joseph W. Fordney (R-MI) and Senator Porter J. McCumber (R-ND). The first tariff to apply a "scientific" method to the calculation of import duties, it was intended to protect American factory and farm output against a feared flood of cheaper products from post-war Europe.

[2] Legislators engage in log rolling when they vote for legislation they normally would not support in exchange for support for their own legislation.

the conclusions of the Commission. Such revision can be accomplished without disturbance to business, as they concern but one item at a time, and the principles laid down assure a protective basis.

The principle of a protective tariff for the benefit of labor, industry, and the farmer is established in the bill by the requirement that the Commission shall adjust the rates so as to cover the differences in cost of production at home and abroad, and it is authorized to increase or decrease the duties by 50 percent to effect this end. The means and methods of ascertaining such differences by the Commission are provided in such fashion as should expedite prompt and effective action if grievances develop.

When the flexible principle was first written into law in 1922, by tradition and force of habit the old conception of legislative revision was so firmly fixed that the innovation was bound to be used with caution and in a restricted field, even had it not been largely inoperative for other reasons. Now, however, and particularly after the record of the last 15 months, there is a growing and widespread realization that in this highly complicated and intricately organized and rapidly shifting modern economic world, the time has come when a more scientific and businesslike method of tariff revision must be devised. Toward this the new flexible provision takes a long step.

These provisions meet the repeated demands of statesmen and industrial and agricultural leaders over the past 25 years. It complies in full degree with the proposals made 20 years ago by President Roosevelt.[3] It now covers proposals which I urged in 1922.

If, however, by any chance the flexible provisions now made should prove insufficient for effective action, I shall ask for further authority for the Commission, for I believe that public opinion will give wholehearted support to the carrying out of such a program on a generous scale to the end that we may develop a protective system free from the vices which have characterized every tariff revision in the past.

The complaints from some foreign countries that these duties have been placed unduly high can be remedied, if justified, by proper application to the Tariff Commission.

It is urgent that the uncertainties in the business world which have been added to by the long-extended debate of the measure should be ended. They can be ended only by completion of this bill. Meritorious demands for further protection to agriculture and labor which have developed since the tariff of 1922 would not end if this bill fails of enactment. Agitation for legislative tariff

---

[3] President Theodore Roosevelt

revision would necessarily continue before the country. ==Nothing would contribute to retard business recovery more than this continued agitation.==

As I have said, I do not assume the rate structure in this or any other tariff bill is perfect, but I am convinced that the disposal of the whole question is urgent. I believe that the flexible provisions can within reasonable time remedy inequalities; that this provision is a progressive advance and gives great hope of taking the tariff away from politics, lobbying, and log rolling; that the bill gives protection to agriculture for the market of its products and to several industries in need of such protection for the wage of their labor; that with returning normal conditions our foreign trade will continue to expand.

- again, this idea that if you disagree, you are essentially the enemy is a recurring theme in major US crises — there is something larger @ stake than the cost of your toilet paper → democratic values

- this is an explanation for something he knows will be unpopular

Document 4

Speech on the Smoot-Hawley Tariff

Representative Jacob Milligan
July 3, 1930

Democrats, who had generally tended to support free trade ever since the days of Thomas Jefferson, were quick to criticize the Smoot-Hawley Tariff, and Hoover in particular for signing it. Critics such as Rep. Jacob Milligan (D-MO) predicted that it would undermine the country's export trade. While that certainly did happen – by the end of the year the value of goods traded internationally had plummeted by $1.5 billion – economists to this day disagree on the extent to which Smoot-Hawley was responsible.

Source: Representative Milligan, speaking on Smoot-Hawley Tariff, on July 3, 1930, 71st Cong., 2d sess., Congressional Record 22, pt. 11: 12675-76.

... [I]t is my opinion that it is most inopportune that the tariff bill should have become a law. We have not only a surplus of farm commodities but also a surplus in all industrial lines, hence must have foreign markets. We can not afford to destroy our foreign trade in order to allow the American manufacturer to plunder the pockets of the consumer. . . .

The tariff bill was under consideration for 17 months. During these 17 months the President had opportunity to inform Congress as to what he meant by "limited tariff revision for the benefit of agriculture." During these 17 months the President remained mute. . . . So the only logical conclusion that can be reached is that the bill was entirely indorsed by the President during its making. So I would not take credit from the President and the "Chief Manipulator" of this legislation in the Senate. I think the bill should be known as the Hoover-Grundy tariff bill.[1] The President assumed full responsibility when he signed the bill, as it could not have become law without his signature.

On the day the tariff bill became a law all grain prices fell to a new low level for the season. Wheat fell to the lowest price in a year, oats to the lowest price in 8 years, rye to the lowest price reached in 30 years. Cotton fell to the lowest price in more than three years.

The steel industry reported a further decline in operations to 69 per cent of capacity.

On the day the bill passed, the Department of Commerce announced that American exports dropped in May to the lowest point in the last six years.

Stocks dropped in value $2,000,000,000 the day the President announced that he would sign the bill.

This tariff law carries a general average increase of 20.4 per cent over the Fordney-McCumber law of 1922,[2] which means an additional burden each year to the consumers of this country. The farmers are told they will benefit by this law. The facts are that every dollar of benefit given the farmer will cost him $10 because of the increase in the rate on the other than the agricultural rates.

…

There is an increase carried in this law upon practically every thing a person uses in everyday life from the swaddling cloth of the newborn babe to the tombstone he erects above his dead. This tariff law means an average increased cost of from fifty to one hundred dollars to every average householder in the United States each year. How the now overburdened masses can carry this additional burden I do not know.

We hear from certain quarters that prosperity is raging rampant in every corner of the land; that we are enjoying this unprecedented prosperity because Mr. Hoover is President. I am willing to give President Hoover full credit for the so-called Hoover prosperity we are not enjoying.

I understand that two new planets have been discovered and that someone suggested one be named "Hoover Prosperity" because it is invisible; the other "Farm Relief" because it is so far away.

---

[1] "Chief Manipulator" refers to Joseph R. Grundy, a Republican senator from Pennsylvania and president of the Pennsylvania Manufacturers' Association. Grundy had allegedly said that anyone who made campaign contributions to Republican candidates was entitled to higher tariffs in return.

[2] a tariff law passed in 1922

Document 5

Press Statement on the Use of Federal Funds for Relief

President Herbert Hoover
February 3, 1931

The deteriorating economy was a major issue in the 1930 midterm elections, and Democrats won major gains. In the House and Senate a coalition of Democrats and progressive Republicans began to demand that federal funds be used to assist those suffering from the effects of the Depression. Hoover objected strenuously. While he had aggressively encouraged the use of public works to provide employment for those out of work, he believed that "charitable purposes" should be left to private organizations such as the Red Cross. For the federal government to get involved, he predicted, would undermine the independence that was necessary to self-government.

Source: Herbert Hoover, "Statement on Public vs. Private Financing of Relief Efforts." Online by Gerhard Peters and John T. Woolley, The American Presidency Project. http://www.presidency.ucsb.edu/ws/?pid=22943.

Certain senators have issued a public statement to the effect that unless the President and the House of Representatives agree to appropriations from the Federal Treasury for charitable purposes they will force an extra session of Congress.

I do not wish to add acrimony to a discussion, but would rather state this case as I see its fundamentals.

This is not an issue as to whether people shall go hungry or cold in the United States. It is solely a question of the best method by which hunger and cold shall be prevented. It is a question as to whether the American people on one hand will maintain the spirit of charity and mutual self-help through voluntary giving and the responsibility of local government, as distinguished on the other hand from appropriations out of the Federal Treasury for such purposes. My own conviction is strongly that if we break down this sense of responsibility of individual generosity to individual and mutual self-help in the country in times of national difficulty and if we start appropriations of this character we have not only impaired something infinitely valuable in the life of the American people but have struck at the roots of self-government. Once this has happened it is not the cost of a few score millions but we are faced with the abyss of reliance in future upon Government charity in some form or another. The money involved is indeed the least of the costs to American ideals and American institutions....

And there is a practical problem to all this. The help being daily extended by neighbors, by local and national agencies, by municipalities, by industry and a great multitude of organizations throughout the country today is many times any appropriation yet proposed. The opening of the doors of the Federal Treasury is likely to stifle this giving and thus destroy far more resources than the proposed charity from the Federal Government.

The basis of successful relief in national distress is to mobilize and organize the infinite number of agencies of self-help in the community. That has been the American way of relieving distress among our own people and the country is successfully meeting its problem in the American way today.

We have two entirely separate and distinct situations in the country; the first is the drought area; the second is the unemployment in our large industrial centers – for both of which these appropriations attempt to make charitable contributions.

Immediately upon the appearance of the drought last August, I convoked a meeting of the governors, the Red Cross and the railways, the bankers and other agencies in the country and laid the foundations of organization and the resources to stimulate every degree of self-help to meet the situation which it was then obvious would develop. The result of this action was to attack the drought problem in a number of directions. The Red Cross established committees in every drought county, comprising the leading citizens of those counties, with instructions to them that they were to prevent starvation among their neighbors and, if the problem went beyond local resources, the Red Cross would support them. *Hoover really just did not get the extent of all of this*

The organization has stretched through the area of suffering, the people are being cared for today through the hands and with sympathetic understanding and upon the responsibility of their neighbors who are being supported in turn by the fine spirit of mutual assistance of the American people. The Red Cross officials whose long devoted service and experience are unchallenged, inform me this morning that except for the minor incidents of any emergency organization, no one is going hungry and no one need go hungry or cold.

To reinforce this work at the opening of Congress I recommended large appropriations for loans to rehabilitate agriculture from the drought and provisions of further large sums for public works and construction in the drought territory which would give employment in further relief to the whole situation. These Federal activities provide for an expenditure of upward of $100,000,000 in this area and it is in progress today.

The Red Cross has always met the situations which it has undertaken. After careful survey and after actual experience of several months with their part of the problem they have announced firmly that they can command the resources with which to meet any call for human relief in prevention of hunger and suffering in drought areas and that they accept this responsibility. They have refused to accept Federal appropriations as not being consonant with either the need or the character of their organization. The Government Departments have given and are giving them every assistance. We possibly need to strengthen the public health service in matters of sanitation and to strengthen the credit facilities of that area through the method approved by the Government departments to divert some existing appropriations to strengthen agricultural credit corporations.

In the matter of unemployment outside of the drought area important economic measures of mutual self-help have been developed such as those to maintain wages, to distribute employment equitably, to increase construction work by industry, to increase Federal construction work from a rate of about $275,000,000 a year prior to the depression to a rate now of over $725,000,000 a year; to expand state and municipal construction – all upon a scale never before provided or even attempted in any depression. But beyond this, to assure that there shall be no suffering, in every town and county voluntary agencies in relief of distress have been strengthened and created and generous funds have been placed at their disposal. They are carrying on their work efficiently and sympathetically.

But after and coincidently with voluntary relief, our American system requires that municipal, county and state governments shall use their own resources and credit before seeking such assistance from the Federal Treasury.

I have indeed spent much of my life in fighting hardship and starvation both abroad and in the southern states. I do not feel that I should be charged with a lack of human sympathy for those who suffer but I recall that in all the organizations with which I have been connected over these many years, the foundation has been to summon the maximum of self-help. I am proud to have sought the help of Congress in the past for nations who were so disorganized by war and anarchy that self-help was impossible. But even these appropriations were but a tithe of that which was coincidently mobilized from the public charity of the United States and foreign countries. There is no such paralysis in the United States and I am confident that our people have the resources, the initiative, the courage, the stamina and kindliness of spirit to meet this situation in the way they have met their problems over generations.

I will accredit to those who advocate Federal charity a natural anxiety for the people of their states. I am willing to pledge myself that if the time should ever come that the voluntary agencies of the country together with the local and state governments are unable to find resources with which to prevent hunger and suffering in my country, I will ask the aid of every resource of the Federal Government because I would no more see starvation amongst our countrymen than would any senator or congressman. I have the faith in the American people that such a day will not come.

The American people are doing their job today. They should be given a chance to show whether they wish to preserve the principles of individual and local responsibility and mutual self-help before they embark on what I believe is a disastrous system. I feel sure they will succeed if given the opportunity.

The whole business situation would be greatly strengthened by the prompt completion of necessary legislation of this session of Congress and thereby the unemployment problem would be lessened, the drought area indirectly benefitted and the resources of self-help in the country strengthened.

Document 6

Veto of the Muscle Shoals Resolution
President Herbert Hoover
March 3, 1931

During World War I the federal government constructed a series of hydroelectric plants on the Tennessee River at Muscle Shoals, Alabama, for the purpose of extracting nitrates for the manufacture of explosives. One of the recurring political battles of the 1920s involved the question of what should be done with those plants. Republicans favored selling them off to private business, but they were repeatedly rebuffed by a coalition of Democrats and progressive Republicans. Their proposal was that the plants continue to be operated by the government, both for the production of nitrates for fertilizer and as a source of cheap electricity for the rural South. Congress in early 1931 approved a bill that would do just that, eliciting a sharp veto message from Hoover. Government, the president insisted, must not conduct business in competition with private concerns.

Source: Herbert Hoover, "Veto of the Muscle Shoals Resolution," March 3, 1931. Online by Gerhard Peters and John T. Woolley, The American Presidency Project. http://www.presidency.ucsb.edu/ws/?pid=23008.

I return herewith, without my approval, Senate Joint Resolution 49, "To provide for the national defense by the creation of a corporation for the operation of the Government properties at and near Muscle Shoals in the State of Alabama; to authorize the letting of the Muscle Shoals properties under certain conditions; and for other purposes."

This bill proposes the transformation of the war plant at Muscle Shoals, together with important expansions, into a permanently operated Government institution for the production and distribution of power and the manufacture of fertilizers....

The purpose of the bill is to provide production and wholesale distribution of surplus power and to give preference to States, municipalities, and cooperative organizations. It further provides that the policy of the

Government must be to distribute the surplus power equitably amongst States, counties, and municipalities within transmission distance of Muscle Shoals and provides for the construction of transmission lines to effect this purpose....

I am firmly opposed to the Government entering into any business the major purpose of which is competition with our citizens. There are national emergencies which require that the Government should temporarily enter the field of business, but they must be emergency actions and in matters where the cost of the project is secondary to much higher considerations. There are many localities where the Federal Government is justified in the construction of great dams and reservoirs, where navigation, flood control, reclamation or stream regulation are of dominant importance, and where they are beyond the capacity or purpose of private or local government capital to construct. In these cases power is often a by-product and should be disposed of by contract or lease. But for the Federal Government deliberately to go out to build up and expand such an occasion to the major purpose of a power and manufacturing business is to break down the initiative and enterprise of the American people; it is destruction of equality of opportunity amongst our people; it is the negation of the ideals upon which our civilization has been based.

This bill raises one of the important issues confronting our people. That is squarely the issue of Federal Government ownership and operation of power and manufacturing business not as a minor by-product but as a major purpose. Involved in this question is the agitation against the conduct of the power industry. The power problem is not to be solved by the Federal Government going into the power business, nor is it to be solved by the project in this bill. The remedy for abuses in the conduct of that industry lies in regulation and not by the Federal Government entering upon the business itself. I have recommended to the Congress on various occasions that action should be taken to establish Federal regulation of interstate power in cooperation with State authorities. This bill would launch the Federal Government upon a policy of ownership and operation of power utilities upon a basis of competition instead of by the proper Government function of regulation for the protection of all the people. I hesitate to contemplate the future of our institutions, of our Government, and of our country if the preoccupation of its officials is to be no longer the promotion of justice and equal opportunity but is to be devoted to barter in the markets. That is not liberalism, it is degeneration....

This bill distinctly proposes to enter the field of powers reserved to the States. It would deprive the adjacent States of the right to control rates for this power and would deprive them of taxes on property within their borders and would invade and weaken the authority of local government....

I sympathize greatly with the desire of the people of Tennessee and Alabama to see this great asset turned to practical use. It can be so turned and to their benefit. I am loath to leave a subject of this character without a suggestion for solution. Congress has been thwarted for 10 years in finding solution, by rivalry of private interests and by the determination of certain groups to commit the Federal Government to Government ownership and operation of power.

The real development of the resources and the industries of the Tennessee Valley can only be accomplished by the people in that valley themselves. Muscle Shoals can only be administered by the people upon the ground, responsible to their own communities, directing them solely for the benefit of their communities and not for purposes of pursuit of social theories or national politics. Any other course deprives them of liberty.

I would therefore suggest that the States of Alabama and Tennessee who are the ones primarily concerned should set up a commission of their own representatives together with a representative from the national farm organizations and the Corps of Army Engineers; that there be vested in that commission full authority to lease the plants at Muscle Shoals in the interest of the local community and agriculture generally. It could lease the nitrate plants to the advantage of agriculture. The power plant is today earning a margin over operating expenses. Such a commission could increase this margin without further capital outlay and should be required to use all such margins for the benefit of agriculture.

The Federal Government should, as in the case of Boulder Canyon, construct Cove Creek Dam as a regulatory measure for the flood protection of the Tennessee Valley and the development of its water resources, but on the same bases as those imposed at Boulder Canyon – that is, that construction should be undertaken at such time as the proposed commission is able to secure contracts for use of the increased water supply to power users or the lease of the power produced as a by-product from such a dam on terms that will return to the Government interest upon its outlay with amortization. On this basis the Federal Government will have cooperated to place the question into the hands of the people primarily concerned. They can lease as their wisdom dictates and for the industries that they deem best in their own interest. It would get a war relic out of politics and into the realm of service.

Document 7

Special Message to the Congress on the Economic Recovery Program
President Herbert Hoover
January 4, 1932

Although the economy showed some signs of improvement in early 1931, developments in Europe – the collapse of several major banks, followed by Great Britain's decision to leave the gold standard – brought another plunge in wholesale prices, and another surge in unemployment. Several of Hoover's closest advisers began to warn him that direct federal intervention was necessary in order to prevent complete financial chaos. Toward the end of the year, therefore, the president and his staff formulated a series of proposals aimed at restoring economic confidence. At the heart of the program was his call for the creation of a Reconstruction Finance Corporation, an agency empowered to make emergency loans to banks, building-and-loan societies, trust companies, credit unions, insurance companies, railroads, and agricultural stabilization corporations. As long as these institutions remained solvent, Hoover reasoned, the economy as a whole could weather the crisis.

Source: Herbert Hoover, "Special Message to the Congress on the Economic Recovery Program," January 4, 1932. Online by Gerhard Peters and John T. Woolley, The American Presidency Project. http://www.presidency.ucsb.edu/ws/?pid=23021.

At the convening of the Congress on December 7, I laid proposals before it designed to check the further degeneration in prices and values, to fortify us against continued shocks from world instability and to unshackle the forces of recovery. The need is manifestly even more evident than at the date of my message a month ago. I should be derelict in my duty if I did not at this time emphasize the paramount importance to the nation of constructive action upon these questions at the earliest possible moment. These recommendations have been largely developed in consultation with leading men of both parties, of agriculture, of labor, of banking and of industry. They furnish the bases for full collaboration to effect these purposes. They have no partisan character. We can and must replace the unjustifiable fear in the country by confidence.

The principal subjects requiring immediate action are:

1. The strengthening of the Federal Land Bank System to the farmer and to maintain at the highest level the credit of these institutions which furnish agriculture with much needed capital. This measure has passed the House of Representatives and is now before the Senate.

2. The creation of a Reconstruction Finance Corporation to furnish during the period of the depression credits otherwise unobtainable under existing circumstances in order to give confidence to agriculture, industry and labor against further paralyzing influences. By such prompt assurance we can reopen many credit channels and reestablish the normal working of our commercial organization and thus contribute greatly to reestablish the resumption of employment and stability in prices and values.

3. The creation of a system of Home Loan Discount Banks in order to revive employment by new construction and to mitigate the difficulties of many of our citizens in securing renewals of mortgages on their homes and farms. It has the further purpose of permanent encouragement of home ownership. To accomplish these purposes we must so liberate the resources of the country banks, the savings banks and the building and loan associations as to restore these institutions to normal functioning. Under the proposal before the Congress the most of the capital of these Discount Banks would be subscribed by the institutions participating in their use and such residue as might be necessary for the federal government to supply temporarily would be repaid in time by such institutions as in the case of the Farm Loan Banks when they were first organized.

4. The discount facilities[1] of our Federal Reserve Banks are restricted by law more than that of the central banks in other countries. This restriction in times such as these limits the liquidity of the banks and tends to increase the forces of deflation, cripples the smaller businesses, stifles new enterprise and thus limits employment. I recommend an enlargement of these discount privileges to take care of emergencies. To meet the needs of our situation it will

---

[1] "Discount facilities" or "discount windows" are terms used to denote the ability of a central bank to lend money to other banks and financial institutions and thus increase their liquidity or cash. When a bank increases its liquidity, it is able to lend more. The term "discount window" derives from the fact that borrowing from the central back originally occurred at a teller window in the bank.

not be necessary to go even as far as the current practice of foreign institutions of similar character. Such a measure has the support of most of the Governors of the Federal Reserve Banks.

5. The development of a plan to assure early distribution to depositors in closed banks is necessary to relieve distress among millions of small depositors and small businesses, and to release vast sums of money now frozen.

6. Revision of the laws relating to transportation in the direction recommended by the Interstate Commerce Commission[2] would strengthen our principal transportation systems and restore confidence in the bonds of our railways. These bonds are held largely by our insurance companies, our savings banks, and benevolent trusts and are therefore the property of nearly every family in the United States. The railways are the largest employers of labor and purchasers of goods.

7. Revision of banking laws in order to better safeguard depositors.

8. The country must have confidence that the credit and stability of the Federal Government will be maintained by drastic economy in expenditure, by adequate increase of taxes, and by restriction of issues of Federal securities. The recent depreciation in prices of government securities is a serious warning which reflects the fear of further large and unnecessary issues of such securities. Promptness in adopting an adequate budget relief to taxpayers by resolute economy and restriction in security issues is essential to remove this uncertainty.

Combating a depression is indeed like a great war in that it is not a battle upon a single front but upon many fronts. These measures are all a necessary addition to the efficient and courageous efforts of our citizens throughout the nation. Our people through voluntary measures and through state and local action are providing for distress. Through the organized action of employers they are securing distribution of employment and thus mitigating the hardships of the depression. Through the mobilization of national credit associations they are aiding the country greatly. Our duty is so to supplement these steps as to make their efforts more fruitful.

The United States has the resources and resilience to make a large measure of recovery independent of the rest of the world. Our internal economy is our primary concern and we must fortify our economic structure in

---

[2] Established in 1887, the Interstate Commerce Commission regulated rates charged for the transport of goods and people between states. Formed primarily to regulate railroad transport, it later regulated trucking and bus transport.

Special Message to the Congress on the Economic Recovery Program 27

order to meet any situation that may arise and by so doing lay the foundations for recovery.

This does not mean that we are insensible to the welfare of other nations or that our own self-interest is not involved in economic rehabilitation abroad which would restore the markets for our agricultural and other commodities. But it is our duty to devote ourselves to the problems of our own internal economy not only as the first necessity to domestic welfare but as our best contribution to the stability of the world as a whole.

Action in these matters by the Congress will go far to reestablish confidence, to restore the functioning of our economic system, and to rebuilding of prices and values and to quickening employment. Our justified hope and confidence for the future rests upon unity of our people and of the government in prompt and courageous action.

Here you can really begin to see Hoover starting to understand that more government intervention might be the only way out → his tone has certainly changed since his initial address.

Document 8

The Norris-La Guardia Act
March 23, 1932

During the first year and a half of the Depression, most companies stood by the promises they had made to the Hoover administration in November 1929 not to reduce wages. However, by the middle of 1931 business owners concluded that they had no choice but to cut pay for workers, and the response was a wave of serious unrest, with workers in many important industries walking out on strike.

Strikes, of course, were not new, and management in the past had frequently stopped them by finding sympathetic judges who were willing to issue court injunctions charging striking workers with violating the antitrust laws by forming "combinations in restraint of trade," and ordering them back to work. Employers, furthermore, sought to head off labor unrest by forcing workers to sign so-called "yellow-dog" contracts, in which they pledged not to join a union. But by 1932 striking workers won the sympathy of Congress, as well as that of President Hoover. In March Hoover signed a law sponsored by Sen. George Norris of Nebraska and Rep. Fiorello La Guardia of New York, which forbade courts from using injunctions to break strikes. It also prohibited them from enforcing yellow-dog contracts (signed agreements between employers and employees who, as a condition for being hired, pledged not to join a union). By removing two of the most commonly used methods for stopping labor disputes, the Norris-La Guardia Act paved the way for a much more aggressive organized labor movement in the 1930s.

Source: 29 U.S. Code Title 29, Chapter 6, §101-110, Online from Legal Information Institute, *Cornell University Law School.* https://www.law.cornell.edu/uscode/text/29/chapter-6.

No court of the United States, as defined in this chapter, shall have jurisdiction to issue any restraining order or temporary or permanent injunction in a case involving or growing out of a labor dispute, except in a strict conformity with the provisions of this chapter; nor shall any such restraining order or temporary or permanent injunction be issued contrary to the public policy declared in this chapter.

In the interpretation of this chapter and in determining the jurisdiction and authority of the courts of the United States, as such jurisdiction and authority are defined and limited in this chapter, the public policy of the United States is declared as follows:

Whereas under prevailing economic conditions, developed with the aid of governmental authority for owners of property to organize in the corporate and other forms of ownership association, the individual unorganized worker is commonly helpless to exercise actual liberty of contract and to protect his freedom of labor, and thereby to obtain acceptable terms and conditions of employment, wherefore, though he should be free to decline to associate with his fellows, it is necessary that he have full freedom of association, self-organization, and designation of representatives of his own choosing, to negotiate the terms and conditions of his employment, and that he shall be free from the interference, restraint, or coercion of employers of labor, or their agents, in the designation of such representatives or in self-organization or in other concerted activities for the purpose of collective bargaining or other mutual aid or protection; therefore, the following definitions of, and limitations upon, the jurisdiction and authority of the courts of the United States are enacted.

Any undertaking or promise, such as is described in this section . . . is declared to be contrary to the public policy of the United States, shall not be enforceable in any court of the United States and shall not afford any basis for the granting of legal or equitable relief by any such court, including specifically the following:

Every undertaking or promise hereafter made, whether written or oral, express or implied, constituting or contained in any contract or agreement of hiring or employment between any individual, firm, company, association, or corporation, and any employee or prospective employee of the same, whereby

(a) Either party to such contract or agreement undertakes or promises not to join, become, or remain a member of any labor organization or of any employer organization; or

(b) Either party to such contract or agreement undertakes or promises that he will withdraw from an employment relation in the event that he joins, becomes, or remains a member of any labor organization or of any employer organization.

No court of the United States shall have jurisdiction to issue any restraining order or temporary or permanent injunction in any case involving or growing out of any labor dispute to prohibit any person or persons participating or interested in such dispute (as these terms are herein defined) from doing, whether singly or in concert, any of the following acts:

(a) Ceasing or refusing to perform any work or to remain in any relation of employment;

(b) Becoming or remaining a member of any labor organization or of any employer organization . . .

(c) Paying or giving to, or withholding from, any person participating or interested in such labor dispute, any strike or unemployment benefits or insurance, or other moneys or things of value;

(d) By all lawful means aiding any person participating or interested in any labor dispute who is being proceeded against in, or is prosecuting, any action or suit in any court of the United States or of any State;

(e) Giving publicity to the existence of, or the facts involved in, any labor dispute, whether by advertising, speaking, patrolling, or by any other method not involving fraud or violence;

(f) Assembling peaceably to act or to organize to act in promotion of their interests in a labor dispute;

(g) Advising or notifying any person of an intention to do any of the acts heretofore specified;

(h) Agreeing with other persons to do or not to do any of the acts heretofore specified; and

(i) Advising, urging, or otherwise causing or inducing without fraud or violence the acts heretofore specified . . .

No court of the United States shall have jurisdiction to issue a restraining order or temporary or permanent injunction upon the ground that any of the persons participating or interested in a labor dispute constitute or are engaged in an unlawful combination or conspiracy because of the doing in concert of the acts enumerated in . . . this title.

No officer or member of any association or organization, and no association or organization participating or interested in a labor dispute, shall be held responsible or liable in any court of the United States for the unlawful acts of individual officers, members, or agents, except upon clear proof of actual participation in, or actual authorization of, such acts, or of ratification of such acts after actual knowledge thereof.

No court of the United States shall have jurisdiction to issue a temporary or permanent injunction in any case involving or growing out of a labor dispute, as defined in this chapter, except after hearing the testimony of witnesses in open court (with opportunity for cross-examination) in support of the allegations of a complaint made under oath, and testimony in opposition thereto, if offered, and except after findings of fact by the court, to the effect—

(a) That unlawful acts have been threatened and will be committed unless restrained or have been committed and will be continued unless restrained, but no injunction or temporary restraining order shall be issued on account of any threat or unlawful act excepting against the person or persons, association, or organization making the threat or committing the unlawful act or actually authorizing or ratifying the same after actual knowledge thereof;

(b) That substantial and irreparable injury to complainant's property will follow;

(c) That as to each item of relief granted greater injury will be inflicted upon complainant by the denial of relief than will be inflicted upon defendants by the granting of relief;

(d) That complainant has no adequate remedy at law; and

(e) That the public officers charged with the duty to protect complainant's property are unable or unwilling to furnish adequate protection.

Such hearing shall be held after due and personal notice thereof has been given, in such manner as the court shall direct, to all known persons against whom relief is sought, and also to the chief of those public officials of the county and city within which the unlawful acts have been threatened or committed charged with the duty to protect complainant's property....

No restraining order or injunctive relief shall be granted to any complainant who has failed to comply with any obligation imposed by law which is involved in the labor dispute in question, or who has failed to make every reasonable effort to settle such dispute either by negotiation or with the aid of any available governmental machinery of mediation or voluntary arbitration....

Document 9

Radio Address on "The Forgotten Man"
Franklin D. Roosevelt
April 7, 1932

By early 1932 a frontrunner had emerged for the Democratic Party's nomination for the presidency: Franklin D. Roosevelt, a fifth cousin of Theodore Roosevelt who had earned a reputation for effectiveness as governor of New York. He also had a natural talent on the radio, which by the late 1920s had become the nation's most common form of mass media. In early April, Roosevelt took to the airwaves to criticize the Republican Party's handling of the economic crisis, and to suggest a new way forward.

Source: Franklin D. Roosevelt, "The Forgotten Man," April 7, 1932, The Public Papers and Addresses of Franklin D. Roosevelt, Vol. 1, 1928-32, (New York City: Random House, 1938), p. 624.

Although I understand that I am talking under the auspices of the Democratic National Committee, I do not want to limit myself to politics. I do not want to feel that I am addressing an audience of Democrats or that I speak merely as a Democrat myself. The present condition of our national affairs is too serious to be viewed through partisan eyes for partisan purposes.

Fifteen years ago my public duty called me to an active part in a great national emergency, the World War. Success then was due to a leadership whose vision carried beyond the timorous and futile gesture of sending a tiny army of 150,000 trained soldiers and the regular navy to the aid of our allies. The generalship of that moment conceived of a whole Nation mobilized for war, [its] economic, industrial, social and military resources gathered into a vast unit capable of and actually in the process of throwing into the scales ten million men equipped with physical needs and sustained by the realization that behind them were the united efforts of 110,000,000 human beings. It was a great plan because it was built from bottom to top and not from top to bottom.

In my calm judgment, the Nation faces today a more grave emergency than in 1917.

This is a good statement

Radio Address on "The Forgotten Man"

It is said that Napoleon lost the battle of Waterloo because he forgot his infantry – he staked too much upon the more spectacular but less substantial cavalry. The present administration in Washington provides a close parallel. It has either forgotten or it does not want to remember the infantry of our economic army.

These unhappy times call for the building of plans that rest upon the forgotten, the unorganized but the indispensable units of economic power, for plans like those of 1917 that build from the bottom up and not from the top down, that put their faith once more in the forgotten man at the bottom of the economic pyramid.

Obviously, these few minutes tonight permit no opportunity to lay down the ten or a dozen closely related objectives of a plan to meet our present emergency, but I can draw a few essentials, a beginning in fact, of a planned program.

It is the habit of the unthinking to turn in times like this to the illusions of economic magic. People suggest that a huge expenditure of public funds by the Federal Government and by State and local governments will completely solve the unemployment problem. But it is clear that even if we could raise many billions of dollars and find definitely useful public works to spend these billions on, even all that money would not give employment to the seven million or ten million people who are out of work. Let us admit frankly that it would be only a stopgap. A real economic cure must go to the killing of the bacteria in the system rather than to the treatment of external symptoms.

How much do the shallow thinkers realize, for example, that approximately one-half of our whole population, fifty or sixty million people, earn their living by farming or in small towns whose existence immediately depends on farms. They have today lost their purchasing power. Why? They are receiving for farm products less than the cost to them of growing these farm products. The result of this loss of purchasing power is that many other millions of people engaged in industry in the cities cannot sell industrial products to the farming half of the Nation. This brings home to every city worker that his own employment is directly tied up with the farmer's dollar. No Nation can long endure half bankrupt. Main Street, Broadway, the mills, the mines will close if half the buyers are broke.

I cannot escape the conclusion that one of the essential parts of a national program of restoration must be to restore purchasing power to the farming half of the country. Without this the wheels of railroads and of factories will not turn.

Closely associated with this first objective is the problem of keeping the home-owner and the farm-owner where he is, without being dispossessed through the foreclosure of his mortgage. His relationship to the great banks of Chicago and New York is pretty remote. The two billion dollar fund which President Hoover and the Congress have put at the disposal of the big banks, the railroads and the corporations of the Nation is not for him.

His is a relationship to his little local bank or local loan company. It is a sad fact that even though the local lender in many cases does not want to evict the farmer or home-owner by foreclosure proceedings, he is forced to do so in order to keep his bank or company solvent. Here should be an objective of Government itself, to provide at least as much assistance to the little fellow as it is now giving to the large banks and corporations. That is another example of building from the bottom up.

One other objective closely related to the problem of selling American products is to provide a tariff policy based upon economic common sense rather than upon politics, hot air, and pull. This country during the past few years, culminating with the Hawley-Smoot Tariff in 1929,[1] has compelled the world to build tariff fences so high that world trade is decreasing to the vanishing point. The value of goods internationally exchanged is today less than half of what it was three or four years ago.

Every man and woman who gives any thought to the subject knows that if our factories run even 80 percent of capacity, they will turn out more products than we as a Nation can possibly use ourselves. The answer is that if they run on 80 percent of capacity, we must sell some goods abroad. How can we do that if the outside Nations cannot pay us in cash? And we know by sad experience that they cannot do that. The only way they can pay us is in their own goods or raw materials, but this foolish tariff of ours makes that impossible.

What we must do is this: revise our tariff on the basis of a reciprocal exchange of goods, allowing other Nations to buy and to pay for our goods by sending us such of their goods as will not seriously throw any of our industries out of balance, and incidentally making impossible in this country the continuance of pure monopolies which cause us to pay excessive prices for many of the necessities of life.

Such objectives as these three, restoring farmers' buying power, relief to the small banks and home-owners and a reconstructed tariff policy, are only a part of ten or a dozen vital factors. But they seem to be beyond the concern of a

---

[1] Document 3

national administration which can think in terms only of the top of the social and economic structure. It has sought temporary relief from the top down rather than permanent relief from the bottom up. It has totally failed to plan ahead in a comprehensive way. It has waited until something has cracked and then at the last moment has sought to prevent total collapse.

It is high time to get back to fundamentals. It is high time to admit with courage that we are in the midst of an emergency at least equal to that of war. Let us mobilize to meet it.

Document 10

Acceptance Speech at the Democratic National Convention
Franklin D. Roosevelt
July 2, 1932

Franklin Roosevelt, then Governor of New York, was not the only candidate for the Democratic nomination in 1932; the 1928 nominee, Al Smith, was also a contender, as was House Speaker John Nance Garner of Texas. Roosevelt was the clear frontrunner, with more pledged delegates than the other two combined, but party rules mandated that the successful candidate win two-thirds of the delegates. As a result, the first three ballots at the Democratic National Convention in Chicago yielded no winner. Finally the Roosevelt team reached an agreement with Garner – if he would instruct his delegates to vote for Roosevelt, Garner would be Roosevelt's pick for vice president. The next ballot, predictably, went for the Governor of New York.

Breaking long-established precedent, Roosevelt chose to be present in Chicago when the nomination was offered to him. In his acceptance speech he insisted that it should be the role of the Democratic Party "to break foolish traditions." He also, in the speech's most memorable line, promised "a new deal for the American people."

Source: Franklin D. Roosevelt, "Address Accepting the Presidential Nomination at the Democratic National Convention in Chicago," July 2, 1932. Online by Gerhard Peters and John T. Woolley, The American Presidency Project. http://www.presidency.ucsb.edu/ws/?pid=75174.

I appreciate your willingness after these six arduous days to remain here, for I know well the sleepless hours which you and I have had. I regret that I am late, but I have no control over the winds of Heaven and could only be thankful for my Navy training.

The appearance before a National Convention of its nominee for President, to be formally notified of his selection, is unprecedented and unusual, but these are unprecedented and unusual times. I have started out on the tasks that lie ahead by breaking the absurd traditions that the candidate should remain in professed ignorance of what has happened for weeks until he is formally notified of that event many weeks later.

My friends, may this be the symbol of my intention to be honest and to avoid all hypocrisy or sham, to avoid all silly shutting of the eyes to the truth in this campaign. You have nominated me and I know it, and I am here to thank you for the honor.

Let it also be symbolic that in so doing I broke traditions. Let it be from now on the task of our Party to break foolish traditions. We will break foolish traditions and leave it to the Republican leadership, far more skilled in that art, to break promises.

Let us now and here highly resolve to resume the country's interrupted march along the path of real progress, of real justice, of real equality for all of our citizens, great and small. Our indomitable leader in that interrupted march is no longer with us, but there still survives today his spirit. Many of his captains, thank God, are still with us, to give us wise counsel. Let us feel that in everything we do there still lives with us, if not the body, the great indomitable, unquenchable, progressive soul of our Commander-in-Chief, Woodrow Wilson.

I have many things on which I want to make my position clear at the earliest possible moment in this campaign. That admirable document, the platform which you have adopted, is clear. I accept it 100 percent.

And you can accept my pledge that I will leave no doubt or ambiguity on where I stand on any question of moment in this campaign.

As we enter this new battle, let us keep always present with us some of the ideals of the Party: The fact that the Democratic Party by tradition and by the continuing logic of history, past and present, is the bearer of liberalism and of progress and at the same time of safety to our institutions. And if this appeal fails, remember well, my friends, that a resentment against the failure of Republican leadership – and note well that in this campaign I shall not use the word "Republican Party," but I shall use, day in and day out, the words, "Republican leadership" – the failure of Republican leaders to solve our troubles may degenerate into unreasoning radicalism.

The great social phenomenon of this depression, unlike others before it, is that it has produced but a few of the disorderly manifestations that too often attend upon such times.

Wild radicalism has made few converts, and the greatest tribute that I can pay to my countrymen is that in these days of crushing want there persists an orderly and hopeful spirit on the part of the millions of our people who have suffered so much. To fail to offer them a new chance is not only to betray their hopes but to misunderstand their patience.

To meet by reaction that danger of radicalism is to invite disaster. Reaction is no barrier to the radical. It is a challenge, a provocation. The way to meet that danger is to offer a workable program of reconstruction, and the party to offer it is the party with clean hands.

This, and this only, is a proper protection against blind reaction on the one hand and an improvised, hit-or-miss, irresponsible opportunism on the other.

There are two ways of viewing the Government's duty in matters affecting economic and social life. The first sees to it that a favored few are helped and hopes that some of their prosperity will leak through, sift through, to labor, to the farmer, to the small business man. That theory belongs to the party of Toryism, and I had hoped that most of the Tories left this country in 1776.

But it is not and never will be the theory of the Democratic Party. This is no time for fear, for reaction or for timidity. Here and now I invite those nominal Republicans who find that their conscience cannot be squared with the groping and the failure of their party leaders to join hands with us; here and now, in equal measure, I warn those nominal Democrats who squint at the future with their faces turned toward the past, and who feel no responsibility to the demands of the new time, that they are out of step with their Party.

Yes, the people of this country want a genuine choice this year, not a choice between two names for the same reactionary doctrine. Ours must be a party of liberal thought, of planned action, of enlightened international outlook, and of the greatest good to the greatest number of our citizens.

Now it is inevitable – and the choice is that of the times – it is inevitable that the main issue of this campaign should revolve about the clear fact of our economic condition, a depression so deep that it is without precedent in modern history. It will not do merely to state, as do Republican leaders to explain their broken promises of continued inaction, that the depression is worldwide. That was not their explanation of the apparent prosperity of 1928. The people will not forget the claim made by them then that prosperity was only a domestic product manufactured by a Republican President and a Republican Congress. If they claim paternity for the one they cannot deny paternity for the other.

I cannot take up all the problems today. I want to touch on a few that are vital. Let us look a little at the recent history and the simple economics, the kind of economics that you and I and the average man and woman talk.

In the years before 1929 we know that this country had completed a vast cycle of building and inflation; for ten years we expanded on the theory of repairing the wastes of the War, but actually expanding far beyond that, and also beyond our natural and normal growth. Now it is worth remembering, and the cold figures of finance prove it, that during that time there was little or no drop in the prices that the consumer had to pay, although those same figures proved that the cost of production fell very greatly; corporate profit resulting from this period was enormous; at the same time little of that profit was devoted to the reduction of prices. The consumer was forgotten. Very little of it went into increased wages; the worker was forgotten, and by no means an adequate proportion was even paid out in dividends – the stockholder was forgotten.

And, incidentally, very little of it was taken by taxation to the beneficent Government of those years.

What was the result? Enormous corporate surpluses piled up – the most stupendous in history. Where, under the spell of delirious speculation, did those surpluses go? Let us talk economics that the figures prove and that we can understand. Why, they went chiefly in two directions: first, into new and unnecessary plants which now stand stark and idle; and second, into the call-money[1] market of Wall Street, either directly by the corporations, or indirectly through the banks. Those are the facts. Why blink at them?

Then came the crash. You know the story. Surpluses invested in unnecessary plants became idle. Men lost their jobs; purchasing power dried up; banks became frightened and started calling loans. Those who had money were afraid to part with it. Credit contracted. Industry stopped. Commerce declined, and unemployment mounted.

And there we are today.

Translate that into human terms. See how the events of the past three years have come home to specific groups of people: first, the group dependent on industry; second, the group dependent on agriculture; third, and made up in large part of members of the first two groups, the people who are called "small investors and depositors." In fact, the strongest possible tie between the first two groups, agriculture and industry, is the fact that the savings and to a degree the security of both are tied together in that third group – the credit structure of the Nation.

Never in history have the interests of all the people been so united in a single economic problem. Picture to yourself, for instance, the great groups of property owned by millions of our citizens, represented by credits issued in the

---

[1] "Call-money" is money loaned by a bank for a very short, unfixed term; the creditor (often a brokerage firm) must repay the loan when the bank recalls it.

form of bonds and mortgages – Government bonds of all kinds, Federal, State, county, municipal; bonds of industrial companies, of utility companies; mortgages on real estate in farms and cities, and finally the vast investments of the Nation in the railroads. What is the measure of the security of each of those groups? We know well that in our complicated, interrelated credit structure if any one of these credit groups collapses they may all collapse. Danger to one is danger to all.

How, I ask, has the present Administration in Washington treated the interrelationship of these credit groups? The answer is clear: It has not recognized that interrelationship existed at all. Why, the Nation asks, has Washington failed to understand that all of these groups, each and every one, the top of the pyramid and the bottom of the pyramid, must be considered together, that each and every one of them is dependent on every other; each and every one of them affecting the whole financial fabric?

Statesmanship and vision, my friends, require relief to all at the same time.

. . .

At last our eyes are open. At last the American people are ready to acknowledge that Republican leadership was wrong and that the Democracy is right.

My program, of which I can only touch on these points, is based upon this simple moral principle: the welfare and the soundness of a Nation depend first upon what the great mass of the people wish and need; and second, whether or not they are getting it.

What do the people of America want more than anything else? To my mind, they want two things: work, with all the moral and spiritual values that go with it; and with work, a reasonable measure of security – security for themselves and for their wives and children. Work and security – these are more than words. They are more than facts. They are the spiritual values, the true goal toward which our efforts of reconstruction should lead. These are the values that this program is intended to gain; these are the values we have failed to achieve by the leadership we now have.

Our Republican leaders tell us economic laws – sacred, inviolable, unchangeable – cause panics which no one could prevent. But while they prate of economic laws, men and women are starving. We must lay hold of the fact that economic laws are not made by nature. They are made by human beings. Yes, when – not if – when we get the chance, the Federal Government will assume bold leadership in distress relief. For years Washington has alternated between putting its head in the sand and saying there is no large number of destitute people in our midst who need food and clothing, and then saying the

States should take care of them, if there are. Instead of planning two and a half years ago to do what they are now trying to do, they kept putting it off from day to day, week to week, and month to month, until the conscience of America demanded action.

I say that while primary responsibility for relief rests with localities now, as ever, yet the Federal Government has always had and still has a continuing responsibility for the broader public welfare. It will soon fulfill that responsibility....

One word more: Out of every crisis, every tribulation, every disaster, mankind rises with some share of greater knowledge, of higher decency, of purer purpose. Today we shall have come through a period of loose thinking, descending morals, an era of selfishness, among individual men and women and among Nations. Blame not Governments alone for this. Blame ourselves in equal share. Let us be frank in acknowledgment of the truth that many amongst us have made obeisance to Mammon,[2] that the profits of speculation, the easy road without toil, have lured us from the old barricades. To return to higher standards we must abandon the false prophets and seek new leaders of our own choosing.

Never before in modern history have the essential differences between the two major American parties stood out in such striking contrast as they do today. Republican leaders not only have failed in material things, they have failed in national vision, because in disaster they have held out no hope, they have pointed out no path for the people below to climb back to places of security and of safety in our American life.

Throughout the Nation, men and women, forgotten in the political philosophy of the Government of the last years, look to us here for guidance and for more equitable opportunity to share in the distribution of national wealth.

On the farms, in the large metropolitan areas, in the smaller cities and in the villages, millions of our citizens cherish the hope that their old standards of living and of thought have not gone forever. Those millions cannot and shall not hope in vain.

I pledge you, I pledge myself, to a new deal for the American people. Let us all here assembled constitute ourselves prophets of a new order of

---

[2] This word for riches or material possessions is used in the Bible; it derives from the Aramaic language spoken at the time of Jesus Christ. Since Jesus said the love of wealth is idolatry, early translators thought of "Mammon" as the demon who lures people into this false worship.

competence and of courage. This is more than a political campaign; it is a call to arms. Give me your help, not to win votes alone, but to win in this crusade to restore America to its own people.

Document 11

Veto of the Emergency Relief and Construction Bill
President Herbert Hoover
July 11, 1932

By mid-1932 the unemployment rate stood at nearly 20 percent of the total labor force. In some industries, such as steel and automobiles, the rate was closer to 50 percent. These were levels unprecedented in U.S. history, and the number of unemployed people overwhelmed the ability of private charities and state and local governments to provide relief. Many Democrats took note of Hoover's willingness to assist banks, railroads, and other large concerns through the Reconstruction Finance Corporation (Document 7); why not, then, allow the RFC to extend loans to state and local governments and private charities so that they could continue their relief efforts and expand public works? The president responded with a stinging veto message; however, just a few weeks later he signed a compromise bill, the Relief and Reconstruction Act, which authorized the RFC to finance up to $15 billion in what Hoover called "self-liquidating" public works – that is, projects such as toll roads, which might at some point pay for themselves. The bill also allowed the RFC to lend up to $300 million to state and local governments to sustain their relief efforts.

Source: Herbert Hoover, "Veto of the Emergency Relief and Construction Bill," July 11, 1932. Online by Gerhard Peters and John T. Woolley, The American Presidency Project. http://www.presidency.ucsb.edu/ws/?pid=23157.

I am returning herewith, without my approval, H. R. 12445, "Emergency relief and construction act of 1932"....

. . . .I have expressed myself at various times upon the extreme undesirability of increasing expenditure on nonproductive public works beyond the $500,000,000 of construction already in the Budget. It is an ultimate burden upon the taxpayer. It unbalances the Budget after all our efforts to attain that object. It does not accomplish the purpose in creating employment for which it is designed, as is shown by the reports of the technical heads of the bureaus concerned that the total annual direct employment under this program would be less than 100,000 out of the 8,000,000 unemployed. Strongly as I feel that this departs from sound public finance, and that it does not accomplish the purpose of which it is instituted, I am not prepared for this reason alone to withhold my assent to the bill provided there is a proper provision that (except for expenditure on public roads which is deductible from future appropriations, together with park and forest roads and trails) these works should not be initiated except on certificate of the Secretary of the Treasury that the moneys necessary for such expenditure are available or can be obtained without interference with current financing operations of the Government. The expression of this principle in the present bill is not in this form and is not adequate....

[This bill represents a] major extension of the authority of the Reconstruction Finance Corporation. The creation of the Reconstruction Finance Corporation itself was warranted only as a temporary measure to safely pass a grave national emergency which would otherwise have plunged us into destructive panic in consequence of the financial collapse in Europe. Its purpose was to preserve the credit structure of the nation and thereby protect every individual in his employment, his farm, his bank deposits, his insurance policy, and his other savings, all of which are directly or indirectly in the safe keeping of the great fiduciary institutions. Its authority was limited practically to loans to institutions which are under Federal or State control or regulation and affected with public interest. These functions were and are in the interest of the whole people....

....[M]y major objection to the measure, as now formulated, lies in the inclusion of an extraordinary extension of authority to the Reconstruction Corporation to make loans to "individuals, to trusts, estates, partnerships, corporations (public or quasi public or private), to associations, joint-stock companies, States, political subdivisions of States, municipalities, or political subdivisions thereof."

The following objections are directed to this particular provision:

First. This expansion of authority of the Reconstruction Corporation would mean loans against security for any conceivable purpose on any conceivable security to anybody who wants money. It would place the Government in private business in such fashion as to violate the very principle of public relations upon which we have builded our Nation, and render insecure its very foundations. Such action would make the Reconstruction Corporation the greatest banking and money-lending institution of all history. It would constitute a gigantic centralization of banking and finance to which the American people have been properly opposed for the past 100 years. The purpose of the expansion is no longer in the spirit of solving a great major emergency but to establish a privilege whether it serves a great national end or not.

Second. One of the most serious objections is that under the provisions of this bill those amongst 16,000 municipalities and the different States that have failed courageously to meet their responsibilities and to balance their own budgets would dump their financial liabilities and problems upon the Federal Government. All proper and insuperable difficulties they may confront in providing relief for distress are fully and carefully met under other provisions in the bill.

Third. The board of directors of the Reconstruction Corporation informed me unanimously that miscellaneous loans under this provision are totally impracticable and unworkable. It would be necessary to set up a huge bureaucracy, to establish branches in every county and town in the United States. The task of organization, of finding competent personnel, would not be a matter of months but of years. Hundreds of thousands of applications representing every diversity of business and interest in the country would immediately flood the board, all of which must be passed upon by seven men. The directors would be dependent upon the ability and integrity of local committees and branch managers. Every political pressure would be assembled for particular persons. It would be within the power of these agencies to dictate the welfare of millions of people, to discriminate between competitive business at will, and to deal favor and disaster amongst them. If it be contended that these hundreds of thousands of miscellaneous loans will be used to increase employment, then an additional bureaucracy for espionage must follow up each case and assure that these funds be used for such purpose.

Fourth. The sole limitation under the bill is that loans shall be secured and that the borrowers shall not have been able to obtain loans from private institutions upon acceptable terms. This at once throws upon the corporation all the doubtful loans in the United States. It would result in every financial institution calling upon their customers whom they regard as less adequately secured to discharge their loans and to demand the money from the Government through the Reconstruction Corporation. The organization would be constantly subjected to conspiracies and raids of predatory interests, individuals, and private corporations. Huge losses and great scandals must inevitably result. It would mean the squandering of hundreds of millions of public funds to be ultimately borne by the taxpayer.

Fifth. The bill provides only the funds to the corporation which the Senate with reason deemed the minimum necessary to aid construction projects and to cover loans to the States in aid of distress. There is, therefore, no provision in the bill for any sum of money for the purpose of these miscellaneous loans. The corporation would thereby be charged with a duty impossible to carry out in practice with no additional funds with which to make loans unless the unemployment projects and the loans to the States are abandoned or seriously curtailed and the fundamental purpose of the legislation defeated.

Sixth. Under the new obligations upon the Reconstruction Corporation to finance the additional construction activities and loans to the States in addition to its present activities it will be necessary for the corporation to place over $3,000,000,000 of securities. It can place these securities only because the credit of the United States is pledged to secure these obligations. To sell any such vast amount of securities at a time like this is a difficult enough task, strong as is the credit of the United States, without having the credit of the Government undermined by the character of use to which it is directed that these moneys should be applied. As long as obligations of the corporation are based on wholly sound securities for self-liquidating purposes, of which early repayment is assured, there is no burden upon the taxpayer. There is an assurance of a strengthening of the economic situation. But if the funds of the corporation are to be squandered by making loans for the purposes here referred to, it will be at once evident that the credit of the Government is being misused and it is not too much to say that if such a measure should become law it further weakens the whole economic situation by threatening the credit of the United States Government with grave consequences of disaster to our people.

CONCLUSION

This proposal violates every sound principle of public finance and of government. Never before has so dangerous a suggestion been seriously made to our country. Never before has so much power for evil been placed at the unlimited discretion of seven individuals.

In view of the short time left to the Congress for consideration of this legislation and of the urgent need for sound relief measures, the necessity of which I have on several occasions urged upon the Congress, I recommend that a compromise should be reached upon terms suggested by members of both Houses and both parties, and that the Congress should not adjourn until this is accomplished. Such compromise proposal should embrace:

First. Title I of H.R. 12445, the act now under consideration, covering provisions for loans to States in amount of $300,000,000 for the care of distress in States where needed.

Second. Title III of this act, with the provision made applicable to all parts of the title except for roads and trails, that such works shall not be initiated except on certificate of the Secretary of the Treasury that the funds necessary are available and can be obtained without interference with the current financing operations of the Government.

Third. That there should be substituted for Title II the substance of the provisions in the substitute bill introduced by Senator Wagner[1] and passed by the Senate, or Senate bill 4822, introduced by Senator Barbour,[2] or section 4 of the substitute bill introduced by Representative Hawley.[3] Among them they provide not only loans for construction work of projects of self-liquidating character but also essential aids to agriculture.

Fourth. That the corporation be authorized to increase its issues of capital by $1,800,000,000 for these purposes.

With the utmost seriousness I urge the Congress to enact a relief measure, but I can not approve the measure before me, fraught as it is with possibilities of misfeasance and special privileges, so impracticable of administration, so dangerous to public credit and so damaging to our whole conception of governmental relations to the people as to bring far more distress than it will cure.

---

[1] Sen. Robert Wagner (D-NY) was the sponsor of the original legislation.
[2] Sen. W. Warren Barbour (R-NJ)
[3] Rep. Willis C. Hawley (R-OR)

Document 12

Statement on the Dispersal of the Bonus Army
President Herbert Hoover
July 29, 1932

One of the most disastrous moments for Hoover's reelection campaign came in late July 1932, when Attorney General William D. Mitchell ordered federal troops to eject a group of World War I veterans and their families from a shantytown they had built in the section of Washington, DC known as Anacostia Flats. They were there to demand the payment of bonuses that had been promised to them at the end of the war, but which they were not scheduled to receive until 1945. The previous year, thanks to the economic hardship brought on the by the Depression, Congress had passed (over Hoover's veto) a bill that would have authorized the government to offer veterans cash advances of up to half the value of their bonuses. Some veterans, however, demanded immediate payment of the entire amount, and organized a "Bonus Army" of roughly 17,000 people that marched on Washington in June 1932 to put pressure on Congress to authorize such a payment. The House agreed, but after the bill failed in the Senate, the Bonus Army refused to leave.

Eventually the administration ordered the eviction of the Bonus Army, but the local police proved unequal to the task and called upon the federal authorities for assistance. The president, while rejecting the advice of some in his administration that he declare martial law, did authorize his secretary of war to have the protesters removed by force. On July 28, units of the U.S. Army under the command of Gen. Douglas MacArthur drove them out of their shanties using tanks and tear gas. The following day Hoover issued the following press statement explaining his actions.

Source: Herbert Hoover, "The President's News Conference," July 29, 1932. Online by Gerhard Peters and John T. Woolley, The American Presidency Project.
http://www.presidency.ucsb.edu/ws/index.php?pid=23189&st=&st1.

THE PRESIDENT said:

A challenge to the authority of the United States Government has been met, swiftly and firmly.

After months of patient indulgence, the Government met overt lawlessness as it always must be met if the cherished processes of self-government are to be preserved. We cannot tolerate the abuse of constitutional rights by those who would destroy all government, no matter who they may be. Government cannot be coerced by mob rule.

The Department of Justice is pressing its investigation into the violence which forced the call for Army detachments, and it is my sincere hope that those agitators who inspired yesterday's attack upon the Federal authority may be brought speedily to trial in the civil courts. There can be no safe harbor in the United States of America for violence.

Order and civil tranquility are the first requisites in the great task of economic reconstruction to which our whole people now are devoting their heroic and noble energies. This national effort must not be retarded in even the slightest degree by organized lawlessness. The first obligation of my office is to uphold and defend the Constitution and the authority of the law. This I propose always to do.

For your own information, while I am on the subject, the National Red Cross has undertaken to send all the women and children out of the District who want to go home, and they are actively in the field this afternoon gathering them up. This is not for publication, just for your own information.

[Note: On the same day, the White House issued a text of the charge given to the grand jury by Judge Oscar R. Luhring of the Supreme Court of the District of Columbia. The charge, dated July 29, 1932, follows:]

The Court must take notice of the startling news appearing in the public press yesterday afternoon and this morning.

It appears that a considerable group of men, styling themselves as bonus marchers, have come to the District of Columbia from all parts of the country for the stated purpose of petitioning Congress for the passage of legislation providing for the immediate payment of the so-called bonus certificates. The number of these men has been variously estimated as from five to ten thousand.

It is reported that certain buildings in this city, belonging to the Government, were in the possession of members of this so-called bonus army, who had been requested to vacate but had declined to do so; that possession of the property by the Government was immediately necessary for the erection of new buildings which Congress had directed built; that yesterday agents of the Treasury, proceeding lawfully, went upon the premises to dispossess the bonus army, and a force of district police was present to afford protection and prevent disorder; that the bonus marchers were removed from one old building which the public contractor was waiting to demolish; that thereupon a mob of several thousand bonus marchers, coming from other quarters, proceeded to this place for the purpose of resisting the officials and of regaining possession of the Government property.

It appears that this mob, incited by some of their number, attacked the police, seriously injured a number of them, and engaged in riot and disorder. Their acts of resistance reached such a point that the police authorities were unable to maintain order and the Commissioners of the District were compelled to call upon the Federal authorities for troops to restore order and protect life and property.

It is obvious that the laws of the District were violated in many respects. You should undertake an immediate investigation of these events with a view to bringing to justice those responsible for this violence, and those inciting it as well as those who took part in acts of violence.

It is reported that the mob guilty of actual violence included few men, and was made up mainly of communists, and other disorderly elements. I hope you will find that is so and that few men who have worn the Nation's uniform engaged in this violent attack upon law and order. In the confusion not many arrests have been made, and it is said that many of the most violent disturbers and criminal elements in the unlawful gathering have already scattered and escaped from the city, but it may be possible yet to identify and apprehend them and bring them to justice.

It is important that this matter be dealt with promptly. The United States Attorney is prepared to assist you in every way you may require.

That is all I have to say. The matter is in your hands.

Document 13

Letter from Bonus Army leader to President Hoover
Philo D. Burke
July 29, 1932

In spite of Hoover's defense of his handling of the Bonus Army, his popularity reached a new low when reports of the "Battle of Anacostia Flats" reached the American public. The president made the situation worse by blurting out at a press conference, "Thank God, you have a government in Washington that knows how to deal with a mob." The timing of the incident – just as the 1932 presidential campaign was getting underway – was particularly damaging to Hoover, as it played into the hands of Democrats seeking to portray him as indifferent to the suffering of the American people. Organizers of the Bonus Army Protesters – or "Bonus Expeditionary Force," as they called themselves, recalling the name given to US troops sent to World War I, the American Expeditionary Force – lent support to the Democratic campaign. The following letter to Hoover from a leading figure in the B. E. F., which was also sent as a press release to the nation's largest newspapers, is a perfect illustration of this.

Source: Letter to President Hoover from Philo D. Burke, Liaison Officer, B. E. F.; July 29, 1932, National Archives and Records Administration, Hoover Museum Digital Archives.
http://www.ecommcode.com/hoover/hooveronline/text/3.html.

President Herbert Hoover,
White House,
Washington, D. C.

Mr. Hoover:

The day of all days in the history of the United States finally arrived yesterday when the President of the United States ordered our soldiers to attack the flag of our country, the symbol of our freedom – the freedom our forefathers gave up their lives to give us. The flag we love and will ever follow, in the hands of the veterans, the most loyal soldiers of the United States, has been attacked at the orders of Andy Mellon's President.[1] Had this cowardly attack occurred in any other country in the world, our government would have justly risen up in protest and, Mr. Hoover, I am not so sure that the people of this fair land of ours will not raise their voices in protest when they understand the truth of yesterday's events.

We, the people of the richest land in the world, have been asleep at the polls too long. During the days before our prosperity was snatched from us by the thieving pack of wolves now in control of our land, we were too busy to care who looked after our affairs of state. Now that the ex-servicemen who came to the seat of our government to peacefully lobby for their just dues and better conditions for the common people of the country have been turned upon by the men at the head of our government I feel safe in predicting that the act of Mellon's President will surely prove to be a boomerang. The people of the United States certainly will not stand by and see these boys who offered their lives and went through a hell known as "no man's land" to protect this country blasted out of their peaceful, dingy shanties, which they so diligently erected for themselves and families while they were awaiting relief from the land they have served.

It is true the President had the power to misdirect our soldiers; the power to have a paid "RED"[2] throw the first missile; the power to have these soldiers and police murder, beat and gas innocent men, women and children; the power to have these soldiers and police burn not only the meager huts and hovels that these patriotic men had constructed for themselves and their families, and also the power to have hundreds of American flags that were lowered to half-mast in honor of their murdered buddy, burned like so many pieces of rags.

He had the power, Mr. Hoover, to follow all this with unsheathed sabers, fixed bayonets, rifles, machine guns, tanks, gas bombs and arson. All directed against these defenseless, unfortunate ex-heroes of our country. During the war these same boys were equipped with gas masks to protect themselves that they might fight to protect the people and the wealth of the nation. They have not stopped fighting for American people and American principals, even though Mellon's President has turned our soldiers against them in their time of need.

Did the President who is a great food administrator and engineer offer these boys or their wives and little children food, shelter or gas masks during

---

[1] Andrew Mellon, Secretary of the Treasury
[2] communist

their stay in Washington or before the disgraceful and cowardly eviction took place?

Most of these people lost their homes through the greed and lust of the few in power. Now these same few drive them out of their crude huts and hovels they had erected for shelter. They were cowardly acts, unpardonable sins, Mr. Hoover; don't forget that, for I am sure the people of the country will be with you in remembering these depredations.

I don't expect that this letter will ever reach your eye, nor do I expect it to be published in the press of our land, but I am giving the press a copy of it and, at the same time, I am dedicating the rest of my life to help put this country back into the hands of the people. I am counting on plenty of help, not as a leader but as a follower.

Since I am a disabled war veteran of the world war and a loyal patriotic citizen of the United States, I stand unafraid of our President and his tactics; his powers and cheap politicians that humble themselves to him, but will loyally support each and every true American who opposes him and the conditions that have been forced upon the people of our country during his administration. I am asking the press to check delivery and receipt of this letter.

Just so you will not mistake me for a "RED" or escaped convict, I am

Philo D. Burke,
Liaison Officer, B. E. F.,
Co. C, 350th Inf. 88th Div., A. E. F.
3228922 -- C-469986,
Official Pilot's License No. 6947
White Water, Cal.

Document 14

Commonwealth Club Address
Franklin D. Roosevelt
September 23, 1932

Thanks to the economic crisis and the deep unpopularity of the Hoover administration, Roosevelt saw little reason for advancing many specific policies in his campaign speeches. His most revealing address came in late September 1932 at San Francisco's Commonwealth Club, where he offered a highly progressive view of U.S. history. The limited federal government that had been sufficient for an agrarian nation with an abundance of cheap land, he argued, was not appropriate for the modern industrial age. Whereas earlier it was enough for the government to remain on the sidelines while the economy grew, the Depression demonstrated that "the day of enlightened administration had come." The immediate task of government, he concluded, must be to build "an economic constitutional order" – a new economic declaration of rights to supplement the older Bill of Rights.

Source: *Samuel I. Rosenman and William D. Hassett, eds.,* The Public Papers and Addresses of Franklin D. Roosevelt, Volume One: The Genesis of the New Deal, 1928 -1932 *(New York: Random House, 1950), volume 1, p. 742-755. Available online from University of Michigan Digital Library:* Public Papers of the Presidents of the United States: Franklin D. Roosevelt, *p. 742 – 755.*

... The issue of Government has always been whether individual men and women will have to serve some system of Government or economics, or whether a system of Government and economics exists to serve individual men and women. This question has persistently dominated the discussion of government for many generations. On questions relating to these things men have differed, and for time immemorial it is probable that honest men will continue to differ.

The final word belongs to no man; yet we can still believe in change and in progress. Democracy, as a dear old friend of mine in Indiana, Meredith Nicholson, has called it, is a quest, a never-ending seeking for better things, and in the seeking for these things and the striving for them, there are many roads to follow. But, if we map the course of these roads, we find that there are only two general directions.

When we look about us, we are likely to forget how hard people have worked to win the privilege of government. The growth of the national Governments of Europe was a struggle for the development of a centralized force in the Nation, strong enough to impose peace upon ruling barons. In many instances the victory of the central Government, the creation of a strong central Government, was a haven of refuge to the individual. The people preferred the master far away to the exploitation and cruelty of the smaller master near at hand.

But the creators of national Government were perforce ruthless men. They were often cruel in their methods, but they did strive steadily toward something that society needed and very much wanted, a strong central State able to keep the peace, to stamp out civil war, to put the unruly nobleman in his place, and to permit the bulk of individuals to live safely. The man of ruthless force had his place in developing a pioneer country, just as he did in fixing the power of the central Government in the development of Nations. Society paid him well for his services and its development. When the development among the Nations of Europe, however, had been completed, ambition and ruthlessness, having served their term, tended to overstep their mark.

There came a growing feeling that Government was conducted for the benefit of a few who thrived unduly at the expense of all. The people sought a balancing – a limiting force. There came gradually, through town councils, trade guilds, national parliaments, by constitution and by popular participation and control, limitations on arbitrary power.

Another factor that tended to limit the power of those who ruled, was the rise of the ethical conception that a ruler bore a responsibility for the welfare of his subjects.

The American colonies were born in this struggle. The American Revolution was a turning point in it. After the Revolution the struggle continued and shaped itself in the public life of the country. There were those who because they had seen the confusion which attended the years of war for American independence surrendered to the belief that popular Government was essentially dangerous and essentially unworkable. They were honest people, my friends, and we cannot deny that their experience had warranted some measure of fear. The most brilliant, honest and able exponent of this point of view was Hamilton. He was too impatient of slow-moving methods. Fundamentally he believed that the safety of the republic lay in the autocratic strength of its Government, that the destiny of individuals was to serve that Government, and that fundamentally a great and strong group of central institutions, guided by a small group of able and public spirited citizens, could best direct all Government.

But Mr. Jefferson, in the summer of 1776, after drafting the Declaration of Independence turned his mind to the same problem and took a different view. He did not deceive himself with outward forms. Government to him was a means to an end, not an end in itself; it might be either a refuge and a help or a threat and a danger, depending on the circumstances. We find him carefully analyzing the society for which he was to organize a Government. "We have no paupers. The great mass of our population is of laborers, our rich who cannot live without labor, either manual or professional, being few and of moderate wealth. Most of the laboring class possess property, cultivate their own lands, have families and from the demand for their labor, are enabled to exact from the rich and the competent such prices as enable them to feed abundantly, clothe above mere decency, to labor moderately and raise their families."[1]

These people, he considered, had two sets of rights, those of "personal competency"[2] and those involved in acquiring and possessing property. By "personal competency" he meant the right of free thinking, freedom of forming and expressing opinions, and freedom of personal living, each man according to his own Rights. To insure the first set of rights, a Government must so order its functions as not to interfere with the individual. But even Jefferson realized that the exercise of the property rights might so interfere with the rights of the individual that the Government, without whose assistance the property rights could not exist, must intervene, not to destroy individualism, but to protect it.

You are familiar with the great political duel which followed; and how Hamilton, and his friends, building toward a dominant centralized power were at length defeated in the great election of 1800, by Mr. Jefferson's party. Out of

---

[1] Roosevelt paraphrases Jefferson's letter to Thomas Cooper, September 10, 1814, *The Papers of Thomas Jefferson*, Retirement Series, vol. 7, *28 November 1813 to 30 September 1814*, ed. J. Jefferson Looney (Princeton: Princeton University Press, 2010), 649–655.

[2] The distinction between "rights of personal competency" and "natural rights," the latter including the right of "acquiring and possessing property," was actually made by Thomas Paine in a 1789 letter he addressed to Jefferson.
Gilbert Chinard, who wrote a biography of Jefferson in 1929, mistakenly attributed the letter to Jefferson. The letter is available online from the Thomas Paine National Historical Association: http://www.thomaspaine.org/letters/thomas-jefferson/to-thomas-jefferson-1789.html.

that duel came the two parties, Republican and Democratic, as we know them today.

So began, in American political life, the new day, the day of the individual against the system, the day in which individualism was made the great watchword of American life. The happiest of economic conditions made that day long and splendid. On the Western frontier, land was substantially free. No one, who did not shirk the task of earning a living, was entirely without opportunity to do so. Depressions could, and did, come and go; but they could not alter the fundamental fact that most of the people lived partly by selling their labor and partly by extracting their livelihood from the soil, so that starvation and dislocation were practically impossible. At the very worst there was always the possibility of climbing into a covered wagon and moving west where the untilled prairies afforded a haven for men to whom the East did not provide a place. So great were our natural resources that we could offer this relief not only to our own people, but to the distressed of all the world; we could invite immigration from Europe, and welcome it with open arms. Traditionally, when a depression came a new section of land was opened in the West; and even our temporary misfortune served our manifest destiny.

It was in the middle of the nineteenth century that a new force was released and a new dream created. The force was what is called the industrial revolution, the advance of steam and machinery and the rise of the forerunners of the modern industrial plant. The dream was the dream of an economic machine, able to raise the standard of living for everyone; to bring luxury within the reach of the humblest; to annihilate distance by steam power and later by electricity, and to release everyone from the drudgery of the heaviest manual toil. It was to be expected that this would necessarily affect Government. Heretofore, Government had merely been called upon to produce conditions within which people could live happily, labor peacefully, and rest secure. Now it was called upon to aid in the consummation of this new dream. There was, however, a shadow over the dream. To be made real, it required use of the talents of men of tremendous will and tremendous ambition, since by no other force could the problems of financing and engineering and new developments be brought to a consummation.

So manifest were the advantages of the machine age, however, that the United States fearlessly, cheerfully, and, I think, rightly, accepted the bitter with the sweet. It was thought that no price was too high to pay for the advantages which we could draw from a finished industrial system. This history of the last half century is accordingly in large measure a history of a group of financial Titans, whose methods were not scrutinized with too much care and who were honored in proportion as they produced the results, irrespective of the means they used. The financiers who pushed the railroads to the Pacific were always ruthless, often wasteful, and frequently corrupt; but they did build railroads, and we have them today. It has been estimated that the American investor paid for the American railway system more than three times over in the process; but despite this fact the net advantage was to the United States. As long as we had free land; as long as population was growing by leaps and bounds; as long as our industrial plants were insufficient to supply our own needs, society chose to give the ambitious man free play and unlimited reward provided only that he produced the economic plant so much desired.

During this period of expansion, there was equal opportunity for all and the business of Government was not to interfere but to assist in the development of industry. This was done at the request of business men themselves. The tariff was originally imposed for the purpose of "fostering our infant industry," a phrase I think the older among you will remember as a political issue not so long ago. The railroads were subsidized, sometimes by grants of money, oftener by grants of land; some of the most valuable oil lands in the United States were granted to assist the financing of the railroad which pushed through the Southwest. A nascent merchant marine was assisted by grants of money, or by mail subsidies, so that our steam shipping might ply the seven seas. Some of my friends tell me that they do not want the Government in business. With this I agree; but I wonder whether they realize the implications of the past. For while it has been American doctrine that the Government must not go into business in competition with private enterprises, still it has been traditional, particularly in Republican administrations, for business urgently to ask the Government to put at private disposal all kinds of Government assistance. The same man who tells you that he does not want to see the Government interfere in business – and he means it, and has plenty of good reasons for saying so – is the first to go to Washington and ask the Government for a prohibitory tariff on his product. When things get just bad enough as they did two years ago, he will go with equal speed to the United States Government and ask for a loan; and the Reconstruction Finance Corporation is the outcome of it. Each group has sought protection from the Government for its own special interests, without realizing that the function of Government must be to favor no small group at the expense of its duty to protect the rights of personal freedom and of private property of all its citizens.

In retrospect we can now see that the turn of the tide came with the turn of the century. We were reaching our last frontier; there was no more free land and our industrial combinations had become great uncontrolled and irresponsible units of power within the State. Clear-sighted men saw with fear the danger that opportunity would no longer be equal; that the growing corporation, like the feudal baron of old, might threaten the economic freedom of individuals to earn a living. In that hour, our antitrust laws were born. The cry was raised against the great corporations. Theodore Roosevelt, the first great Republican Progressive, fought a Presidential campaign on the issue of "trust busting" and talked freely about malefactors of great wealth. If the government had a policy it was rather to turn the clock back, to destroy the large combinations and to return to the time when every man owned his individual small business.

This was impossible; Theodore Roosevelt, abandoning the idea of "trust busting," was forced to work out a difference between "good" trusts and "bad" trusts. The Supreme Court set forth the famous "rule of reason" by which it seems to have meant that a concentration of industrial power was permissible if the method by which it got its power, and the use it made of that power, were reasonable.[3]

Woodrow Wilson, elected in 1912, saw the situation more clearly. Where Jefferson had feared the encroachment of political power on the lives of individuals, Wilson knew that the new power was financial. He saw, in the highly centralized economic system, the despot of the twentieth century, on whom great masses of individuals relied for their safety and their livelihood, and whose irresponsibility and greed (if they were not controlled) would reduce them to starvation and penury. The concentration of financial power had not proceeded so far in 1912 as it has today; but it had grown far enough for Mr. Wilson to realize fully its implications. It is interesting, now, to read his speeches. What is called "radical" today (and I have reason to know whereof I speak) is mild compared to the campaign of Mr. Wilson. "No man can deny," he said, "that the lines of endeavor have more and more narrowed and stiffened; no man who knows anything about the development of industry in this country can have failed to observe that the larger kinds of credit are more and more difficult to obtain unless you obtain them upon terms of uniting your efforts with those who already control the industry of the country, and nobody can fail to observe that every man who tries to set himself up in competition with any process of manufacture which has taken place under the control of large combinations of capital will presently find himself either squeezed out or

---

[3] The rule of reason is a judicial principle used in anti-trust or monopoly cases. It holds that a trade practice violates the Sherman Anti-Trust Act (1890) if that practice is, based on economic considerations, an unreasonable constraint on trade.

obliged to sell and allow himself to be absorbed."[4] Had there been no World War – had Mr. Wilson been able to devote eight years to domestic instead of to international affairs – we might have had a wholly different situation at the present time. However, the then distant roar of European cannon, growing ever louder, forced him to abandon the study of this issue. The problem he saw so clearly is left with us as a legacy; and no one of us on either side of the political controversy can deny that it is a matter of grave concern to the Government.

A glance at the situation today only too clearly indicates that equality of opportunity as we have known it no longer exists. Our industrial plant is built; the problem just now is whether under existing conditions it is not overbuilt. Our last frontier has long since been reached, and there is practically no more free land. More than half of our people do not live on the farms or on lands and cannot derive a living by cultivating their own property. There is no safety valve in the form of a Western prairie to which those thrown out of work by the Eastern economic machines can go for a new start. We are not able to invite the immigration from Europe to share our endless plenty. We are now providing a drab living for our own people.

Our system of constantly rising tariffs has at last reacted against us to the point of closing our Canadian frontier on the north, our European markets on the east, many of our Latin-American markets to the south, and a goodly proportion of our Pacific markets on the west, through the retaliatory tariffs of those countries. It has forced many of our great industrial institutions which exported their surplus production to such countries, to establish plants in such countries, within the tariff walls. This has resulted in the reduction of the operation of their American plants, and opportunity for employment.

Just as freedom to farm has ceased, so also the opportunity in business has narrowed. It still is true that men can start small enterprises, trusting to native shrewdness and ability to keep abreast of competitors; but area after area has been pre-empted altogether by the great corporations, and even in the fields which still have no great concerns, the small man starts under a handicap. The unfeeling statistics of the past three decades show that the independent business man is running a losing race. Perhaps he is forced to the wall; perhaps he cannot command credit; perhaps he is "squeezed out," in Mr. Wilson's words, by highly organized corporate competitors, as your corner grocery man

---

[4] This passage is from Woodrow Wilson's "The Old Order Changeth," which is the first chapter in his book, *The New Freedom*. The book is a collection of campaign speeches Wilson made while running for President in 1912.

can tell you. Recently a careful study was made of the concentration of business in the United States. It showed that our economic life was dominated by some six hundred odd corporations who controlled two-thirds of American industry. Ten million small business men divided the other third. More striking still, it appeared that if the process of concentration goes on at the same rate, at the end of another century we shall have all American industry controlled by a dozen corporations, and run by perhaps a hundred men. Put plainly, we are steering a steady course toward economic oligarchy, if we are not there already.

Clearly, all this calls for a re-appraisal of values. A mere builder of more industrial plants, a creator of more railroad systems, an organizer of more corporations, is as likely to be a danger as a help. The day of the great promoter or the financial Titan, to whom we granted anything if only he would build, or develop, is over. Our task now is not discovery or exploitation of natural resources, or necessarily producing more goods. It is the soberer, less dramatic business of administering resources and plants already in hand, of seeking to reestablish foreign markets for our surplus production, of meeting the problem of underconsumption, of adjusting production to consumption, of distributing wealth and products more equitably, of adapting existing economic organizations to the service of the people. The day of enlightened administration has come.

Just as in older times the central Government was first a haven of refuge, and then a threat, so now in a closer economic system the central and ambitious financial unit is no longer a servant of national desire, but a danger. I would draw the parallel one step farther. We did not think because national Government had become a threat in the 18th century that therefore we should abandon the principle of national Government. Nor today should we abandon the principle of strong economic units called corporations, merely because their power is susceptible of easy abuse. In other times we dealt with the problem of an unduly ambitious central Government by modifying it gradually into a constitutional democratic Government. So today we are modifying and controlling our economic units.

As I see it, the task of Government in its relation to business is to assist the development of an economic declaration of rights, an economic constitutional order. This is the common task of statesman and business man. It is the minimum requirement of a more permanently safe order of things.

Happily, the times indicate that to create such an order not only is the proper policy of Government, but it is the only line of safety for our economic structures as well. We know, now, that these economic units cannot exist unless prosperity is uniform, that is, unless purchasing power is well distributed throughout every group in the Nation. That is why even the most selfish of corporations for its own interest would be glad to see wages restored and unemployment ended and to bring the Western farmer back to his accustomed level of prosperity and to assure a permanent safety to both groups. That is why some enlightened industries themselves endeavor to limit the freedom of action of each man and business group within the industry in the common interest of all; why business men everywhere are asking a form of organization which will bring the scheme into balance, even though it may in some measure qualify the freedom of action of individual units within the business.

The exposition need not further be elaborated. It is brief and incomplete, but you will be able to expand it in terms of your own business or occupation without difficulty. I think everyone who has actually entered the economic struggle – which means everyone who was not born to safe wealth – knows in his own experience and his own life that we have now to apply the earlier concepts of American Government to the conditions of today.

The Declaration of Independence discusses the problem of Government in terms of a contract. Government is a relation of give and take, a contract, perforce, if we would follow the thinking out of which it grew. Under such a contract rulers were accorded power, and the people consented to that power on consideration that they be accorded certain rights. The task of statesmanship has always been the re-definition of these rights in terms of a changing and growing social order. New conditions impose new requirements upon Government and those who conduct Government. . . .

I feel that we are coming to a view through the drift of our legislation and our public thinking in the past quarter century that private economic power is, to enlarge an old phrase, a public trust as well. I hold that continued enjoyment of that power by any individual or group must depend upon the fulfillment of that trust. The men who have reached the summit of American business life know this best; happily, many of these urge the binding quality of this greater social contract.

The terms of that contract are as old as the Republic, and as new as the new economic order.

Every man has a right to life; and this means that he has also a right to make a comfortable living. He may by sloth or crime decline to exercise that right; but it may not be denied him. We have no actual famine or dearth; our industrial and agricultural mechanism can produce enough and to spare. Our Government formal and informal, political and economic, owes to everyone an avenue to possess himself of a portion of that plenty sufficient for his needs, through his own work.

Every man has a right to his own property; which means a right to be assured, to the fullest extent attainable, in the safety of his savings. By no other means can men carry the burdens of those parts of life which, in the nature of things, afford no chance of labor: childhood, sickness, old age. In all thought of property, this right is paramount; all other property rights must yield to it. If, in accord with this principle, we must restrict the operations of the speculator, the manipulator, even the financier, I believe we must accept the restriction as needful, not to hamper individualism but to protect it.

These two requirements must be satisfied, in the main, by the individuals who claim and hold control of the great industrial and financial combinations which dominate so large a part of our industrial life. They have undertaken to be, not business men, but princes of property. I am not prepared to say that the system which produces them is wrong. I am very clear that they must fearlessly and competently assume the responsibility which goes with the power. So many enlightened business men know this that the statement would be little more than a platitude, were it not for an added implication.

This implication is, briefly, that the responsible heads of finance and industry instead of acting each for himself, must work together to achieve the common end. They must, where necessary, sacrifice this or that private advantage; and in reciprocal self-denial must seek a general advantage. It is here that formal Government – political Government, if you choose – comes in. Whenever in the pursuit of this objective the lone wolf, the unethical competitor, the reckless promoter, the Ishmael[5] or Insull[6] whose hand is against every man's, declines to join in achieving an end recognized as being for the public welfare, and threatens to drag the industry back to a state of anarchy, the Government may properly be asked to apply restraint. Likewise,

---

[5] This is a curious application of the story of Ishmael, told in Genesis (see especially 16:11-13 and 21:1-20). Ismael roamed in the wilderness as a hunter, untamed by tribal customs, because Sarah's jealousy of Hagar, Ishmael's mother (Abraham's concubine) resulted in Ishmael and Hagar being cast out of the family.

[6] Here Roosevelt is referring to Samuel Insull, a financier who had built up a massive empire of utility companies and railroads through the use of holding companies. When the Great Depression caused the structure to collapse, some 600,000 stockholders lost their investments. Fearing prosecution, Insull fled to France, but his name was frequently invoked by supporters of the New Deal who argued for greater government oversight of securities trading.

should the group ever use its collective power contrary to the public welfare, the Government must be swift to enter and protect the public interest.

The Government should assume the function of economic regulation only as a last resort, to be tried only when private initiative, inspired by high responsibility, with such assistance and balance as Government can give, has finally failed. As yet there has been no final failure, because there has been no attempt; and I decline to assume that this Nation is unable to meet the situation.

The final term of the high contract was for liberty and the pursuit of happiness. We have learned a great deal of both in the past century. We know that individual liberty and individual happiness mean nothing unless both are ordered in the sense that one man's meat is not another man's poison. We know that the old "rights of personal competency," the right to read, to think, to speak, to choose and live a mode of life, must be respected at all hazards. We know that liberty to do anything which deprives others of those elemental rights is outside the protection of any compact; and that Government in this regard is the maintenance of a balance, within which every individual may have a place if he will take it; in which every individual may find safety if he wishes it; in which every individual may attain such power as his ability permits, consistent with his assuming the accompanying responsibility.

All this is a long, slow talk. Nothing is more striking than the simple innocence of the men who insist, whenever an objective is present, on the prompt production of a patent scheme guaranteed to produce a result. Human endeavor is not so simple as that. Government includes the art of formulating a policy, and using the political technique to attain so much of that policy as will receive general support; persuading, leading, sacrificing, teaching always, because the greatest duty of a statesman is to educate. But in the matters of which I have spoken, we are learning rapidly, in a severe school. The lessons so learned must not be forgotten, even in the mental lethargy of a speculative upturn. We must build toward the time when a major depression cannot occur again; and if this means sacrificing the easy profits of inflationist booms, then let them go; and good riddance.

Faith in America, faith in our tradition of personal responsibility, faith in our institutions, faith in ourselves demand that we recognize the new terms of the old social contract. We shall fulfill them, as we fulfilled the obligation of the apparent Utopia which Jefferson imagined for us in 1776, and which Jefferson, Roosevelt and Wilson sought to bring to realization. We must do so, lest a rising tide of misery, engendered by our common failure, engulf us all. But failure is not an American habit; and in the strength of great hope we must all shoulder our common load.

Document 15

Consequences of the Proposed "New Deal"
President Herbert Hoover
October 31, 1932

As the 1932 presidential campaign drew to a close, Hoover fired back against his Democratic challenger in a speech at Madison Square Garden in New York City. He seized on proposals made by Democratic leaders in Congress, and Roosevelt's own words from the Commonwealth Club address, to portray the opposition as dangerously irresponsible and committed to a philosophy at odds with that of the American Founding. The president reminded his listeners of the progress made in the past thirty years, and while he admitted that the past three years had brought considerable distress, he asserted that the system established by the Founders in the Constitution had proven capable of weathering the worst of the crisis.

Source: "Address at Madison Square Garden in New York City," October 31, 1932. Online by Gerhard Peters and John T. Woolley, The American Presidency Project. http://www.presidency.ucsb.edu/ws/?pid=23317.

This campaign is more than a contest between two men. It is more than a contest between two parties. It is a contest between two philosophies of government.

We are told by the opposition that we must have a change, that we must have a new deal. It is not the change that comes from normal development of national life to which I object or you object, but the proposal to alter the whole foundations of our national life which have been builded through generations of testing and struggle, and of the principles upon which we have made this Nation. The expressions of our opponents must refer to important changes in our economic and social system and our system of government; otherwise they would be nothing but vacuous words. And I realize that in this time of distress many of our people are asking whether our social and economic system is incapable of that great primary function of providing security and comfort of life to all of the firesides of 25 million homes in America, whether our social system provides for the fundamental development and progress of our people, and whether our form of government is capable of originating and sustaining that security and progress.

This question is the basis upon which our opponents are appealing to the people in their fear and their distress. They are proposing changes and so-called new deals which would destroy the very foundations of the American system of life.

Our people should consider the primary facts before they come to the judgment – not merely through political agitation, the glitter of promise, and the discouragement of temporary hardships – whether they will support changes which radically affect the whole system which has been builded during these six generations of the toil of our fathers. They should not approach the question in the despair with which our opponents would clothe it.

Our economic system has received abnormal shocks during the last three years which have temporarily dislocated its normal functioning. These shocks have in a large sense come from without our borders, and I say to you that our system of government has enabled us to take such strong action as to prevent the disaster which would otherwise have come to this Nation. It has enabled us further to develop measures and programs which are now demonstrating their ability to bring about restoration and progress.

We must go deeper than platitudes and emotional appeals of the public platform in the campaign if we will penetrate to the full significance of the changes which our opponents are attempting to float upon the wave of distress and discontent from the difficulties through which we have passed. We can find what our opponents would do after searching the record of their appeals to discontent, to group and sectional interest. To find that, we must search for them in the legislative acts which they sponsored and passed in the Democratic-controlled House of Representatives in the last session of Congress. We must look into both the measures for which they voted and in which they were defeated. We must inquire whether or not the Presidential and Vice-Presidential candidates have disavowed those acts. If they have not, we must conclude that they form a portion and are a substantial indication of the profound changes in the new deal which is proposed.

And we must look still further than this as to what revolutionary changes have been proposed by the candidates themselves.

We must look into the type of leaders who are campaigning for the Democratic ticket, whose philosophies have been well known all their lives and whose demands for a change in the American system are frank and forceful. I can respect the sincerity of these men in their desire to change our form of government and our social and our economic system, though I shall do my best tonight to prove they are wrong. I refer particularly to Senator Norris,[1] Senator La Follette,[2] Senator Cutting,[3] Senator Huey Long,[4] Senator Wheeler,[5] William Randolph Hearst,[6] and other exponents of a social philosophy different from the traditional philosophies of the American people. Unless these men have felt assurance of support to their ideas they certainly would not be supporting these candidates and the Democratic Party. The zeal of these men indicates that they must have some sure confidence that they will have a voice in the administration of this Government.

I may say at once that the changes proposed from all these Democratic principals and their allies are of the most profound and penetrating character. If they are brought about, this will not be the America which we have known in the past....

Now, our American system is founded on a peculiar conception of self-government designed to maintain an equality of opportunity to the individual, and through decentralization it brings about and maintains these responsibilities. The centralization of government will undermine these responsibilities and will destroy the system itself.

Our Government differs from all previous conceptions, not only in the decentralization but also in the independence of the judicial arm of the Government.

Our Government is founded on a conception that in times of great emergency, when forces are running beyond the control of individuals or cooperative action, beyond the control of local communities or the States, then the great reserve powers of the Federal Government should be brought into action to protect the people. But when these forces have ceased there must be a return to State, local, and individual responsibility.

The implacable march of scientific discovery with its train of new inventions presents every year new problems to government and new problems to the social order. Questions often arise whether, in the face of the

---

[1] George W. Norris (R-NE)
[2] Robert M. La Follette, Jr. (R-WI)
[3] Bronson M. Cutting (R-NM)
[4] Huey Long (D-LA)
[5] Burton K. Wheeler (D-MT)
[6] William Randolph Hearst was a highly influential newspaper publisher of progressive views. Although ambitious for a leading role in New York Democratic politics, he was far more successful as a media magnate, and by the 1920s owned twenty daily and eleven Sunday newspapers in thirteen American cities.

growth of these new and gigantic tools, democracy can remain master in its own house and can preserve the fundamentals of our American system. I contend that it can, and I contend that this American system of ours has demonstrated its validity and superiority over any system yet invented by human mind. It has demonstrated it in the face of the greatest test of peacetime history – that is the emergency which we have passed in the last three years.

When the political and economic weakness of many nations of Europe, the result of the World War and its aftermath, finally culminated in the collapse of their institutions, the delicate adjustments of our economic and social and governmental life received a shock unparalleled in our history. No one knows that better than you of New York. No one knows its causes better than you. That the crisis was so great that many of the leading banks sought directly or indirectly to convert their assets into gold or its equivalent with the result that they practically ceased to function as credit institutions is known to you; that many of our citizens sought flight for their capital to other countries; that many of them attempted to hoard gold in large amounts you know. These were but superficial indications of the flight of confidence and the belief that our Government could not overcome these forces.

Yet these forces were overcome – perhaps by narrow margins – and this demonstrates that our form of government has the capacity. It demonstrates what the courage of a nation can accomplish under the resolute leadership of the Republican Party. And I say the Republican Party because our opponents, before and during the crisis, proposed no constructive program, though some of their members patriotically supported ours for which they deserve on every occasion the applause of patriotism. Later on in the critical period, the Democratic House of Representatives did develop the real thought and ideas of the Democratic Party. They were so destructive that they had to be defeated. They did delay the healing of our wounds for months.

Now, in spite of all these obstructions we did succeed. Our form of government did prove itself equal to the task. We saved this Nation from a generation of chaos and degeneration; we preserved the savings, the insurance policies, gave a fighting chance to men to hold their homes. We saved the integrity of our Government and the honesty of the American dollar. And we installed measures which today are bringing back recovery. Employment, agriculture, and business – all of these show the steady, if slow, healing of an enormous wound.

As I left Washington, our Government departments communicated to me the fact that the October statistics on employment show that since the first day of July, the men returned to work in the United States exceed one million.

I therefore contend that the problem of today is to continue these measures and policies to restore the American system to its normal functioning, to repair the wounds it has received, to correct the weaknesses and evils which would defeat that system. To enter upon a series of deep changes now, to embark upon this inchoate new deal which has been propounded in this campaign would not only undermine and destroy our American system but it will delay for months and years the possibility of recovery....

Now, to go back to my major thesis – the thesis of the longer view. Before we enter into courses of deep-seated change and of the new deal, I would like you to consider what the results of this American system have been during the last 30 years – that is, a single generation. For if it can be demonstrated that by this means, our unequaled political, social, and economic system, we have secured a lift in the standards of living and the diffusion of comfort and hope to men and women, the growth of equality of opportunity, the widening of all opportunity such as had never been seen in the history of the world, then we should not tamper with it and destroy it, but on the contrary we should restore it and, by its gradual improvement and perfection, foster it into new performance for our country and for our children.

Now, if we look back over the last generation we find that the number of our families and, therefore, our homes, has increased from about 16 to about 25 million, or 62 percent. In that time we have builded for them 15 million new and better homes. We have equipped 20 million out of these 25 million homes with electricity; thereby we have lifted infinite drudgery from women and men. The barriers of time and space have been swept away in this single generation. Life has been made freer, the intellectual vision of every individual has been expanded by the installation of 20 million telephones, 12 million radios, and the service of 20 million automobiles. Our cities have been made magnificent with beautiful buildings, parks, and playgrounds. Our countryside has been knit together with splendid roads. We have increased by 12 times the use of electrical power and thereby taken sweat from the backs of men. In the broad sweep real wages and purchasing power of men and women have steadily increased. New comforts have steadily come to them. The hours of labor have decreased, the 12-hour day has disappeared, even the 9-hour day has almost gone. We are now advocating the 5-day week. During this generation the portals of opportunity to our children have ever widened. While our population grew by but 62 percent, yet we have increased the number of children in high schools by 700 percent, and those in institutions of higher learning by 300 percent. With all our spending, we multiplied by six times the savings in our banks and in our building and loan associations. We multiplied by 1,200 percent the amount of our life insurance. With the enlargement of our leisure we have come to a fuller life; we have gained new visions of hope; we are more nearly realizing our national aspirations and giving increased scope to the creative power of every individual and expansion of every man's mind.

Now, our people in these 30 years have grown in the sense of social responsibility. There is profound progress in the relation of the employer to the employed. We have more nearly met with a full hand the most sacred obligation of man, that is, the responsibility of a man to his neighbor. Support to our schools, hospitals, and institutions for the care of the afflicted surpassed in totals by billions the proportionate service in any period in any nation in the history of the world.

Now, three years ago there came a break in this progress. A break of the same type we have met 15 times in a century and yet have recovered from. But 18 months later came a further blow by the shocks transmitted to us from earthquakes of the collapse of nations throughout the world as the aftermath of the World War. The workings of this system of ours were dislocated. Businessmen and farmers suffered, and millions of men and women are out of jobs. Their distress is bitter. I do not seek to minimize it, but we may thank God that in view of the storm that we have met that 30 million still have jobs, and yet this does not distract our thoughts from the suffering of the 10 million.

But I ask you what has happened. This 30 years of incomparable improvement in the scale of living, of advance of comfort and intellectual life, of security, of inspiration, and ideals did not arise without right principles animating the American system which produced them. Shall that system be discarded because vote-seeking men appeal to distress and say that the machinery is all wrong and that it must be abandoned or tampered with? Is it not more sensible to realize the simple fact that some extraordinary force has been thrown into the mechanism which has temporarily deranged its operation? Is it not wiser to believe that the difficulty is not with the principles upon which our American system is founded and designed through all these generations of inheritance? Should not our purpose be to restore the normal working of that system which has brought to us such immeasurable gifts, and not to destroy it?

Now, in order to indicate to you that the proposals of our opponents will endanger or destroy our system, I propose to analyze a few of them in their relation to these fundamentals which I have stated.

First: A proposal of our opponents that would break down the American system is the expansion of governmental expenditure by yielding to sectional and group raids on the Public Treasury. The extension of governmental expenditures beyond the minimum limit necessary to conduct the proper functions of the Government enslaves men to work for the Government. If we combine the whole governmental expenditures – national, State, and municipal – we will find that before the World War each citizen worked, theoretically, 25 days out of each year for the Government. In 1924, he worked 46 days out of the year for the Government. Today he works, theoretically, for the support of all forms of Government 61 days out of the year.

No nation can conscript its citizens for this proportion of men's and women's time without national impoverishment and without the destruction of their liberties. Our Nation cannot do it without destruction to our whole conception of the American system. The Federal Government has been forced in this emergency to unusual expenditure, but in partial alleviation of these extraordinary and unusual expenditures the Republican administration has made a successful effort to reduce the ordinary running expenses of the Government....

Second: Another proposal of our opponents which would destroy the American system is that of inflation of the currency. The bill which passed the last session of the Democratic House called upon the Treasury of the United States to issue $2,300 million in paper currency that would be unconvertible into solid values. Call it what you will, greenbacks or fiat money. It was the same nightmare which overhung our own country for years after the Civil War. . . .

The use of this expedient by nations in difficulty since the war in Europe has been one of the most tragic disasters to equality of opportunity and the independence of man....

Third: In the last session of the Congress, under the personal leadership of the Democratic Vice-Presidential candidate, and their allies in the Senate, they enacted a law to extend the Government into personal banking business. I know it is always difficult to discuss banks. There seems to be much prejudice against some of them, but I was compelled to veto that bill out of fidelity to the whole American system of life and government....

They failed to pass this bill over my veto. But you must not be deceived. This is still in their purposes as a part of the new deal, and no responsible candidate has yet disavowed it.

Fourth: Another proposal of our opponents which would wholly alter our American system of life is to reduce the protective tariff to a competitive tariff for revenue....

Fifth: Another proposal is that the Government go into the power business....

I have stated unceasingly that I am opposed to the Federal Government going into the power business. I have insisted upon rigid regulation. The Democratic candidate has declared that under the same conditions which may make local action of this character desirable, he is prepared to put the Federal Government into the power business. He is being actively supported by a score of Senators in this campaign, many of whose expenses are being paid by the Democratic National Committee, who are pledged to Federal Government development and operation of electrical power....

Sixth: I may cite another instance of absolutely destructive proposals to our American system by our opponents, and I am talking about fundamentals and not superficialities.

Recently there was circulated through the unemployed in this city and other cities, a letter from the Democratic candidate in which he stated that he would support measures for the inauguration of self-liquidating public works such as the utilization of water resources, flood control, land reclamation, to provide employment for all surplus labor at all times.

I especially emphasize that promise to promote "employment for all surplus labor at all times" – by the Government. I at first could not believe that anyone would be so cruel as to hold out a hope so absolutely impossible of realization to those 10 million who are unemployed and suffering. But the authenticity of that promise has been verified. And I protest against such frivolous promises being held out to a suffering people. It is easy to demonstrate that no such employment can be found. But the point that I wish to make here and now is the mental attitude and spirit of the Democratic Party that would lead them to attempt this or to make a promise to attempt it. That is another mark of the character of the new deal and the destructive changes which mean the total abandonment of every principle upon which this Government and this American system are founded. If it were possible to give this employment to 10 million people by the Government – at the expense of the rest of the people – it would cost upwards of $9 billion a year.

The stages of this destruction would be first the destruction of Government credit, then the destruction of the value of Government securities, the destruction of every fiduciary trust in our country, insurance policies and all. It would pull down the employment of those who are still at work by the high taxes and the demoralization of credit upon which their employment is dependent. It would mean the pulling and hauling of politics for projects and measures, the favoring of localities and sections and groups. It would mean the growth of a fearful bureaucracy which, once established, could never be dislodged. If it were possible, it would mean one-third of the electorate would have Government jobs, earnest to maintain this bureaucracy and to control the political destinies of the country....

I have said before, and I want to repeat on this occasion, that the only method by which we can stop the suffering and unemployment is by returning our people to their normal jobs in their normal homes, carrying on their normal functions of living. This can be done only by sound processes of protecting and stimulating recovery of the existing system upon which we have built our progress thus far – preventing distress and giving such sound employment as we can find in the meantime....

In order that we may get at the philosophical background of the mind which pronounces the necessity for profound change in our economic system and a new deal, I would call your attention to an address delivered by the Democratic candidate in San Francisco early in October.[7]

He said:

> Our industrial plant is built. The problem just now is whether under existing conditions it is not overbuilt. Our last frontier has long since been reached. There is practically no more free land. There is no safety valve in the Western prairies where we can go for a new start. . . . The mere building of more industrial plants, the organization of more corporations is as likely to be as much a danger as a help.... Our task now is not the discovery of natural resources or necessarily the production of more goods, it is the sober, less dramatic business of administering the resources and plants already in hand. . . . establishing markets for surplus production, of meeting the problem of under-consumption, distributing the wealth and products more equitably and adopting the economic organization to the service of the people....

Now, there are many of these expressions with which no one would quarrel. But I do challenge the whole idea that we have ended the advance of America, that this country has reached the zenith of its power and the height of its development. That is the counsel of despair for the future of America. That is not the spirit by which we shall emerge from this depression. That is not the

---

[7] Franklin Roosevelt's "Commonwealth Address" (Document 14)

spirit which has made this country. If it is true, every American must abandon the road of countless progress and countless hopes and unlimited opportunity. I deny that the promise of American life has been fulfilled, for that means we have begun the decline and the fall. No nation can cease to move forward without degeneration of spirit.

I could quote from gentlemen who have emitted this same note of profound pessimism in each economic depression going back for 100 years. What the Governor[8] has overlooked is the fact that we are yet but on the frontiers of development of science and of invention. I have only to remind you that discoveries in electricity, the internal-combustion engine, the radio – all of which have sprung into being since our land was settled – have in themselves represented the greatest advances made in America. This philosophy upon which the Governor of New York proposes to conduct the Presidency of the United States is the philosophy of stagnation and of despair. It is the end of hope. The destinies of this country cannot be dominated by that spirit in action. It would be the end of the American system.

I have recited to you some of the items in the progress of this last generation. Progress in that generation was not due to the opening up of new agricultural land; it was due to the scientific research, the opening of new invention, new flashes of light from the intelligence of our people. These brought the improvements in agriculture and in industry. There are a thousand inventions for comfort and the expansion of life yet in the lockers of science that have not yet come to light. We are only upon their frontiers. As for myself, I am confident that if we do not destroy our American system, if we continue to stimulate scientific research, if we continue to give it the impulse of initiative and enterprise, if we continue to build voluntary cooperation instead of financial concentration, if we continue to build into a system of free men, my children will enjoy the same opportunity that has come to me and to the whole 120 million of my countrymen. I wish to see American Government conducted in that faith and hope....

My countrymen, the proposals of our opponents represent a profound change in American life – less in concrete proposal, bad as that may be, than by implication and by evasion. Dominantly in their spirit they represent a radical departure from the foundations of 150 years which have made this the greatest Nation in the world. This election is not a mere shift from the ins to the outs. It means the determining of the course of our Nation over a century to come.

---

[8] Franklin D. Roosevelt

Now, my conception of America is a land where men and women may walk in ordered liberty, where they may enjoy the advantages of wealth not concentrated in the hands of a few but diffused through the opportunity of all, where they build and safeguard their homes, give to their children the full opportunities of American life, where every man shall be respected in the faith that his conscience and his heart direct him to follow, and where people secure in their liberty shall have leisure and impulse to seek a fuller life. That leads to the release of the energies of men and women, to the wider vision and higher hope. It leads to opportunity for greater and greater service not alone of man to man in our country but from our country to the world. It leads to health in body and a spirit unfettered, youthful, eager with a vision stretching beyond the farthest horizons with a mind open and sympathetic and generous. But that must be builded upon our experience with the past, upon the foundations which have made this country great. It must be the product of the development of our truly American system.

Document 16

Letter to Senator Simeon Fess
President Herbert Hoover
February 21, 1933

In his final weeks in the Oval Office, as the economic crisis reached its most severe stage, Hoover traced the following brief history of the Depression. There were, Hoover claimed, two periods of economic improvement in 1932, but in each case irresponsible proposals by the Democrats undermined the business confidence necessary to sustain the recovery. Now, according to Hoover, President-elect Roosevelt had made the situation worse by refusing to commit himself to balancing the budget and maintaining a sound currency. Hoover first offered his account verbally to one of his closest political allies, Republican Senator Simeon Fess of Ohio. At Fess's request, Hoover put his remarks in writing in a letter he sent the Senator. In an accompanying letter, Hoover asked Fess to keep his remarks confidential, "unless the Democratic leaders at some future time should endeavor to mislead the American people as to the origins of the present situation."

Source: "Herbert Hoover analyzes 5 periods in the development of the history of the Depression," Simeon D. Fess Papers, 1933, National Archives Catalog, https://catalog.archives.gov/id/187086.

... Today we are on the verge of financial panic and chaos. Fear for the policies of the new administration has gripped the country. People do not await events, they act. Hoarding of currency, and of gold, has risen to a point never before known; banks are suspending [their activities] not only in isolated instances, but in one case an entire state. Prices have fallen since last autumn below the levels which debtors and creditors can meet. Men over large areas are unable or are refusing to pay their debts. Hundreds of millions of orders placed before election have been cancelled. Unemployment is increasing, there are evidences of the flight of capital from the United States to foreign countries, men have abandoned all sense of new enterprise and are striving to put their affairs in defense against disaster.

Some days before election the whole economic machine began to hesitate from the upward movement of last summer and fall. For some time after election it continued to hesitate but hoped for the best. As time has gone on, however, every development has stirred the fear and apprehension of the people. They have begun to realize what the abandonment of a successful program of this administration which was bringing rapid recovery last summer and fall now means and they are alarmed at possible new deal policies indicated by the current events. It is this fear that now dominates the national situation. It is not lack of resources, currency or credit.

The incidents which have produced this fear are clear. There was a delay by the President-elect of over two months in willingness to cooperate with us to bring about order from confusion in our foreign economic relations. There have been a multitude of speeches, bills, and statements of democratic members of Congress and others proposing inflation or tinkering with the currency. My proposals for reduction of expenditures have been ignored to the extent of over $200,000,000 by the Democratic House of Representatives. The differences between Democratic leaders and the President-elect over the basis of taxation with which to balance the budget caused them to reject the balancing of the budget. The publication by Democratic leaders of the House of the Reconstruction Corporation loans has caused runs on hundreds of banks, failures of many of them, and hoarding on a wide scale. There have been proposed in the Congress by Democratic leaders and publicly even by the President-elect, projects involving federal expenditure of tremendous dimensions which would obviously lie beyond the capacity of the federal government to borrow without tremendous depreciation in government securities. Such proposals as the bills to assume Federal responsibility for billions of mortgages, loans to municipalities for public works, the Tennessee improvement and Muscle Shoals, are all of this order.[1] The proposals of Speaker Garner[2] that a constitutional government should be abandoned because the Congress, in which there will be an overwhelming [Democratic] majority, is unable to face reduction of expenses, has started a chatter of dictatorship. The President-elect has done nothing publicly to disavow any of these proposals.

The Democratic House has defeated a measure to increase tariffs so as to prevent invasion of goods from depreciated currency countries, thus estopping increased unemployment from this source. There have been interminable

---

[1] See Document 6.
[2] John N. Garner (D-TX), the Vice-President-elect

delays and threatened defeat of the Glass Banking Bill,[3] and the Bankruptcy bill.[4]

How much this whole situation is the result of fear of the policies of the new administration is further indicated by a short review of the five distinct periods in recent economic history.

The first period began with the financial and monetary collapse of Europe in the last half of 1931 culminating in October, bringing contraction of credit and reduction of exports, falling prices of both commodities and securities, followed by great fear and apprehension in the people which was promptly represented by hoarding, bank failures, flight of capital, withdrawal of foreign gold balances with final interpretation in decreased employment, demoralization of agriculture and general stagnation.

The second period following the approval by Congress of our measures of reconstruction in early February 1932 was a period of sharp recovery over a period between 60 and 90 days; during this period public confidence was restored, prices of commodities and securities rose, currency began to return from hoarding, gold shipments abroad were greatly lessened, bank failures practically ceased and the whole country moved upward.

The third period began in April and continued through July. This was a period of a sharp debacle which was brought about by the Democratic House by the same character of proposals we now see again, that is by the original failure of the revenue bill, the failure to reduce expenditures recommended by the Executive with consequent fear that the movement toward balancing the budget would not be successful; the passage of a group of inflationary measures including the Patman Bill,[5] the Goldsborough Bill,[6] etc. The passage of a series of projects which would have required greater issues of government securities than the Treasury could support including the Garner Bills for gigantic public works and unlimited loans by the Reconstruction Corporation, etc. Public confidence was destroyed; hoarding, withdrawal of foreign gold,

---

[3] Hoover refers probably to the legislation that became the Banking Bill of 1933. This bill prohibited banks from engaging in both commercial and investment banking and established a system of insurance for bank deposits. The bill passed June 16, 1933.

[4] Hoover's reference is not clear, but may be to the Hastings-Michener Bill of 1932. See, Vincent L. Leibel, "The Chandler Act: Its Effect Upon the Law of Bankruptcy," *Fordham Law Review* 9, 3 (1940), 380–409.

[5] A bill proposed by Congressman Wright Patman (D-TX) in 1932 authorizing payment of bonuses to veterans.

[6] Thomas A. Goldsborough (D-MD) proposed a bill in 1932 to require the Federal Reserve to restore the purchasing power of the dollar to its average level in the 1920s.

decrease in employment, falling prices and general economic demoralization took place.

The fourth period began about [the time of] the adjournment of Congress when it was assured that these destructive measures were defeated and that constructive measures would be held. This period extended from July until October and was a period of even more definite march out of the depression. Employment was increasing at the rate of half a million men a month, bank failures ceased, hoarded currency was flowing back steadily and gold was returning from abroad, car loadings, commodity and security prices and all the other proofs of emergence from the depression were visible to every one. Fear and despair had again been replaced by hope and confidence.

The fifth period began shortly before election when the outcome became evident, and has lasted until today. I have already recited its events.

The causes of this terrible retrogression and fear in this fifth period have an exact parallel in the third period of last spring. The fact that there was no disavowal of the actions of last spring by the Democratic candidates during the campaign lends added color and alarm that the same actions and proposals which are now repeated in this period positively represent the policies of the new administration – and the people are seeking to protect themselves individually but with national damage. The movement forward in recovery of our people is again defeated by precisely the same factors as last spring and again emanating from the Democratic leaders.

In the interest of every man, woman and child, the President-elect has, during the past week, been urged by the saner leaders of his own party such as Senator Glass[7] and others, by myself, and by Democratic bankers and economists whom he has called on for advice, to stop the conflagration before it becomes uncontrollable, by announcing firmly and at once (a) that the budget will be balanced even if it means increased taxation; (b) new projects will be so restricted that government bond issues will not in any way endanger stability of government finances; (c) there will be no inflation or tampering with the currency; to which some have added that as the Democratic party [is] coming in with an overwhelming majority in both houses, there can be no excuse for abandonment of Constitutional processes.

The President-elect is the only man who has the power to give assurances which will stabilize [the] public mind as he alone can execute them. Those assurances should have been given before now but must be given at once if the

---

[7] Carter Glass (D-VA)

situation is to be greatly helped. It would allay some fear and panic whereas delay will make the situation more acute.

The present administration is devoting its days and nights to put out the fires or to localize them. I have scrupulously refrained from criticism which is well merited, but have instead been giving repeated assurances to the country of our desire to cooperate and help the new administration.

What is needed, if the country is not to drift into great grief, is the immediate and emphatic restoration of confidence in the future. The resources of the country are incalculable, the available credit is ample but lenders will not lend, and men will not borrow unless they have confidence. Instead they are withdrawing their resources and their energies. The courage and enterprise of the people still exist and only await release from fears and apprehension.

The day will come when the Democratic Party will endeavor to place the responsibility for the events of this Fifth period on the Republican Party. When that day comes I hope you will invite the attention of the American people to the actual truth.

Document 17

First Inaugural Address
President Franklin D. Roosevelt
March 4, 1933

Franklin D. Roosevelt's first inaugural address is perhaps the most famous speech of its kind in American history, with its memorable phrase, "the only thing we have to fear is fear itself." In it he diagnosed the Depression as a symptom of moral decay, and promised to set things right now that the "money changers have fled from their high seats in the temple of our civilization." This would mean a far more activist federal government, and, in particular, a far stronger presidency. Indeed, he told his listeners that if Congress did not respond quickly and forcefully enough to his initiatives, he would ask for "broad Executive power to wage a war against the emergency, as great as the power that would be given to me if we were in fact invaded by a foreign foe."

Source: Samuel Rosenman, ed., The Public Papers of Franklin D. Roosevelt, Volume Two: The Year of Crisis, 1933, (Ann Arbor, Michigan: University of Michigan Library, 2005), pp. 11–16.

I am certain that my fellow Americans expect that on my induction into the Presidency I will address them with a candor and a decision which the present situation of our Nation impels. This is preeminently the time to speak the truth, the whole truth, frankly and boldly. Nor need we shrink from honestly facing conditions in our country today. This great Nation will endure as it has endured, will revive and will prosper. So, first of all, let me assert my firm belief that the only thing we have to fear is fear itself – nameless, unreasoning, unjustified terror which paralyzes needed efforts to convert retreat into advance. In every dark hour of our national life a leadership of frankness and vigor has met with that understanding and support of the people themselves which is essential to victory. I am convinced that you will again give that support to leadership in these critical days.

In such a spirit on my part and on yours we face our common difficulties. They concern, thank God, only material things. Values have shrunken to fantastic levels; taxes have risen; our ability to pay has fallen; government of all kinds is faced by serious curtailment of income; the means of exchange are frozen in the currents of trade; the withered leaves of industrial enterprise lie on every side; farmers find no markets for their produce; the savings of many years in thousands of families are gone.

More important, a host of unemployed citizens face the grim problem of existence, and an equally great number toil with little return. Only a foolish optimist can deny the dark realities of the moment.

Yet our distress comes from no failure of substance. We are stricken by no plague of locusts. Compared with the perils which our forefathers conquered because they believed and were not afraid, we have still much to be thankful for. Nature still offers her bounty and human efforts have multiplied it. Plenty is at our doorstep, but a generous use of it languishes in the very sight of the supply. Primarily this is because the rulers of the exchange of mankind's goods have failed, through their own stubbornness and their own incompetence, have admitted their failure, and abdicated. Practices of the unscrupulous money changers stand indicted in the court of public opinion, rejected by the hearts and minds of men.

True they have tried, but their efforts have been cast in the pattern of an outworn tradition. Faced by failure of credit they have proposed only the lending of more money. Stripped of the lure of profit by which to induce our people to follow their false leadership, they have resorted to exhortations, pleading tearfully for restored confidence. They know only the rules of a generation of self-seekers. They have no vision, and when there is no vision the people perish.[1]

The money changers have fled from their high seats in the temple of our civilization.[2] We may now restore that temple to the ancient truths. The measure of the restoration lies in the extent to which we apply social values more noble than mere monetary profit.

Happiness lies not in the mere possession of money; it lies in the joy of achievement, in the thrill of creative effort. The joy and moral stimulation of work no longer must be forgotten in the mad chase of evanescent profits. These dark days will be worth all they cost us if they teach us that our true

---

[1] A reference to Proverbs 29:18, "Where there is no vision, the people perish: but he that keepeth the law, happy is he."

[2] Roosevelt is alluding to the story of Jesus throwing the money changers out of the temple in Jerusalem. The story is in Matthew 21:12-17, Mark 11:15-19, Luke 19: 45:48, and John 2:13-16.

destiny is not to be ministered unto but to minister to ourselves and to our fellow men.

Recognition of the falsity of material wealth as the standard of success goes hand in hand with the abandonment of the false belief that public office and high political position are to be valued only by the standards of pride of place and personal profit; and there must be an end to a conduct in banking and in business which too often has given to a sacred trust the likeness of callous and selfish wrongdoing. Small wonder that confidence languishes, for it thrives only on honesty, on honor, on the sacredness of obligations, on faithful protection, on unselfish performance; without them it cannot live.

Restoration calls, however, not for changes in ethics alone. This Nation asks for action, and action now.

Our greatest primary task is to put people to work. This is no unsolvable problem if we face it wisely and courageously. It can be accomplished in part by direct recruiting by the Government itself, treating the task as we would treat the emergency of a war, but at the same time, through this employment, accomplishing greatly needed projects to stimulate and reorganize the use of our natural resources.

Hand in hand with this we must frankly recognize the overbalance of population in our industrial centers and, by engaging on a national scale in a redistribution, endeavor to provide a better use of the land for those best fitted for the land. The task can be helped by definite efforts to raise the values of agricultural products and with this the power to purchase the output of our cities. It can be helped by preventing realistically the tragedy of the growing loss through foreclosure of our small homes and our farms. It can be helped by insistence that the Federal, State, and local governments act forthwith on the demand that their cost be drastically reduced. It can be helped by the unifying of relief activities which today are often scattered, uneconomical, and unequal. It can be helped by national planning for and supervision of all forms of transportation and of communications and other utilities which have a definitely public character. There are many ways in which it can be helped, but it can never be helped merely by talking about it. We must act and act quickly.

Finally, in our progress toward a resumption of work we require two safeguards against a return of the evils of the old order; there must be a strict supervision of all banking and credits and investments; there must be an end to speculation with other people's money, and there must be provision for an adequate but sound currency.

There are the lines of attack. I shall presently urge upon a new Congress in special session detailed measures for their fulfillment, and I shall seek the immediate assistance of the several States.

Through this program of action we address ourselves to putting our own national house in order and making income balance outgo. Our international trade relations, though vastly important, are in point of time and necessity secondary to the establishment of a sound national economy. I favor as a practical policy the putting of first things first. I shall spare no effort to restore world trade by international economic readjustment, but the emergency at home cannot wait on that accomplishment.

The basic thought that guides these specific means of national recovery is not narrowly nationalistic. It is the insistence, as a first consideration, upon the interdependence of the various elements in all parts of the United States – a recognition of the old and permanently important manifestation of the American spirit of the pioneer. It is the way to recovery. It is the immediate way. It is the strongest assurance that the recovery will endure.

In the field of world policy I would dedicate this Nation to the policy of the good neighbor – the neighbor who resolutely respects himself and, because he does so, respects the rights of others – the neighbor who respects his obligations and respects the sanctity of his agreements in and with a world of neighbors.

If I read the temper of our people correctly, we now realize as we have never realized before our interdependence on each other; that we can not merely take but we must give as well; that if we are to go forward, we must move as a trained and loyal army willing to sacrifice for the good of a common discipline, because without such discipline no progress is made, no leadership becomes effective. We are, I know, ready and willing to submit our lives and property to such discipline, because it makes possible a leadership which aims at a larger good. This I propose to offer, pledging that the larger purposes will bind upon us all as a sacred obligation with a unity of duty hitherto evoked only in time of armed strife.

With this pledge taken, I assume unhesitatingly the leadership of this great army of our people dedicated to a disciplined attack upon our common problems.

Action in this image and to this end is feasible under the form of government which we have inherited from our ancestors. Our Constitution is so simple and practical that it is possible always to meet extraordinary needs by changes in emphasis and arrangement without loss of essential form. That is why our constitutional system has proved itself the most superbly enduring political mechanism the modern world has produced. It has met every stress of vast expansion of territory, of foreign wars, of bitter internal strife, of world relations.

It is to be hoped that the normal balance of executive and legislative authority may be wholly adequate to meet the unprecedented task before us. But it may be that an unprecedented demand and need for undelayed action may call for temporary departure from that normal balance of public procedure.

I am prepared under my constitutional duty to recommend the measures that a stricken nation in the midst of a stricken world may require. These measures, or such other measures as the Congress may build out of its experience and wisdom, I shall seek, within my constitutional authority, to bring to speedy adoption.

But in the event that the Congress shall fail to take one of these two courses, and in the event that the national emergency is still critical, I shall not evade the clear course of duty that will then confront me. I shall ask the Congress for the one remaining instrument to meet the crisis – broad Executive power to wage a war against the emergency, as great as the power that would be given to me if we were in fact invaded by a foreign foe.

For the trust reposed in me I will return the courage and the devotion that befit the time. I can do no less.

We face the arduous days that lie before us in the warm courage of the national unity; with the clear consciousness of seeking old and precious moral values; with the clean satisfaction that comes from the stern performance of duty by old and young alike. We aim at the assurance of a rounded and permanent national life.

We do not distrust the future of essential democracy. The people of the United States have not failed. In their need they have registered a mandate that they want direct, vigorous action. They have asked for discipline and direction under leadership. They have made me the present instrument of their wishes. In the spirit of the gift I take it.

In this dedication of a Nation we humbly ask the blessing of God. May He protect each and every one of us. May He guide me in the days to come.

Document 18

Call for Legislation to Create the Tennessee Valley Authority
President Franklin D. Roosevelt
April 10, 1933

Immediately upon taking office, Roosevelt called Congress into special session, and over the next hundred days it approved 15 major pieces of legislation aimed at restoring the solvency of the nation's banking system, raising prices for agricultural products and manufactured goods, and providing relief for the unemployed. The president conveyed information about all of these to the American people through regular radio broadcasts from the White House, which he called "Fireside Chats." One of the top priorities of his administration was the development of the Tennessee Valley, and in a speech before Congress in early April Roosevelt proposed going farther than simply providing rural residents with subsidized electricity from the hydroelectric works. He envisioned a comprehensive plan for the region, encompassing "flood control, soil erosion, reforestation, elimination from agricultural use of marginal lands, and distribution and diversification of industry." Further, he believed that this sort of planning could serve as a model for other parts of the nation.

Southern Democrats and Progressive Republicans enthusiastically embraced Roosevelt's call for a Tennessee Valley Authority, and it was quickly implemented. The TVA still exists today as a government-run corporation whose reach encompasses most of Tennessee, as well as parts of Alabama, Mississippi, Kentucky, Georgia, North Carolina, and Virginia.

Source: "Message to Congress Suggesting the Tennessee Valley Authority," April 10, 1933. Online by Gerhard Peters and John T. Woolley, The American Presidency Project. http://www.presidency.ucsb.edu/ws/?pid=14614.

The continued idleness of a great national investment in the Tennessee Valley leads me to ask the Congress for legislation necessary to enlist this project in the service of the people.

It is clear that the Muscle Shoals development is but a small part of the potential public usefulness of the entire Tennessee River.[1] Such use, if envisioned in its entirety, transcends mere power development; it enters the wide fields of flood control, soil erosion, reforestation, elimination from agricultural use of marginal lands, and distribution and diversification of industry. In short, this power development of war days leads logically to national planning for a complete river watershed involving many States and the future lives and welfare of millions. It touches and gives life to all forms of human concerns.

I, therefore, suggest to the Congress legislation to create a Tennessee Valley Authority, a corporation clothed with the power of Government but possessed of the flexibility and initiative of a private enterprise. It should be charged with the broadest duty of planning for the proper use, conservation and development of the natural resources of the Tennessee River drainage basin and its adjoining territory for the general social and economic welfare of the Nation. The Authority should also be clothed with the necessary power to carry these plans into effect. Its duty should be the rehabilitation of the Muscle Shoals development and the coordination of it with the wider plan.

Many hard lessons have taught us the human waste that results from lack of planning. Here and there a few wise cities and counties have looked ahead and planned. But our Nation has "just grown." It is time to extend planning to a wider field, in this instance comprehending in one great project many States directly concerned with the basin of one of our greatest rivers.

This in a true sense is a return to the spirit and vision of the pioneer. If we are successful here we can march on, step by step, in a like development of other great natural territorial units within our borders.

---

[1] See Document 6.

Document 19

"Fireside Chat" on the Purposes and Foundations of the Recovery Program

President Franklin D. Roosevelt
July 24, 1933

In late July, after an exceptionally busy special session of Congress, Roosevelt took to the airwaves to speak to the American people about the policies that had just been enacted. He discussed his successful handling of the bank crisis, as well as the $3 billion committed to public works projects. He then moved on to explain the Agricultural Adjustment Act (which he refers to here as the "Farm Act"), which sought to force agricultural prices higher by getting farmers – in return for government subsidies – to grow less of certain commodities.

Most of this "Fireside Chat," however, is dedicated to the centerpiece of Roosevelt's program for industrial recovery, the National Industrial Recovery Act (NIRA). This bill aimed at eliminating "unfair trading practices" through a partnership among government, business, and labor. It called for the creation of codes of "fair competition" to eliminate price-cutting and overproduction. Each industry would form a committee made up of business owners, labor leaders, and government employees that would then be charged with drafting the code for that industry. While the codes varied from industry to industry, all of them were to include a minimum hourly wage, a maximum number of hours worked per week, and a ban on child labor. A special feature of the NIRA was Section 7(a), which guaranteed the right of workers to organize and bargain collectively. Although adherence to the codes was technically voluntary, the law also included provisions authorizing the president to impose codes where industries failed to draft them voluntarily.

Source: "Fireside Chat (Recovery Program)," July 24, 1933. Online by Gerhard Peters and John T. Woolley, The American Presidency Project. http://presidency.proxied.lsit.ucsb.edu/ws/index.php?pid=14488.

After the adjournment of the historical special session of the Congress five weeks ago I purposely refrained from addressing you for two very good reasons.

First, I think that we all wanted the opportunity of a little quiet thought to examine and assimilate in a mental picture the crowding events of the hundred days which had been devoted to the starting of the wheels of the New Deal.

Secondly, I wanted a few weeks in which to set up the new administrative organization and to see the first fruits of our careful planning.

I think it will interest you if I set forth the fundamentals of this planning for national recovery; and this I am very certain will make it abundantly clear to you that all of the proposals and all of the legislation since the fourth day of March have not been just a collection of haphazard schemes but rather the orderly component parts of a connected and logical whole.

Long before Inauguration Day I became convinced that individual effort and local effort and even disjointed Federal effort had failed and of necessity would fail and, therefore, that a rounded leadership by the Federal Government had become a necessity both of theory and of fact. Such leadership, however, had its beginning in preserving and strengthening the credit of the United States Government, because without that no leadership was a possibility. For years the Government had not lived within its income. The immediate task was to bring our regular expenses within our revenues. That has been done.

It may seem inconsistent for a government to cut down its regular expenses and at the same time to borrow and to spend billions for an emergency. But it is not inconsistent because a large portion of the emergency money has been paid out in the form of sound loans which will be repaid to the Treasury over a period of years; and to cover the rest of the emergency money we have imposed taxes to pay the interest and the installments on that part of the debt.

So you will see that we have kept our credit good. We have built a granite foundation in a period of confusion. That foundation of the Federal credit stands there broad and sure. It is the base of the whole recovery plan.

Then came the part of the problem that concerned the credit of the individual citizens themselves. You and I know of the banking crisis and of the great danger to the savings of our people. On March sixth every national bank was closed. One month later 90 per cent of the deposits in the national banks had been made available to the depositors. Today only about 5 per cent of the deposits in national banks are still tied up. The condition relating to state banks, while not quite so good on a percentage basis, is showing a steady reduction in the total of frozen deposits – a result much better than we had expected three months ago.

The problem of the credit of the individual was made more difficult because of another fact. The dollar was a different dollar from the one with which the average debt had been incurred. For this reason large numbers of people were actually losing possession of and title to their farms and homes. All of you know the financial steps which have been taken to correct this inequality. In addition the Home Loan Act, the Farm Loan Act and the Bankruptcy Act were passed.[1]

It was a vital necessity to restore purchasing power by reducing the debt and interest charges upon our people, but while we were helping people to save their credit it was at the same time absolutely essential to do something about the physical needs of hundreds of thousands who were in dire straits at that very moment. Municipal and State aid were being stretched to the limit. We appropriated half a billion dollars to supplement their efforts and in addition, as you know, we have put 300,000 young men into practical and useful work in our forests and to prevent flood and soil erosion. The wages they earn are going in greater part to the support of the nearly one million people who constitute their families.

In this same classification we can properly place the great public works program running to a total of over three billion dollars – to be used for highways and ships and flood prevention and inland navigation and thousands of self-sustaining state and municipal improvements. Two points should be made clear in the allotting and administration of these projects – first, we are using the utmost care to choose labor-creating quick-acting, useful projects, avoiding the smell of the pork barrel; and secondly, we are hoping that at least half of the money will come back to the government from projects which will pay for themselves over a period of years.

Thus far I have spoken primarily of the foundation stones – the measures that were necessary to re-establish credit and to head people in the opposite direction by preventing distress and providing as much work as possible through governmental agencies. Now I come to the links which will build us a more lasting prosperity. I have said that we cannot attain that in a nation half boom and half broke. If all of our people have work and fair wages and fair

---

[1] As Roosevelt noted in his talk, these were all acts intended to restore credit by providing mortgage assistance to homeowners in danger of defaulting on their mortgages, loans for agricultural purposes, and relief for debtors, especially farmers in debt.

profits, they can buy the products of their neighbors and business is good. But if you take away the wages and the profits of half of them, business is only half as good. It doesn't help much if the fortunate half is very prosperous – the best way is for everybody to be reasonably prosperous.

For many years the two great barriers to a normal prosperity have been low farm prices and the creeping paralysis of unemployment. These factors have cut the purchasing power of the country in half. I promised action. Congress did its part when it passed the farm and the industrial recovery acts. Today we are putting these two acts to work and they will work if people understand their plain objectives.

First, the Farm Act: It is based on the fact that the purchasing power of nearly half our population depends on adequate prices for farm products. We have been producing more of some crops than we consume or can sell in a depressed world market. The cure is not to produce so much. Without our help the farmers cannot get together and cut production, and the Farm Bill gives them a method of bringing their production down to a reasonable level and of obtaining reasonable prices for their crops. I have clearly stated that this method is in a sense experimental, but so far as we have gone we have reason to believe that it will produce good results.

It is obvious that if we can greatly increase the purchasing power of the tens of millions of our people who make a living from farming and the distribution of farm crops, we will greatly increase the consumption of those goods which are turned out by industry.

That brings me to the final step – bringing back industry along sound lines.

Last Autumn, on several occasions, I expressed my faith that we can make possible by democratic self-discipline in industry general increases in wages and shortening of hours sufficient to enable industry to pay its own workers enough to let those workers buy and use the things that their labor produces. This can be done only if we permit and encourage cooperative action in industry because it is obvious that without united action a few selfish men in each competitive group will pay starvation wages and insist on long hours of work. Others in that group must either follow suit or close up shop. We have seen the result of action of that kind in the continuing descent into the economic Hell of the past four years.

There is a clear way to reverse that process: If all employers in each competitive group agree to pay their workers the same wages – reasonable wages – and require the same hours – reasonable hours – then higher wages and shorter hours will hurt no employer. Moreover, such action is better for the employer than unemployment and low wages, because it makes more buyers for his product. That is the simple idea which is the very heart of the Industrial Recovery Act.

On the basis of this simple principle of everybody doing things together, we are starting out on this nationwide attack on unemployment. It will succeed if our people understand it – in the big industries, in the little shops, in the great cities and in the small villages. There is nothing complicated about it and there is nothing particularly new in the principle. It goes back to the basic idea of society and of the nation itself that people acting in a group can accomplish things which no individual acting alone could even hope to bring about.

Here is an example. In the Cotton Textile Code and in other agreements already signed, child labor has been abolished. That makes me personally happier than any other one thing with which I have been connected since I came to Washington. In the textile industry – an industry which came to me spontaneously and with a splendid cooperation as soon as the recovery act was signed, – child labor was an old evil. But no employer acting alone was able to wipe it out. If one employer tried it, or if one state tried it, the costs of operation rose so high that it was impossible to compete with the employers or states which had failed to act. The moment the Recovery Act was passed, this monstrous thing which neither opinion nor law could reach through years of effort went out in a flash. As a British editorial put it, we did more under a Code in one day than they in England had been able to do under the common law in eighty-five years of effort. I use this incident, my friends, not to boast of what has already been done but to point the way to you for even greater cooperative efforts this summer and autumn.

We are not going through another winter like the last. I doubt if ever any people so bravely and cheerfully endured a season half so bitter. We cannot ask America to continue to face such needless hardships. It is time for courageous action, and the Recovery Bill gives us the means to conquer unemployment with exactly the same weapon that we have used to strike down Child Labor.

The proposition is simply this:

If all employers will act together to shorten hours and raise wages we can put people back to work. No employer will suffer, because the relative level of competitive cost will advance by the same amount for all. But if any considerable group should lag or shirk, this great opportunity will pass us by and we will go into another desperate winter. This must not happen.

We have sent out to all employers an agreement which is the result of weeks of consultation. This agreement checks against the voluntary codes of nearly all the large industries which have already been submitted. This blanket agreement carries the unanimous approval of the three boards which I have appointed to advise in this, boards representing the great leaders in labor, in industry and in social service. The agreement has already brought a flood of approval from every State, and from so wide a cross-section of the common calling of industry that I know it is fair for all. It is a plan – deliberate, reasonable and just – intended to put into effect at once the most important of the broad principles which are being established, industry by industry, through codes. Naturally, it takes a good deal of organizing and a great many hearings and many months, to get these codes perfected and signed, and we cannot wait for all of them to go through. The blanket agreements, however, which I am sending to every employer will start the wheels turning now, and not six months from now.

There are, of course, men, a few of them, who might thwart this great common purpose by seeking selfish advantage. There are adequate penalties in the law, but I am now asking the cooperation that comes from opinion and from conscience. These are the only instruments we shall use in this great summer offensive against unemployment. But we shall use them to the limit to protect the willing from the laggard and to make the plan succeed.

In war, in the gloom of night attack, soldiers wear a bright badge on their shoulders to be sure that comrades do not fire on comrades. On that principle, those who cooperate in this program must know each other at a glance. That is why we have provided a badge of honor for this purpose, a simple design with a legend, "We do our part," and I ask that all those who join with me shall display that badge prominently. It is essential to our purpose.

Already all the great, basic industries have come forward willingly with proposed codes, and in these codes they accept the principles leading to mass reemployment. But, important as is this heartening demonstration, the richest field for results is among the small employers, those whose contribution will give new work for from one to ten people. These smaller employers are indeed a vital part of the backbone of the country, and the success of our plans lies largely in their hands.

Already the telegrams and letters are pouring into the White House – messages from employers who ask that their names be placed on this special Roll of Honor. They represent great corporations and companies, and partnerships and individuals. I ask that even before the dates set in the agreements which we have sent out, the employers of the country who have not already done so – the big fellows and the little fellows – shall at once write or telegraph to me personally at the White House, expressing their intention of going through with the plan. And it is my purpose to keep posted in the post office of every town, a Roll of Honor of all those who join with me.

I want to take this occasion to say to the twenty-four governors who are now in conference in San Francisco, that nothing thus far has helped in strengthening this great movement more than their resolutions adopted at the very outset of their meeting, giving this plan their instant and unanimous approval, and pledging to support it in their states.

To the men and women whose lives have been darkened by the fact or the fear of unemployment, I am justified in saying a word of encouragement because the codes and the agreements already approved, or about to be passed upon, prove that the plan does raise wages, and that it does put people back to work. You can look on every employer who adopts the plan as one who is doing his part, and those employers deserve well of everyone who works for a living. It will be clear to you, as it is to me, that while the shirking employer may undersell his competitor, the saving he thus makes is made at the expense of his country's welfare.

While we are making this great common effort there should be no discord and dispute. This is no time to cavil or to question the standard set by this universal agreement. It is time for patience and understanding and cooperation. The workers of this country have rights under this law which cannot be taken from them, and nobody will be permitted to whittle them away, but, on the other hand, no aggression is now necessary to attain those rights. The whole country will be united to get them for you. The principle that applies to the employers applies to the workers as well, and I ask you workers to cooperate in the same spirit.

When Andrew Jackson, "Old Hickory," died, someone asked, "Will he go to Heaven?" and the answer was, "He will if he wants to." If I am asked whether the American people will pull themselves out of this depression, I answer, "They will if they want to." The essence of the plan is a universal limitation of hours of work per week for any individual by common consent, and a universal payment of wages above a minimum, also by common consent. I cannot guarantee the success of this nationwide plan, but the people of this country can guarantee its success. I have no faith in "cure-alls" but I believe that we can greatly influence economic forces. I have no sympathy with the professional economists who insist that things must run their course and that human agencies can have no influence on economic ills. One reason is that I happen to know that professional economists have changed their definition of economic laws every five or ten years for a very long time, but I do have faith, and retain faith, in the strength of common purpose, and in the strength of unified action taken by the American people.

That is why I am describing to you the simple purposes and the solid foundations upon which our program of recovery is built. That is why I am asking the employers of the Nation to sign this common covenant with me – to sign it in the name of patriotism and humanity. That is why I am asking the workers to go along with us in a spirit of understanding and of helpfulness.

Document 20

"Black Labor and the Codes"
August 1933

Just as was the case with organized labor, the relationship between the Roosevelt administration and African-Americans was complicated. Thousands of blacks benefited from New Deal programs, particularly public works projects, so that Roosevelt in 1936 would become the first presidential candidate of the Democratic Party to receive a majority of the black vote. Nevertheless, the president feared alienating southern whites, and therefore refused to challenge discrimination in federal relief programs, or to endorse legislation that would have made lynching a federal crime (thus taking lynching cases out of local courts, where perpetrators were likely to be acquitted). Moreover, the interests of African-Americans were frequently ignored in the crafting of New Deal legislation. For example, as this editorial in Opportunity – the magazine of the National Urban League – makes clear, the new codes mandated by the National Industrial Recovery Act often allowed blacks to be paid lower wages than whites. The National Urban League, founded in 1910, united organizations established earlier in the twentieth century to defend the economic interests of urban blacks.

Source: Opportunity: A Journal of Negro Life, 11:8 (August 1933), p. 231.

If there were those who supposed for a moment that the identity of interests of black and white labor would be recognized in the codes submitted by Industry in accordance with the provisions of the National Industrial Recovery Act, by this time they must be aware, to say the least, that their hopes were ill founded. For in the Textile Code, the first code accepted by the government and apparently approved by organized labor, Negro unskilled labor, classified as cleaners, outside workers, etc., was ruthlessly excluded from the benefits of the minimum wage provision and that of the limitation of hours of work. So glaring was this ill-concealed discrimination on the basis of race that the President himself in his acceptance of the code demanded that on January first, these classes of labor admittedly composed for the most part of Negroes should be especially considered so as to be included in the general purposes of the Act.

It would seem that in the codes proposed thus far, those industries in which the bulk of the unskilled labor is black have made an adroit attempt to establish a differential wage based on race. In the proposed lumber and steel codes the wide disparity in the wages, especially of the unskilled in the North and in the South, which appears to be merely geographical, is in reality an effort to perpetuate the wage inequalities current in the South. Only where the threat of organized labor menaces the company union and the open shop has there been any effort to protect the interest of the black worker, and in the Steel Code this alone inspired a section against discrimination of Negro workers.

The manipulation of wage scales on the basis of race is fraught with danger to all workers. The consequences which will flow from reducing black workers to a wage which does not insure "decent living" must inevitably be felt by millions of unskilled whites, whose wage will tend to approach that of the despised blacks. A labor policy which condones such a practice or is without voice when it is perpetrated must be condemned as short sighted, stupid and woefully lacking in knowledge of the historic mission of the labor movement.

The blanket code recently promulgated by the President will be hailed by millions of black workers who will come under its provisions. But there is no reason to believe that the same tendencies which have appeared in the codes – will be absent in the operation of the code in the industries of the South. Only sincere, vigorous, unceasing vigilance on the part of the Department of Labor will be able to prevent such discrimination against Negro workers in the South as will practically nullify the intent and purpose of the National Industrial Recovery Act for the American Negro.

Document 21

"The Right to Strike"
Mauritz A. Hallgren
November 8, 1933

Labor disputes continued to multiply during the first year of the Roosevelt administration. Much of the unrest centered on the formation of so-called industrial unions, which under the leadership of the Congress of Industrial Organizations aggressively sought to organize unskilled and semi-skilled factory workers. This was in sharp contrast to traditional "craft unionism" represented by the older American Federation of Labor. The unions affiliated with the AFL tended to represent skilled workers such as carpenters and electricians, and they emphasized cooperation over confrontation in its relationship with management. However, as the left-wing journalist Mauritz Hallgren pointed out in this article, the relationship between the White House and organized labor was complicated. There is no question that the Roosevelt administration was friendlier to industrial unions than its predecessor, and that Section 7(a) of the National Industrial Recovery Act (Document 19) gave a tremendous boost to organizing efforts. In a single month, 100,000 men joined the United Mine Workers, while another 50,000 joined unions for rubber tire workers. On the other hand, many leading members of the administration worried that labor unrest could impede economic recovery, and sought to discourage strikes.

Source: The Nation, 137: 3566 (November 8, 1933) p. 530 - 531.

Nearly a million American workers have gone out on strike since the New Deal began. Probably as many as l00,000 men are out today, the total rising or falling as old disputes are adjusted and new strikes begin. The number of disputes brought to the attention of the Bureau of Labor Statistics has increased fourfold in the last six months and more than 500 per cent as compared with the average for 1932. While not all these controversies result in strikes or lockouts, a large majority of them do. Even those that are settled peaceably reflect the unrest which is spreading among American workers.

This unrest has taken a violent turn in many communities. It has resulted not only in the usual wholesale arrests of strikers and strike pickets but in the destruction of property: in the coal country mine tipples[1] have been dynamited and bridges and miners' homes blown up, and in Philadelphia motor trucks laden with goods have been set afire. It has also led to numerous riots, from which both workers and police have come away with bruised heads and broken limbs, when no more serious injuries have been inflicted. Indeed, press dispatches show that some hundreds of strikers have been wounded and perhaps a dozen killed in clashes with factory guards, deputy sheriffs, and city police.

It is true that, measured either numerically or in terms of violence, the present wave of strikes seems mild and peaceful compared with similar series of outbreaks in the past. In 1919, for example, there were 2,665 labor disputes, strikes, and lockouts, involving no fewer than 4,160,348 workers – three times as many as had ever before or have since participated in such disputes in any one year. This period, which saw the rise of a militant revolutionary movement and also witnessed the notorious Palmer red raids, was doubtless the most turbulent in recent labor history.

The revolutionary fervor that gripped a section of the working class in 1919 is absent today, and there is no indication of a trend toward extreme violence on the part either of the workers or of the authorities. Yet it is well to remember that the present labor unrest is far from having run its course. And it must also be remembered that there is in the present situation a factor that did not exist in 1919 or in the seventies and eighties of the last century. In the past the workers had always to fight on their own. They had to contend not only with an antagonistic employing class and an apathetic public but with a government that was at least unsympathetic when it was not openly hostile. The attitude of the government has now been changed, or so we may presume from the language of the recovery act and the utterances of Administration officials. Under the New Deal the government is actively supporting the cause of the working class. At least many workers believe this, whether or not it is actually true. Whatever the ultimate effect of the apparent combination between government and labor may be, it is clear that it has introduced a new and uncertain factor. Hence it is difficult, if not quite impossible, to compare the present strike movement with similar movements in the past.

It is probable that the summer and autumn of 1933 would in any case have seen an outbreak of labor troubles. There were portents of a minor upturn in business even before Franklin Roosevelt took office. Such upturns have in the past invariably been accompanied by labor unrest, for it is when economic

---

[1] where coal is loaded for transport

recovery begins and prices start to climb that the divergence between living costs and wage-income is brought into sharpest focus for the average workingman and his wife. But the number of strikes was undoubtedly increased by the brisk but basically unsound boom in industry that took place from May to August. Production indices soared almost to normal and retail prices started upward, but the employment index was left far behind and the payroll totals showed hardly any change at all. That this boom, largely the product of the government's currency policy, was an important factor in stirring up the workers cannot be questioned.

However, other and perhaps more important factors have been at work. For not all the strikes called to date have had higher wages or improved working conditions as their principal objectives. In fact, a majority of the strikes have been started with a view to compelling employers to recognize and deal with labor unions. There have been few strikes and few signs of unrest in the organized industries – for example, in the printing trades, among the railroad workers, and in the building trades. On the other hand, many controversies have arisen in open-shop[2] industries, such as steel and automobiles, and in loosely integrated industries – bituminous[3] mining and the clothing and needle trades, for instance – where internal conditions have been such as to make the organization of labor difficult. Labor unions have been active in these latter industries for many years, but in no case have they been wholly successful. On the contrary, the United Mine Workers, which even at the zenith of its power had been unable to penetrate the important Appalachian or Southern fields, was literally falling to pieces when the recovery act came to its rescue. In the clothing industry such organizations as the Amalgamated Clothing Workers did much better, but even these unions, alert and progressive as they were, had difficulty in keeping up with the shifting of sweatshops across State lines and with the other rapid changes so easily effected in an industry made up of small, mobile units.

It may be noted that most of the strike activity has been confined to industries where progressive or radical unions had been at work or where industrial unionism had gained a foothold. This has been true especially of the clothing and textile industries, in which the Amalgamated Clothing Workers, the unions of the Conference for Progressive Labor Action, and the Communists have been active; and also of the bituminous industry, in which the United Mine Workers, the largest industrial union in the country, seems

---

[2] a place of employment where workers are not required to join a union
[3] black coal

once again to be fairly well established. It has been less true of the steel and automobile industries, which the craft unionists of the A. F. of L. appear to have marked out for themselves. Most of the recent steel strikes have been inspired or openly called by the Communists rather than by the A. F. of L. unions, while the few automobile strikes that have taken place have been more or less spontaneous. The A. F. of L. has been active in building up its membership, but it has been far behind the progressives and radicals both in its militancy and in its willingness to expand into new fields. There are numerous industries, not included in the list above, which are either entirely unorganized or at best inadequately organized, and in which there have been very few labor disputes. The absence of such controversies does not necessarily mean that the workers are satisfied with conditions in these industries, for the contrary is more likely to be the case; it suggests rather that union organizers have as yet made no serious attempt to enter these industries. Why the A. F. of L. has made no determined effort to organize a field which is practically virgin territory may perhaps be ascribed in part to its refusal to abandon the principle of craft unionism, and in part to the fact, as expressed by J. B. S. Hardman in *The Nation* of December 21, 1932, that for the federation leaders it would mean "going out of well-appointed offices into the field, jeopardizing accumulated resources, sometimes taking a chance with life itself."

To sum up, recognition by employers of established or new unions has been the chief objective of the strike movement as a whole. American labor is again in the midst of one of its periodic struggles to get itself organized. Whether it will be any more successful than it has been in the past remains to be seen. This time, in any event, it appears to have the support of the government. Section 7a of the recovery act, which President Roosevelt has called labor's "new charter of rights," frankly says to the workers in the unorganized industries: Go ahead and form your unions; the government guarantees that they will be protected and recognized. This guaranty is obviously worthless in fact unless it can be enforced, and the workers, facing a hostile employing class, have thus far found no way to enforce it except by resort to strikes.

One concrete result of the wave of strikes has been to arouse apprehensions concerning its effect on the Roosevelt recovery program. Already many voices have been raised to suggest or demand that the right to strike be suppressed in the interest of economic recovery. Ida M. Tarbell[4] has

---

[4] Tarbell (1857–1944) was a leading "muckraking" or investigative journalist during the Progressive era.

denounced the strikes as antiquated and barbaric. The Paul Block newspapers[5] recently published an editorial declaring that the "hundreds of strikes throughout the country are largely responsible for the retardment of business programs.... Business is ready to start upward, and no one, either employer or employee, should be allowed to stand in the way." Edward F. McGrady, Assistant Secretary of Labor and formerly chief Washington lobbyist for the A. F. of L., asserted that there is "no doubt that the public sentiment of the country is almost unanimously behind the President. Unnecessary strikes will turn that sentiment against organized labor." Leo Wolman, chairman of the Labor Advisory Board,[6] contended that it is "unnecessary to call strikes to enforce" the labor provisions of the recovery law. "Labor," he said, "cannot afford to endanger the success of the NRA." Senator Wagner,[7] chairman of the National Labor Board,[8] has several times spoken in the same vein. General Hugh Johnson, head of the NRA,[9] went so far in his speech before the A. F. of L. convention as to call the strike a form of "economic sabotage." He openly hinted at government control of the labor unions should the strike movement continue.

There can be no question that any cessation of effort on the part of the workers will impede the Roosevelt program. With this in mind the Administration is hastily setting up extensive machinery for the purpose of intervening in labor disputes. The National Labor Board has been formed in Washington, and this body is organizing district branches in various parts of the country. The use of such machinery is understandable enough in cases where the disputes or strikes are of the usual sort having to do with wages and working conditions. But a large majority of the strikes today are designed to obtain that recognition for labor organizations which the recovery act presumes to guarantee the workers. In other words, no mediation or arbitration is necessary to settle these disputes. All that the Roosevelt

---

[5] Paul Block (1877–1941) published the Pittsburgh *Post-Gazette* and the Toledo *Blade*.
[6] The Labor Advisory Board represented labor's interests in the National Recovery Administration.
[7] Robert F. Wagner (D-NY). See Document 24.
[8] Established on August 5, 1933, the National Labor Board was to resolve labor disputes arising under the National Industry Recovery Act.
[9] Established by the National Industrial Recovery Act (Document 19) in 1933, the National Recovery Administration sought to coordinate the activities of labor, industry and government through codes to reduce what the Roosevelt administration thought was harmful or inefficient competition. The codes set work hours and prices. The Supreme Court ruled the NRA unconstitutional in 1935 (Document 28).

Administration need do is to enforce the law of which it is itself the author. Hence it is strange to find even the labor representatives in the Administration speaking in terms of arbitration when discussing the labor disputes that have arisen.

It is likely, however, that the erection of this elaborate mediation machinery is not entirely without meaning. Granted that it was sincerely devised with a view to helping labor, the fact remains that it can be turned against labor. One notes, for example, that the National Labor Board contains what the suspicious-minded might consider an anti-working-class majority. Four of the seven members of the board are employing-class representatives, and if a real clash between the economic interests of capital and labor is brought before the board, this factor may make itself felt, even though at the moment two or three of the employing-class members appear to be sympathetically inclined toward the interests of the workers. In addition, two of the three labor representatives on the board, William Green[10] and John L. Lewis,[11] are notorious reactionaries.

It is still a moot question whether the workers, feeling that there is now a friendly Administration in Washington and that their interests are adequately protected by the recovery act, will now sit back and let the government do their fighting for them, or will instead be encouraged by the Administration's support to redouble their own efforts out in the field. If they choose the former course, as many of them seem to have done, they will probably be doomed to disappointment. For General Johnson and other high Administration officials have repeatedly said that it is not a part of the government's task to help organize labor unions. That the workers will have to do for themselves. If, on the other hand, they choose the latter path, they will encounter other and no less serious obstacles. Employers in general seem determined not to extend recognition to the unions without a struggle. Therefore the workers are virtually compelled to fight, that is, to strike, to obtain such recognition. But with the economic crisis actually deepening, despite surface indications to the contrary, the Administration finds itself under increasing pressure to extend its control over all factors affecting its recovery program. One of the most important of these factors is obviously the right of the workers to withhold their labor in order to gain their own ends. If the strike movement continues to spread through the coming winter, we shall probably see the National Labor

---

[10] William Green (1873–1952) was an American labor leader.
[11] John L. Lewis (1880–1969) was President of the United Mine Workers of America, 1920–1960.

Board being used not only to settle wage disputes but also, though perhaps not openly, as a device for the suppression of the right to strike.

Document 22

Speech to Congress on Foreign Trade
President Franklin D. Roosevelt
March 2, 1934

Ever since the days of Jefferson and Jackson, Democrats had favored a policy of free trade. During the 1932 campaign Roosevelt frequently denounced the Smoot-Hawley tariff, and upon becoming president he tapped as secretary of state Cordell Hull, a Tennessee senator who had based much of his political career on fighting against trade barriers. Nevertheless, Roosevelt moved slowly on trade, fearing (as Hoover did) that an influx of inexpensive goods from abroad would impede economic recovery.

Finally, at Hull's insistence, the president unveiled in early 1934 a major trade proposal – the Reciprocal Trade Agreement Act. Like most of the legislation proposed by Roosevelt during his first term, it passed quickly, but it dramatically altered the way the U.S. government concluded trade deals with other countries. The RTAA empowered the president to negotiate commercial treaties that could reduce tariffs by up to 50 percent from their prevailing rates (which were, at the time, those set by Smoot-Hawley – Document 3) without consulting Congress. Practically overnight, much of the legislative branch's authority to determine trade policy was transferred to the executive – where it remains to this day.

There is no doubt that U.S. foreign trade increased in the years that followed. By 1941 the total value of both the country's imports and exports had doubled. While some of this no doubt was the result of the general recovery of the global economy in the late 1930s, at least some of the credit must go to the ability of the executive to negotiate bilateral trade deals independently of Congress.

Source: "Message to Congress Requesting Authority Regarding Foreign Trade," March 2, 1934. Online by Gerhard Peters and John T. Woolley, The American Presidency Project. http://www.presidency.ucsb.edu/ws/?pid=14817.

I am requesting the Congress to authorize the Executive to enter into executive commercial agreements with foreign Nations; and in pursuance thereof, within carefully guarded limits, to modify existing duties and import restrictions in such a way as will benefit American agriculture and industry. This action seems opportune and necessary at this time for several reasons.

First, world trade has declined with startling rapidity. Measured in terms of the volume of goods in 1933, it has been reduced to approximately 70 percent of its 1929 volume; measured in terms of dollars, it has fallen to 35 percent. The drop in the foreign trade of the United States has been even sharper. Our exports in 1933 were but 52 percent of the 1929 volume, and 32 percent of the 1929 value.

This has meant idle hands, still machines, ships tied to their docks, despairing farm households, and hungry industrial families. It has made infinitely more difficult the planning for economic readjustment in which the Government is now engaged.

You and I know that the world does not stand still; that trade movements and relations once interrupted can with the utmost difficulty be restored; that even in tranquil and prosperous times there is a constant shifting of trade channels.

How much greater, how much more violent is the shifting in these times of change and of stress is clear from the record of current history. Every Nation must at all times be in a position quickly to adjust its taxes and tariffs to meet sudden changes and avoid severe fluctuations in both its exports and its imports.

You and I know, too, that it is important that the country possess within its borders a necessary diversity and balance to maintain a rounded national life, that it must sustain activities vital to national defense and that such interests cannot be sacrificed for passing advantage. Equally clear is the fact that a full and permanent domestic recovery depends in part upon a revived and strengthened international trade and that American exports cannot be permanently increased without a corresponding increase in imports.

Second, other Governments are to an ever-increasing extent winning their share of international trade by negotiated reciprocal trade agreements. If American agricultural and industrial interests are to retain their deserved place in this trade, the American Government must be in a position to bargain for that place with other Governments by rapid and decisive negotiation based upon a carefully considered program, and to grant with discernment corresponding opportunities in the American market for foreign products supplementary to our own.

If the American Government is not in a position to make fair offers for fair opportunities, its trade will be superseded. If it is not in a position at a given moment rapidly to alter the terms on which it is willing to deal with other countries, it cannot adequately protect its trade against discriminations and against bargains injurious to its interests. Furthermore a promise to which prompt effect cannot be given is not an inducement which can pass current at par in commercial negotiations.

For this reason, any smaller degree of authority in the hands of the Executive would be ineffective. The executive branches of virtually all other important trading countries already possess some such power.

I would emphasize that quick results are not to be expected. The successful building up of trade without injury to American producers depends upon a cautious and gradual evolution of plans.

The disposition of other countries to grant an improved place to American products should be carefully sounded and considered; upon the attitude of each must somewhat depend our future course of action. With countries which are unwilling to abandon purely restrictive national programs, or to make concessions toward the reestablishment of international trade, no headway will be possible.

The exercise of the authority which I propose must be carefully weighed in the light of the latest information so as to give assurance that no sound and important American interest will be injuriously disturbed. The adjustment of our foreign trade relations must rest on the premise of undertaking to benefit and not to injure such interests. In a time of difficulty and unemployment such as this, the highest consideration of the position of the different branches of American production is required.

From the policy of reciprocal negotiation which is in prospect, I hope in time that definite gains will result to American agriculture and industry.

Important branches of our agriculture, such as cotton, tobacco, hog products, rice, cereal and fruit-raising, and those branches of American industry whose mass production methods have led the world, will find expanded opportunities and productive capacity in foreign markets, and will thereby be spared in part, at least, the heartbreaking readjustments that must be necessary if the shrinkage of American foreign commerce remains permanent.

A resumption of international trade cannot but improve the general situation of other countries, and thus increase their purchasing power. Let us well remember that this in turn spells increased opportunity for American sales.

Legislation such as this is an essential step in the program of national economic recovery which the Congress has elaborated during the past year. It is part of an emergency program necessitated by the economic crisis through which we are passing. It should provide that the trade agreements shall be terminable within a period not to exceed three years; a shorter period probably would not suffice for putting the program into effect. In its execution, the Executive must, of course, pay due heed to the requirements of other branches of our recovery program, such as the National Industrial Recovery Act.[1]

I hope for early action. The many immediate situations in the field of international trade that today await our attention can thus be met effectively and with the least possible delay.

---

[1] See Document 19.

Document 23

Speech to Congress on Social Security
President Franklin D. Roosevelt
January 17, 1935

Democrats made impressive gains in the midterm elections of 1934, which Roosevelt interpreted as a popular mandate for the New Deal. In 1935, therefore, he moved even more boldly, placing before Congress a new series of measures on a wide variety of subjects in what has become known as the "Second New Deal." Perhaps the most important of these was the Social Security Act, which provided for unemployment insurance and old-age pensions to be paid through a 6 percent payroll tax divided between employers and employees. The revenues generated from these payroll taxes would be more than sufficient to provide for the current elderly; the surplus would be deposited in a special fund that would – theoretically, at least – maintain the program in perpetuity. Other aspects of the plan directed that federal money would also be passed along to the states to support assistance programs for the blind, the disabled, and families with dependent children. While the benefits to the elderly would be managed at the federal level by a Social Security Administration, unemployment insurance and other assistance programs would remain under the control of the states.

The Social Security Act fell far short of what liberals in the administration had in mind. They had hoped that the program would be funded from revenues generated by the income tax, so that it might redistribute wealth from rich to poor. However, Roosevelt recognized that such a provision was unlikely to win the support of Congress. As he later explained, funding Social Security through payroll taxes gave recipients "a legal, moral, and political right to collect their pensions and their unemployment benefits. With those [payroll] taxes in there, no damn politician can ever scrap my social security program."

Source: The Public Papers and Addresses of Franklin D. Roosevelt, Volume Four, The Court Disapproves, 1935 *(New York: Random House, 1938), pp. 43 - 46.*

In addressing you on June 8, 1934, I summarized the main objectives of our American program. Among these was, and is, the security of the men, women, and children of the Nation against certain hazards and vicissitudes of life. This purpose is an essential part of our task. In my annual message to you I promised to submit a definite program of action. This I do in the form of a report to me by a Committee on Economic Security, appointed by me for the purpose of surveying the field and of recommending the basis of legislation....

It is my best judgment that this legislation should be brought forward with a minimum of delay. Federal action is necessary to, and conditioned upon, the action of States. Forty-four legislatures are meeting or will meet soon. In order that the necessary State action may be taken promptly it is important that the Federal Government proceed speedily.

The detailed report of the Committee sets forth a series of proposals that will appeal to the sound sense of the American people. It has not attempted the impossible, nor has it failed to exercise sound caution and consideration of all of the factors concerned: the national credit, the rights and responsibilities of States, the capacity of industry to assume financial responsibilities and the fundamental necessity of proceeding in a manner that will merit the enthusiastic support of citizens of all sorts....

Three principles should be observed in legislation on this subject. First, the system adopted, except for the money necessary to initiate it, should be self-sustaining in the sense that funds for the payment of insurance benefits should not come from the proceeds of general taxation. Second, excepting in old-age insurance, actual management should be left to the States subject to standards established by the Federal Government. Third, sound financial management of the funds and the reserves, and protection of the credit structure of the Nation should be assured by retaining Federal control over all funds through trustees in the Treasury of the United States.

At this time, I recommend the following types of legislation looking to economic security:

1. Unemployment compensation.

2. Old-age benefits, including compulsory and voluntary annuities.

3. Federal aid to dependent children through grants to States for the support of existing mothers' pension systems and for services for the protection and care of homeless, neglected, dependent, and crippled children.

4. Additional Federal aid to State and local public-health agencies and the strengthening of the Federal Public Health Service. I am not at this time recommending the adoption of so-called "health insurance," although groups representing the medical profession are cooperating with the Federal Government in the further study of the subject and definite progress is being made.

With respect to unemployment compensation, I have concluded that the most practical proposal is the levy of a uniform Federal payroll tax, 90 percent of which should be allowed as an offset to employers contributing under a compulsory State unemployment compensation act. The purpose of this is to afford a requirement of a reasonably uniform character for all States cooperating with the Federal Government and to promote and encourage the passage of unemployment compensation laws in the States. The 10 percent not thus offset should be used to cover the costs of Federal and State administration of this broad system. Thus, States will largely administer unemployment compensation, assisted and guided by the Federal Government. An unemployment compensation system should be constructed in such a way as to afford every practicable aid and incentive toward the larger purpose of employment stabilization. This can be helped by the intelligent planning of both public and private employment. It also can be helped by correlating the system with public employment so that a person who has exhausted his benefits may be eligible for some form of public work as is recommended in this report. Moreover, in order to encourage the stabilization of private employment, Federal legislation should not foreclose the States from establishing means for inducing industries to afford an even greater stabilization of employment.

In the important field of security for our old people, it seems necessary to adopt three principles: First, noncontributory old-age pensions for those who are now too old to build up their own insurance. It is, of course, clear that for perhaps 30 years to come funds will have to be provided by the States and the Federal Government to meet these pensions. Second, compulsory contributory annuities which in time will establish a self-supporting system for those now young and for future generations. Third, voluntary contributory annuities by which individual initiative can increase the annual amounts received in old age. It is proposed that the Federal Government assume one-half of the cost of the old-age pension plan, which ought ultimately to be supplanted by self-supporting annuity plans....

The establishment of sound means toward a greater future economic security of the American people is dictated by a prudent consideration of the hazards involved in our national life. No one can guarantee this country against the dangers of future depressions but we can reduce these dangers. We can eliminate many of the factors that cause economic depressions, and we can provide the means of mitigating their results. This plan for economic security is at once a measure of prevention and a method of alleviation.

We pay now for the dreadful consequence of economic insecurity – and dearly. This plan presents a more equitable and infinitely less expensive means of meeting these costs. We cannot afford to neglect the plain duty before us. I strongly recommend action to attain the objectives sought in this report.

if this ever happens again, we will already have taken the steps to head it off early.

Document 24

Speech on the National Labor Relations Act
Senator Robert F. Wagner
February 21, 1935

One of the most important pieces of legislation to come out of the Second New Deal originated not with the Roosevelt administration, but with supporters of organized labor in the House and Senate. The impetus for the National Labor Relations Act – sometimes called the Wagner Act after its primary sponsor, Sen. Robert F. Wagner (D-NY) – lay in disillusionment with Section 7(a) of the National Industrial Recovery Act (NIRA) that guaranteed the right of labor to organize (Document 19). Union leaders complained that many employers simply ignored it, or set up company unions subservient to management. At the same time, labor unrest continued to escalate through 1934, with particularly serious disputes in the trucking, coal mining, textile and shipping industries. One walkout by longshoremen in San Francisco led to a general strike in which thousands of workers throughout the city left their jobs.

The National Labor Relations Act called for the strengthening of the National Labor Relations Board (originally created under Section 7[a] of the NIRA), empowering that body to mediate labor disputes and enforce its decisions in the courts. The bill also laid out procedures by which workers could choose which union (if any) would represent them, and required that employers bargain in good faith with any union so chosen. Republicans objected, claiming that it would lead to even further labor unrest, and enough southern Democrats joined them that President Roosevelt decided to remain silent on the issue. Two days before the bill came to a vote in the Senate, in fact, he told reporters that he had not "given it any thought one way or the other." After it passed both houses of Congress, however, the president quickly signed it into law.

Source: Congressional Record, 74th Cong., 1st sess., Vol. 79, pt. 8 (February 21, 1935), pp. 2371-72.

The recovery program has sought to bestow upon the business man and the worker a new freedom to grapple with the great economic challenges of our times. We have released the business man from the undiscriminating enforcement of the antitrust laws, which had been subjecting him to the attacks of the price cutters and wage reducers – the pirates of industry. In order to deal out the equal treatment upon which a just democratic society must rest, we at the same time guaranteed the freedom of action of the worker. In fact, the now famous section 7(a), by stating that employees should be allowed to cooperate among themselves if they desired to do so, merely restated principles that Congress has avowed for half a century.

Congress is familiar with the events of the past 2 years. While industry's freedom of action has been encouraged until the trade association movement has blanketed the entire country, employees attempting in good faith to exercise their liberties under section 7(a) have met with repeated rebuffs. It was to check this evil that the President in his wisdom created the National Labor Board in August 1933, out of which has emerged the present National Labor Relations Board.

The Board has performed a marvelous service in composing disputes and sending millions of workers back to their jobs upon terms beneficial to every interest. But it was handicapped from the beginning, and it is gradually but surely losing its effectiveness, because of the practical inability to enforce its decisions. At present it may refer its findings to the National Recovery Administration[1] and await some action by that agency, such as the removal of the Blue Eagle. We all know that the entire enforcement procedure of the N.R.A. is closely interlinked with the voluntary spirit of the codes. Business in the large is allowed to police itself through the code authorities. This voluntarism is without question admirable in respect to provisions for fair competition that have been written by industry and with which business is in complete accord. But it is wholly unadapted to the enforcement of a specific law of Congress which becomes a crucial issue only in those very cases where it is opposed by the guiding spirits of the code authorities. Secondly, the Board may refer a case to the Department of Justice. But since the Board has no power to subpoena records or witnesses, its hearings are largely ex parte[2] and its records so infirm that the Department of Justice is usually unable to act.

---

[1] Established by the National Industrial Recovery Act (Document 19) in 1933, the National Recovery Administration sought to coordinate the activities of labor, industry and government through voluntary codes to reduce what the Roosevelt administration thought was inefficient competition. Its symbol was a blue eagle. The Supreme Court ruled the NRA unconstitutional in 1935 (Document 28).

[2] A legal term referring to a court procedure at which all concerned parties are not present.

Finally, the existence of numerous industrial boards whose interpretations of section 7(a) are not subject to the coordinating influence of a supreme National Labor Relations Board, is creating a maze of confusion and contradictions. While there is a different code for each trade, there is only one section 7(a), and no definite law written by Congress can mean something different in each industry. These difficulties are reducing section 7(a) to a sham and a delusion.

The break-down of section 7(a) brings results equally disastrous to industry and to labor. Last summer it led to a procession of bloody and costly strikes, which in some cases swelled almost to the magnitude of national emergencies. It is not material at this time to inquire where the balance of right and wrong rested in respect to these various controversies. If it is true that employees find it difficult to remain acquiescent when they lose the main privilege promised them by the Recovery Act, it is equally true that employers are tremendously handicapped when it is impossible to determine exactly what their rights are. Everybody needs a law that is precise and certain.

There has been a second and even more serious consequence of the break-down of section 7(a). When employees are denied the freedom to act in concert even when they desire to do so, they cannot exercise a restraining influence upon the wayward members of their own groups, and they cannot participate in our national endeavor to coordinate production and purchasing power. The consequences are already visible in the widening gap between wages and profits. If these consequences are allowed to produce their full harvest, the whole country will suffer from a new economic decline.

The national labor relations bill which I now propose is novel neither in philosophy nor in content. It creates no new substantive rights. It merely provides that employees, if they desire to do so, shall be free to organize for their mutual protection or benefit. Quite aside from section 7(a), this principle has been embodied in the Norris-LaGuardia Act,[3] in amendments to the Railway Labor Act[4] passed last year, and in a long train of other enactments of Congress.

There is not a scintilla of truth in the wide-spread propaganda to the effect that this bill would tend to create a so-called "labor dictatorship." It does not encourage national unionism. It does not favor any particular union. It does

---

[3] Passed in 1932, this act gave certain protections to labor unions and those trying to organize them.

[4] Passed in 1926 and amended in 1934, this act encouraged the resolution of labor disputes through mediation.

not display any preference toward craft or industrial organizations. Most important of all, it does not force or even counsel any employee to join any union if he prefers to deal directly or individually with his employers. It seeks merely to make the worker a free man in the economic as well as the political field. Certainly the preservation of long-recognized fundamental rights is the only basis for frank and friendly relations in industry.

The erroneous impression that the bill expresses a bias for some particular form of union organization probably arises because it outlaws the company-dominated union. Let me emphasize that nothing in the measure discourages employees from uniting on an independent- or company-union basis, if by these terms we mean simply an organization confined to the limits of one plant or one employer. Nothing in the bill prevents employers from maintaining free and direct relations with their workers or from participating in group insurance, mutual welfare, pension systems, and other such activities. The only prohibition is against the sham or dummy union which is dominated by the employer, which is supported by the employers, which cannot change its rules or regulations without his consent, and which cannot live except by the grace of the employer's whims. To say that that kind of a union must be preserved in order to give employees freedom of selection is a contradiction in terms. There can be no freedom in an atmosphere of bondage. No organization can be free to represent the workers when it is the mere creature of the employer.

Equally erroneous is the belief that the bill creates a closed shop for all industry. It does not force any employer to make a closed-shop agreement.[5] It does not even state that Congress favors the policy of the closed shop. It merely provides that employers and employees may voluntarily make closed-shop agreements in any State where they are now legal. Far from suggesting a change, it merely preserves the status quo.

A great deal of interest centers around the question of majority rule. The national labor relations bill provides that representatives selected by the majority of employees in an appropriate unit shall represent all the employees within that unit for the purposes of collective bargaining. This does not imply that an employee who is not a member of the majority group can be forced to enter the union which the majority favors. It means simply that the majority may decide who are to be the spokesmen for all in making agreements concerning wages, hours, and other conditions of employment. Once such agreements are made the bill provides that their terms must be applied without

---

[5] An agreement between union and management mandating that new employees join the union as a condition of employment.

favor or discrimination to all employees. These provisions conform to the democratic procedure that is followed in every business and in our governmental life, and that was embodied by Congress in the Railway Labor Act last year. Without them the phrase "collective bargaining" is devoid of meaning, and the very few unfair employers are encouraged to divide their workers against themselves.

Finally, the National Labor Relations Board is established permanently, with jurisdiction over other boards dealing with cases under section 7(a) or under its equivalent as written into this bill. Nothing could be more unfounded than the charges that the Board would be invested with arbitrary or dictatorial or even unusual powers. Its powers are modeled upon those of the Federal Trade Commission[6] and numerous other governmental agencies. Its orders would be enforceable not by the Board, but by recourse to the courts of the United States, with every affected party entitled to all the safeguards of appeal.

The enactment of this measure will clarify the industrial atmosphere and reduce the likelihood of another conflagration of strife such as we witnessed last summer. It will stabilize and improve business by laying the foundations for the amity and fair dealing upon which permanent progress must rest. It will give notice to all that the solemn pledge made by Congress when it enacted section 7(a) cannot be ignored with impunity, and that a cardinal principle of the new deal for all and not some of our people is going to be supported and preserved by the Government.

---

[6] Established in 1914, the Commission seeks to prevent anti-competitive business practices, such as monopolies.

Document 25

"Black Cotton Farmers and the AAA"
E.E. Lewis
March 1935

One of the greatest complaints made by rural blacks toward the Agricultural Adjustment Administration was the effect that its policies had on southern – largely African-American – sharecroppers. The AAA had been formed under the 1933 Agricultural Adjustment Act; its purpose was to implement a "domestic allotment" plan to raise the price of farm products by paying farmers to produce less. This proved a great deal for farmers who owned their own land. However, for those who lived and worked on land owned by others – particularly black sharecroppers in the South – the results were often disastrous, as landowners simply informed them that their labor was no longer necessary, and evicted them from the land. A few members of the AAA tried to fight this, but were soon dismissed after encountering objections from southern Democrats. Black journalist E.E. Lewis took to the pages of Opportunity *to express his dissatisfaction with the AAA. (*Opportunity *was the magazine of the National Urban League, an organization founded in 1910 to defend the interests of urban African-Americans.) Lewis acknowledges the racial prejudice affecting black sharecroppers, but emphasizes the underlying economic and technological conditions of southern agriculture affecting both blacks and whites.*

Source: Opportunity: A Journal of Negro Life, *13:3 (March 1935), p. 72. Available at* http://newdeal.feri.org/opp/opp3572.htm.

The avowed aim of the new deal is to enhance the well being of the masses, but matching this aim with the actual achievements of the Administration is not a very happy occupation. Nowhere is the discrepancy between aim and achievement more disconcerting than in the case of the Negro cotton producer. The natural reaction of those interested in the economic problems of the Negro is to pass judgment upon the personal character of the individual members of the Administration. A much wiser plan is to forget personalities and concentrate our attention upon basic social and economic forces which are so largely responsible for the present federal program and for the present and probable changes in the cotton growing industry itself. In so doing one is likely to make a shrewder guess as to the future, and hence it is in these terms that I should like to respond to Mr. Carter's[1] request for comment on the prospect of the Negro agricultural worker.

While the agricultural "adjustment" program is, broadly speaking, the result of a very real need for some form of farm relief, the specific program in force represents the government's response to a particular kind of political pressure. The fundamental fact to bear in mind in examining the present set-up (or in fact the whole story of agrarian revolt from the days of Greenbackism[2] to Mr. Hoover's Federal Farm Board[3]) is that the "farmer" for the purpose of politics is not simply an individual cultivating the soil but the independent business man in agriculture. The independent farm owner and the richer farm tenant are and always have been the vocal element in our farm population, and hence the class to obtain concessions from the government. The character of the farmer lobby is of fundamental importance in understanding the present program.

The basic purpose of agricultural adjustment as conceived by the present administration runs in terms of farm prices, if we leave aside the supplementary credit program (the farmer's R. F. C.).[4] Increase the value of farm products (by raising prices) and add to these market prices certain benefit payments – that is to say, enhance the total income on individual farms, but take no thought concerning the distribution of these increased returns. Now this is a business man's solution of farm relief; whereas a program aimed at the relief of our farm population as a whole would run thus: Increase the total income of each individual farm, and see to it that both farm capital and farm labor benefit from the same individual, receives the entire increased income [as in the original].

As a matter of fact, these two programs come to about the same thing under certain conditions. If American agriculture were carried on entirely by small independent farmers, owning their land or renting on some equitable basis, and performing most of the labor, then a program such as we have would

---

[1] perhaps Elmer Anderson Carter, the editor of *Opportunity* from 1928 to 1945
[2] a movement of the 1870s popular among farmers and in the South advocating a greater supply of paper money
[3] Established in 1929, the Federal Farm Board sought to stabilize prices for agricultural products.
[4] a reference to the Reconstruction Finance Corporation, a New Deal agency established in 1932 that made loans to businesses (see Document 19)

be truly "democratic." For if . . . the same family, receives the entire farm income we should have no reason to worry about the division of benefits as between profits and wages. No doubt one can explain much of the inconsistencies between the apparently sincere expressions of "good will" emanating so frequently from members of the Agricultural Adjustment Administration and the actual concentration of benefits by the fact that Mr. Wallace[5] and his aides have in mind just this type of farm organization. But, the program as formulated at present is truly democratic only if and where agriculture is so organized.

Taking the Cotton Belt[6] as a whole, however, we find a sharp degree of economic stratification. It is best illustrated by the large plantations with their concentration of wealth and power in the hands of the planter, but the plantation system also colors the relationship between the tenant and landlord on non-plantation land, and for that matter the small farmer (renter or owner) and the credit-granting merchant or banker generally. This is not to say, of course, that there are no truly independent small farmers in the South, but simply that concentration of control is very much more prevalent there than elsewhere.

What happens when a program designed merely to increase the total income of each individual producing unit is applied to a section where the control over these producing units is concentrated in a relatively few hands? Just what is happening in the South today. Any other result would simply indicate that Southern planters, unlike the rest of us, are not actuated by self-interest. If the government were really bent on a democratic type of rehabilitation for all cotton producers, it would be compelled by one means or another to put its power behind the Southern share-cropper to force a more favorable division of benefits. The principle that force must be met with force in economic as well as military affairs is one to which the Administration has paid at least lip service in the case of labor relations in industry, but not in agriculture – a fact attested by the complete exclusion of the farm laborer from the program and the highly unsatisfactory provisions affecting share-croppers.

With respect to the agricultural program as a whole, this is, as has been said, a reflection of the type of political interests behind the farm relief program. With respect to the Cotton Belt itself, there are further complicating factors. To begin with, cheap labor has been the life-blood of the plantation

---

[5] Henry Wallace, Secretary of Agriculture, 1933–40
[6] the area of the southeastern United States where cotton was grown, stretching from Maryland to eastern Texas

system and an attack on low labor incomes in the South would be interpreted by the Southern planters not as merely one more thorn in the flesh, but as a mortal blow. The aristocracy of the South is not going to put up with any nonsense about share-croppers' unions and the like. Moreover, it happens that the present national administration is Democratic – in party if not in policy – and must rely to a large extent upon the support of the dominant class of the South. If one expects the Roosevelt administration to "smash" the Southern labor system or to modify it appreciably, one is leaving out of the picture some of its most essential details.

An additional complicating circumstance in the Cotton Belt is the existence of the race issue, both as it appears today and as it reflects the unique historical forces which have shaped the Southern system. For the bi-racial character of the labor force of the Cotton Belt on the one hand renders more stubborn the resistance to any sort of economic change, and on the other makes the resistance so much the more effective. A concession to the share-cropper class is not only one to labor but one to the Negro as well. And such a concession is thereby made more distasteful, and less necessary.

One may disagree perhaps that the race issue fits in here, for it seems to imply that the race issue is relatively minor. In a sense it is just that, and it will be well to examine the question rather carefully. When we look at the problem of the Negro farmer, the feature which stands out most sharply is his handicaps as compared with his white neighbor. Sources of credit available to the white man are closed. The credit that he does get is much more expensive than that of the white man. Legal redress in matters of contracts are beyond his reach. One may cite any number of difficulties which he encounters solely because of his race. All this is most unjust, and any fair-minded observer will immediately conclude that these racial differentials ought to be wiped out. And yet, if all these matters of racial discriminations could be eliminated, a real question would remain. How much would the lot of the Negro farmer actually be improved if he were put on a par with the white man? Is the small white farmer living in an economic paradise? To one familiar with the facts, the answer to the last question is all too obvious. Whether we like it or not, the basic problem of the South is fundamentally economic and not racial – the problem of the poor man (white and black) and not the problem solely of the underprivileged Negro. Any program of economic betterment of the mass of cotton producers must run in terms of a general economic reorganization of cotton production as a whole, and not merely in terms of a purely racial program aimed at eliminating the differentials between Negro and white. The latter type of program is of course most desirable as far as it goes, but after all an intelligent traveller makes sure not only that he is headed in the right direction but also that he has the proper means of really getting to his destination. Thus, if we regard the race question, not just as a matter of discrimination against the colored man, but in its broader aspects as a deterrent to effective reorganization of Southern agriculture, we are likely to be guided into a much more serviceable program for the colored man himself in the long run.

If we look beyond the immediate government program, we find certain other forces which are likely sooner or later to change the entire situation of the small cotton producer of either race. Traditionally, cotton farming has postulated a supply of extremely cheap labor, for the picking and hence most of the other operations, must be done purely by hand. But the shift to mechanized production through the introduction of the mechanical picker, if not just around the proverbial corner, seems at least definitely in the offing, awaiting the development of favorable economic conditions. Now cotton raising through the use of a mechanical picker is likely to be much more efficient than the old "hand" methods, because picking cost itself will be reduced, and also because the introduction of machinery at this point will make it profitable to use mechanical power down the whole line of pre-picking operations. As a result, the competition of mechanized plantations is likely to prove fatal to the older kind of cotton farming. What will this mean for the mass of workers in the Cotton Belt?

Obviously, the old story of "technological unemployment" will be repeated in the South – the planter who cultivates a thousand acres in cotton by machinery will need fewer workers than he needs now. But the introduction of the mechanical picker will mean more than this. In the first place it will mean a substantial change in location of cotton farming. Experts tell us that the use of a mechanical picker is much more feasible on flat lands such as one finds in the western part of the Cotton Belt, than in the hilly country of Georgia and surrounding states – indeed it is extremely doubtful that the mechanical picker can be used to any great extent in this territory. The shift to mechanization will be a shift to the West. And this in turn will be a shift from the Negro, for there is plenty of non-Negro labor in the West to meet the demand of mechanized production. The same holds true of course with respect to white labor east of the Mississippi River.

But why cannot the Negro follow this trend and go in for mechanized cotton production himself? Such a development would take care of only a small proportion of our present agricultural population, but at least it would be an item on the other side of the ledger. This brings us to the second feature of the change to mechanical picking – namely, that cotton farming will necessitate larger capital outlays than at present. Not only will the machinery itself be more expensive, but its use will involve much larger tracts of land. For the machinery will not pay for itself unless the farm is sufficiently large so that the machine is occupied to a maximum degree. (An idle tractor in the barn eats up profits as effectively as an idle mule.) This means that the new type of cotton farm will become inaccessible to the man of small means. In this respect the Negro takes his place beside the vast majority of white men – the days of the "little fellow" (white or black) seem to be numbered.

If the present administration seems such a poor source of immediate benefit, and if the longer prospects in the Cotton Belt are even darker, one is perhaps tempted to accept the defeat and be done with it. For after all, Southern agriculture has in the past been a place of refuge (however shabby) for the Negro American, and the prospects of curtailed opportunities in this field must certainly be "viewed with alarm." Without minimizing the serious dangers inherent to the situation, however, one may still find . . . a flicker of light ahead. Certainly we have in this country the material basis for a good life for all our population, white and black, and who knows but that we shall turn the trick! It is in that happy consummation that hope lies for the vast majority of Negroes and whites. Just where that larger problem will lead us is another story, but the first chapters seem pretty clear and they concern such things as social security, shorter hours, collective bargaining, and related programs. It is primarily along such lines that those interested in the welfare of the Negro must direct their efforts. Once these broader objectives are set, the purely racial elements in a program for Negro betterment become really significant. For if the standard of living of workers in general is being substantially raised, the fight against racial discrimination in matters of pay and other working conditions will mean real improvement for the Negro himself. The achievement of these ends involves something more than a reformulation of aims on the part of the Negro. It necessitates as well among both Negroes and whites a deeper realization of the community of their interests and of the necessity of cooperative action.

Document 26

Speech on Social Security
Representative James W. Wadsworth
April 19, 1935

The Social Security Act (Document 23), which went before Congress in spring 1935, appeared sufficiently moderate that it aroused little real opposition, except from a few die-hard conservatives such as Republican Representative James W. Wadsworth of New York, who feared that it would destroy incentives to work and save. Others claimed that the proposed payroll tax was excessive; not only would it retard recovery, but they feared that the resulting surplus might be used to fund other attempts at New Deal "social engineering." In spite of such criticism the bill passed both houses by wide margins, and Roosevelt signed it into law on August 14, 1935.

Social Security has been one of the most enduring legacies of the New Deal. It was and remains one of Roosevelt's most popular accomplishments, but in many ways it has also proved the most troublesome. When the program began paying out old-age benefits in 1940, there were 159.2 taxpayers for every recipient. By 2013, however, according to the Social Security Administration, demographic patterns and longer life expectancy had changed the ratio to 2.8 taxpayers for every recipient. Some have suggested that without major changes, the Social Security system cannot remain solvent.

Source: Congressional Record, 74th Cong., 1st sess., Vol. 79, pt. 6, pp. 6060-6061.

. . . I realize perfectly well that this bill is going to pass the House of Representatives . . . without any substantial change, and nothing that I can say will prevent it or even tend to prevent it, in view of the determination of the majority.

It is not my purpose to discuss it in detail . . . but I am going to endeavor to glance a little toward the far future and analyze some one or two things which seem to me to be susceptible of analysis, and certainly worth serious thought on the part of Members of the House regardless of their political affiliations.

First, as to the financing of the major portion of this program. As I understand it . . . these funds are to be established in the Treasury Department, through the collection of payroll taxes. . . . The bill provides in general that those moneys shall be invested solely in the bonds of the Government of the United States or bonds guaranteed as to the principal and interest by the Government. As I read the report and have listened to the discussion on the floor, it is apparent that the proponents of this bill expect that this fund will grow from time to time, year after year, until about 1970, if I am not mistaken, the fund will approximate $32,000,000,000, every penny of which must be invested in government bonds.

It is apparent that unless the national debt of the United States goes far, far beyond $32,000,000,000 in the time over which this calculation is extended, by the time this fund has been built up to any considerable degree it will become a fund large enough to absorb at least a major portion of the national debt, and finally absorb it all. . . .

Now, that may seem an effective and adequate way to finance the Government's financial activities in all the years to come. I am trying to look to the future. Heretofore the Government has financed its undertakings primarily and fundamentally as a result of the confidence of the individual citizen in the soundness of the Government's undertaking, but from this point on we are apparently going to abandon that philosophy of public confidence and resort to a very different practice. The Government is to impose a payroll tax through one of its agencies, collect the money into the Treasury Department, then the Treasury Department with its left hand on the proceeds of these taxes is to turn around and buy bonds of the United States Government issued by the right hand of the Treasury Department. Thus the Government of the United States, after this thing gets going, is no longer to be financed directly by its citizens, confident in the soundness of the Government, but it is to be financed instead by arrangements made within the bureaucracy – an undemocratic and dangerous undertaking. . . .

Now, this may not seem important at this moment. I may be old-fashioned. . . . It seems to me that we are moving away from democracy in this new and manipulative method of financing the obligations of the United States. I do not question the integrity and the honor of the men who are going to manage this fund or the men who will be Secretaries of the Treasury down through the years to come, but there is something offensive to me in the spectacle of one branch of the Treasury Department having collected a fund by taxing the working people of America, and then using that money for the floating of its own bonds. It seems to me to present the possibility of a vicious circle, and is certainly removing the financial support of the Government of the United States far from the people themselves and confining it to an inner ring, bureaucratic in character. I am trying to look ahead and visualize what that may mean in the preservation of democracy....

One other thing looking toward the future.... I know the appeal this bill has to every human being, that it appeals to the humane instincts of men and women everywhere. We will not deny, however, that it constitutes an immense, immense departure from the traditional functions of the Federal Government for it to be projected into the field of pensioning the individual citizens of the several States. It launches the Federal Government into an immense undertaking which in the aggregate will reach dimensions none of us can really visualize and which in the last analysis, you will admit, affects millions and millions of individuals. Remember, once we pay pensions and supervise annuities, we cannot withdraw from the undertaking no matter how demoralizing and subversive it may become. Pensions and annuities are never abandoned; nor are they ever reduced. The recipients ever clamor for more. To gain their ends they organize politically. They may not constitute a majority of the electorate, but their power will be immense. On more than one occasion we have witnessed the political achievements of organized minorities. This bill opens the door and invites the entrance into the political field of a power so vast, so powerful as to threaten the integrity of our institutions and so pull the pillars of the temple down upon the heads of our descendants.

We are taking a step here today which may well be fateful. I ask you to consider it, to reexamine the fundamental philosophy of this bill, to estimate the future and ask yourselves the questions, "In what sort of country shall our grandchildren live? Shall it be a free country or one in which the citizen is a subject taught to depend upon government?"

Document 27

Statement on the Share Our Wealth Society
Senator Huey P. Long
May 23, 1935

One of Roosevelt's most prominent opponents was Huey P. Long, who as a popular and reform-minded Democratic governor of Louisiana took on the oil industry and built a powerful state political organization. After being elected to the U.S. Senate (in 1930, although he did not take his seat until 1932), he used his national standing to issue frequent denunciations of the wealthy and the banking system. In 1932 he supported Roosevelt's presidential campaign, and supported most of the measures of the early New Deal. However, the personalities of the two men immediately clashed, and the New York patrician and the colorful, rural senator known as the "Kingfish" (after a character in the popular radio show Amos & Andy) came to loathe one another.

Long's greatest complaint with the New Deal was that to his mind it did not go far enough in reducing the great inequalities of wealth in American society. In March 1933 he proposed a series of bills that would have seized all fortunes greater than $100 million, as well as all annual income in excess of $1 million. When these laws failed – as did, indeed, everything Long proposed as senator – he established a national organization called the Share Our Wealth Society. By 1935 the society boasted 27,000 chapters nationwide, with a total membership of 7.5 million. Long hoped to use this group as a launching pad for a presidential run in 1936; however, in September 1935 he was assassinated by the son of one of his many political enemies.

Source: Congressional Record, 74th Cong., 1st sess., Vol. 79 (May 23, 1935), pp. 8040-43.

The Share Our Wealth Society proposes to enforce the traditions on which this country was founded, rather than to have them harmed; we aim to carry out the guaranties of our immortal Declaration of Independence and our Constitution of the United States, as interpreted by our forefathers who wrote them and who gave them to us; we will make the works and compacts of the Pilgrim fathers, taken from the Laws of God, from which we were warned never to depart, breathe into our Government again that spirit of liberty, justice, and mercy which they inspired in our founders in the days when they gave life and hope to our country. God has beckoned fullness and peace to our land; our forefathers have set the guide stakes so that none need fail to share in this abundance. Will we now have our generation, and the generations which are to come, cheated of such heritage because of the greed and control of wealth and opportunity by 600 families?

To members and well-wishers of the Share Our Wealth Society:

For 20 years I have been in the battle to provide that, so long as America has, or can produce, an abundance of the things which make life comfortable and happy, that none should own such much [sic] of the things which he does not need and cannot use as to deprive the balance of the people of a reasonable proportion of the necessities and conveniences of life. The whole line of any political thought has always been that America must face the time when the whole country would shoulder the obligation which it owes to every child born on earth – that is, a fair chance to life, liberty, and happiness. . . .

It is not out of place for me to say that the support which I brought to Mr. Roosevelt to secure his nomination and election as President – and without which it was hardly probabl[e] he would ever have been nominated – was on the assurances which I had that he would take the proper stand for the redistribution of wealth in the campaign. He did that much in the campaign; but after his election, what then? I need not tell you the story. We have not time to cry over our disappointments, over promises which others did not keep, and over pledges which were broken. . . .

It is impossible for the United States to preserve itself as a republic or as a democracy when 600 families own more of this Nation's wealth – in fact, twice as much – as all the balance of the people put together. Ninety-six percent of our people live below the poverty line, while 4 percent own 87 percent of the wealth. America can have enough for all to live in comfort and still permit millionaires to own more than they can ever spend and to have more money than they can ever use; but America cannot allow the multimillionaires and the billionaires, a mere handful of them, to own everything unless we are willing to inflict starvation upon 125,000,000 people.

We looked upon the year 1929 as the year when too much was produced for the people to consume. We were told, and we believed, that the farmers raised too much cotton and wool for the people to wear and too much food for the people to eat. Therefore, much of it went to waste, some rotted, and much of it was burned or thrown into the river or into the ocean. But, when we picked up the bulletin of the Department of Agriculture for that year 1929, we found that, according to the diet which they said everyone should eat in order to be healthy, multiplying it by 120,000,000, the number of people we had in 1929, had all of our people had the things which the Government said that [they] should eat in order to live well[? W]e did not have enough even in 1929 to feed the people. In fact, these statistics show that in some instances we had from one-third to one-half less than the people needed, particularly of milk, eggs, butter, and dried fruits.

But why in the year 1929 did it appear we had too much? Because the people could not buy the things they wanted to eat, and needed to eat. That showed the need for and duty of the Government then and there, to have forced a sharing of our wealth, and a redistribution, and Roosevelt was elected on the pledge to do that very thing.

But what was done? Cotton was plowed under the ground. Hogs and cattle were burned by the millions. The same was done to wheat and corn, and farmers were paid starvation money not to raise and not to plant because of the fact that we did not want so much because of people having no money with which to buy. Less and less was produced, when already there was less produced than the people needed if they ate what the Government said they needed to sustain life. God forgive those rulers who burned hogs, threw milk in the river, and plowed under cotton while little children cried for meat and milk and something to put on their naked backs!

But the good God who placed this race on earth did not leave us without an understanding of how to meet such problems; nor did the Pilgrim fathers who landed at Plymouth in 1620 fail to set an example as to how a country and a nation of people should act under such circumstances, and our great statesman like Thomas Jefferson, Daniel Webster, Abraham Lincoln, Theodore Roosevelt, and Ralph Waldo Emerson did not fail to explain the need and necessity for following the precedents and purposes, which are necessary, even in a land of abundance, if all the people are to share the fruits produced therein. God's law commanded that the wealth of the country should be redistributed ever so often, so that none should become too rich and none should become too poor; it commanded that debts should be canceled and released ever so often, so that the human race would not be loaded with a burden which it could never pay. When the Pilgrims landed at Plymouth in 1620, they established their law by compact, signed by everyone who was on board the Mayflower, and it provided that at the end of every 7 years the finances of their newly formed country would be readjusted and that all debts would be released and property redistributed, so that none should starve in the land of plenty, and none should have an abundance of more than he needed.

These principles were preserved in the Declaration of Independence, signed in 1776, and in our Constitution. Our great statesmen, such men as James Madison, who wrote the Constitution of the United States, and Daniel Webster, its greatest exponent, admonished the generations of America to come that they must never forget to require the redistribution of wealth if they desire that their Republic should live.

And, now, what of America? Will we allow the political sports, the high heelers, the wiseacres, and those who ridicule us in our misery and poverty to keep us from organizing these societies in every hamlet so that they may bring back to life this law and custom of God and of this country? Is there a man or woman with a child born on the earth, or who expects ever to have a child born on earth, who is willing to have it raised under the present-day practices of piracy, where it comes into life burdened with debt, condemned to a system of slavery by which the sweat of its brow throughout its existence must go to satisfy the vanity and the luxury of a leisurely few, who can never be made to see that they are destroying the root and branch of the greatest country ever to have risen? Our country is calling; the laws of the Lord are calling; the graces of our forefathers would open today if their occupants could see the bloom and flower of their creation withering and dying because the greed of the financial masters of this country has starved and withheld from mankind those things produced by his own labor. To hell with the ridicule of the wise street-corner politician. Pay no attention to any newspaper or magazine that has sold its columns to perpetuate this crime against the people of America. Save this country. Save mankind. Who can be wrong in such a work, and who cares what consequences may come following the mandates of the Lord, of the Pilgrims, of Jefferson, Webster, and Lincoln? He who falls in this fight falls in the radiance of the future. Better to make this fight and lose than to be a party to a system that strangles humanity.

It took the genius of labor and the lives of all Americans to produce the wealth of this land. If any man, or 100 men, wind up with all that has been produced by 120,000,000 people, that does not mean that those 100 men produced the wealth of the country; it means that those 100 men stole, directly or indirectly, what 125,000,000 people produced. Let no one tell you that the money masters made this country. They did [no] such thing. Very few of them ever hewed the forest; very few ever hacked a crosstie; very few ever nailed a board; fewer of them ever laid a brick. Their fortunes came from manipulated finance, control of government, rigging of markets, the spider webs that have grabbed all businesses; they grab the fruits of the land, the conveniences and the luxuries that are intended for 125,000,000 people, and run their heelers to our meetings to set up the cry. "We earned it honestly." The Lord says they did no such thing. The voices of our forefathers say they did no such thing. In this land of abundance, they have no right to impose starvation, misery, and pestilence for the purpose of vaunting their own pride and greed....

Here is the whole sum and substance of the share-our-wealth movement:

1. Every family to be furnished by the Government a homestead allowance, free of debt, of not less than one-third the average family wealth of the country, which means, at the lowest, that every family shall have the reasonable comforts of life up to a value of from $5,000 to $6,000. No person to have a fortune of more than 100 to 300 times the average family fortune, which means that the limit to fortunes is between $1,500,000 and $5,000,000, with annual capital levy taxes imposed on all above $1,000,000.

2. The yearly income of every family shall be not less than one-third of the average family income, which means that, according to the estimates of the statisticians of the United States Government and Wall Street, no family's annual income would be less than from $2,000 to $[2,500]. No yearly income shall be allowed to any person larger than from 100 to 300 times the size of the average family income, which means that no person would be allowed to earn in any year more than from $600,000 to $1,800,000, all to be subject to present income-tax laws.

3. To limit or regulate the hours of work to such an extent as to prevent overproduction; the most modern and efficient machinery would be encouraged, so that as much would be produced as possible so as to satisfy all demands of the people, but to also allow the maximum time to the workers for recreation, convenience, education, and luxuries of life.

4. An old-age pension to the persons over 60.

5. To balance agricultural production with what can be consumed according to the laws of God, which includes the preserving and storage of surplus commodities to be paid for and held by the Government for the emergencies when such are needed. Please bear in mind, however, that when the people of America have had money to buy things they needed, we have never had a surplus of any commodity. This plan of God does not call for destroying any of the things raised to eat or wear, nor does it countenance wholesale destruction of hogs, cattle, or milk.

6. To pay the veterans of our wars what we owe them and to care for their disabled.

7. Education and training for all children to be equal in opportunity in all schools, colleges, universities, and other institutions for training in the professions and vocations of life; to be regulated on the capacity of children to

learn, and not on the ability of parents to pay the costs. Training for life's work to be as much universal and thorough for all walks in life as has been the training in the arts of killing.

8. The raising of revenue and taxes for the support of this program to come from the reduction of swollen fortunes from the top, as well as for the support of public works to give employment whenever there may be any slackening necessary in private enterprise.

I now ask those who read this circular to help us at once in this work of giving life and happiness to our people – not a starvation dole upon which someone may live in misery from week to week. Before this miserable system of wreckage has destroyed the life germ of respect and culture in our American people let us save what was here, merely by having none too poor and none too rich. The theory of the Share Our Wealth Society is to have enough for all, but not to have one with so much that less than enough remains for the balance of the people.

Please, therefore, let me ask you who read this document – please help this work before it is too late for us to be of help to our people. We ask you now, (1) help to get your neighbor into the work of this society and (2) help get other Share Our Wealth societies started in your county and in adjoining counties and get them to go out to organize other societies.

To print and mail out this circular costs about 60 cents per hundred, or $6 per thousand. Anyone who reads this and wants more circulars of this kind to use in the work, can get them for that price by sending the money to me, and I will pay the printer for him. Better still, if you can have this circular reprinted in your own town or city.

Let everyone who feels he wishes to help in our work start right out and go ahead. One man or woman is as important as any other. Take up the fight! Do not wait for someone else to tell you what to do. There are no high lights in this effort. We have no State managers and no city managers. Everyone can take up the work, and as many societies can be organized as there are people to organize them. One is the same as another. The reward and compensation is the salvation of humanity. Fear no opposition. "He who fails in this fight falls in the radiance of the future!"

Document 28

Schechter Poultry Corp. v. United States
Chief Justice Charles Evans Hughes
May 27, 1935

The Roosevelt administration was dealt a stunning setback in late May 1935 when the Supreme Court found the National Industrial Recovery Act (NIRA; see Document 19) to be unconstitutional. The decision stemmed from a case in which a small family-owned poultry business in New York City was prosecuted for violating the National Recovery Administration (NRA) code for the poultry industry. Established by the NIRA in 1933, the NRA sought to coordinate the activities of labor, industry and government through voluntary codes to reduce what the Roosevelt administration thought was harmful competition. In a unanimous opinion written by Chief Justice Charles Evans Hughes, the Court denied the administration's claim that the economic crisis justified stretching the ordinary constitutional restraints on federal power. The NIRA, the justices asserted, by giving an executive agency the power to define "fair competition," unlawfully granted legislative authority to the executive branch. Moreover, the Court dismissed the administration's contention that this particular business could be regulated by the federal government under the interstate commerce clause of the Constitution. Although the chickens might have originally come from outside New York, the Schechters sold them exclusively to butchers within the state, hence it was not part of the "stream of interstate commerce."

President Roosevelt was outraged by the ruling, which he claimed was based on an antiquated reading of the Constitution. He was particularly disturbed by the fact that even the Supreme Court's liberals, such as the venerable progressive Justice Louis Brandeis, signed on to the decision. Brandeis told a group of the president's aides to "go back and tell the president that we're not going to let this government centralize everything."

Source: Online from "FDR and the Supreme Court," The New Deal Network (Columbia University: Institute for Learning Technologies), http://newdeal.feri.org/court/295US495.htm.

First. Two preliminary points are stressed by the government with respect to the appropriate approach to the important questions presented. We are told that the provision of the statute authorizing the adoption of codes must be viewed in the light of the grave national crisis with which Congress was confronted. Undoubtedly, the conditions to which power is addressed are always to be considered when the exercise of power is challenged. Extraordinary conditions may call for extraordinary remedies. But the argument necessarily stops short of an attempt to justify action which lies outside the sphere of constitutional authority. Extraordinary conditions do not create or enlarge constitutional power. The Constitution established a national government with powers deemed to be adequate, as they have proved to be both in war and peace, but these powers of the national government are limited by the constitutional grants. Those who act under these grants are not at liberty to transcend the imposed limits because they believe that more or different power is necessary. Such assertions of extraconstitutional authority were anticipated and precluded by the explicit terms of the Tenth Amendment – 'The powers not delegated to the United States by the Constitution, nor prohibited by it to the States, are reserved to the States respectively, or to the people.'

The further point is urged that the national crisis demanded a broad and intensive co-operative effort by those engaged in trade and industry, and that this necessary co-operation was sought to be fostered by permitting them to initiate the adoption of codes. But the statutory plan is not simply one for voluntary effort. It does not seek merely to endow voluntary trade or industrial associations or groups with privileges or immunities. It involves the coercive exercise of the lawmaking power. The codes of fair competition which the statute attempts to authorize are codes of laws. If valid, they place all persons within their reach under the obligation of positive law, binding equally those who assent and those who do not assent. Violations of the provisions of the codes are punishable as crimes.

Second. The Question of the Delegation of Legislative Power. . . . The Constitution provides that 'All legislative powers herein granted shall be vested in a Congress of the United States, which shall consist of a Senate and House of Representatives.' Article 1, 1. And the Congress is authorized 'To make all Laws which shall be necessary and proper for carrying into Execution' its general powers. Article 1, 8, par. 18. The Congress is not permitted to abdicate or to transfer to others the essential legislative functions with which it is thus vested. We have repeatedly recognized the necessity of adapting legislation to complex conditions involving a host of details with which the national

Legislature cannot deal directly.... But we said that the constant recognition of the necessity and validity of such provisions, and the wide range of administrative authority which has been developed by means of them, cannot be allowed to obscure the limitations of the authority to delegate, if our constitutional system is to be maintained....

Accordingly, we look to the statute to see whether Congress has overstepped these limitations – whether Congress in authorizing 'codes of fair competition' has itself established the standards of legal obligation, thus performing its essential legislative function, or, by the failure to enact such standards, has attempted to transfer that function to others....

What is meant by 'fair competition' as the term is used in the act? Does it refer to a category established in the law, and is the authority to make codes limited accordingly? Or is it used as a convenient designation for whatever set of laws the formulators of a code for a particular trade or industry may propose and the President may approve (subject to certain restrictions), or the President may himself prescribe, as being wise and beneficent provisions for the government of the trade or industry in order to accomplish the broad purposes of rehabilitation, correction, and expansion which are stated in the first section of title 1?

The act does not define 'fair competition.' 'Unfair competition,' as known to the common law, is a limited concept. Primarily, and strictly, it relates to the palming off of one's goods as those of a rival trader.... Unfairness in competition has been predicated of acts which lie outside the ordinary course of business and are tainted by fraud or coercion or conduct otherwise prohibited by law.... But it is evident that in its widest range, 'unfair competition,' as it has been understood in the law, does not reach the objectives of the codes which are authorized by the National Industrial Recovery Act. The codes may, indeed, cover conduct which existing law condemns, but they are not limited to conduct of that sort. The government does not contend that the act contemplates such a limitation. It would be opposed both to the declared purposes of the act and to its administrative construction....

.... The government urges that the codes will 'consist of rules of competition deemed fair for each industry by representative members of that industry – by the persons most vitally concerned and most familiar with its problems.' Instances are cited in which Congress has availed itself of such assistance; as, e.g., in the exercise of its authority over the public domain, with respect to the recognition of local customs or rules of miners as to mining claims, or, in matters of a more or less technical nature, as in designating the standard height of drawbars. But would it be seriously contended that Congress could delegate its legislative authority to trade or industrial associations or groups so as to empower them to enact the laws they deem to be wise and beneficent for the rehabilitation and expansion of their trade or industries? Could trade or industrial associations or groups be constituted legislative bodies for that purpose because such associations or groups are familiar with the problems of their enterprises? And could an effort of that sort be made valid by such a preface of generalities as to permissible aims as we find in section 1 of title 1? The answer is obvious. Such a delegation of legislative power is unknown to our law, and is utterly inconsistent with the constitutional prerogatives and duties of Congress.

The question, then, turns upon the authority which section 3 of the Recovery Act vests in the President to approve or prescribe. If the codes have standing as penal statutes, this must be due to the effect of the executive action. But Congress cannot delegate legislative power to the President to exercise an unfettered discretion to make whatever laws he thinks may be needed or advisable for the rehabilitation and expansion of trade or industry....

To summarize and conclude upon this point: Section 3 of the Recovery Act is without precedent. It supplies no standards for any trade, industry, or activity. It does not undertake to prescribe rules of conduct to be applied to particular states of fact determined by appropriate administrative procedure. Instead of prescribing rules of conduct, it authorizes the making of codes to prescribe them. For that legislative undertaking, section 3 sets up no standards, aside from the statement of the general aims of rehabilitation, correction, and expansion described in section 1. In view of the scope of that broad declaration and of the nature of the few restrictions that are imposed, the discretion of the President in approving or prescribing codes, and thus enacting laws for the government of trade and industry throughout the country, is virtually unfettered. We think that the code-making authority thus conferred is an unconstitutional delegation of legislative power.

Third. The Question of the Application of the Provisions of the Live Poultry Code to Intrastate Transactions....

Were these transactions 'in' interstate commerce? Much is made of the fact that almost all the poultry coming to New York is sent there from other states. But the code provisions, as here applied, do not concern the transportation of the poultry from other states to New York, or the transactions of the commission men or others to whom it is consigned, or the sales made by such consignees to defendants. When defendants had made their purchases, whether at the West Washington Market in New York City or at the railroad terminals serving the city, or elsewhere, the poultry was trucked to their slaughterhouses in Brooklyn for local disposition. The interstate transactions in relation to that poultry then ended. Defendants held the poultry at their slaughterhouse markets for slaughter and local sale to retail dealers and butchers who in turn sold directly to consumers. Neither the slaughtering nor the sales by defendants were transactions in interstate commerce. . . .

The undisputed facts thus afford no warrant for the argument that the poultry handled by defendants at their slaughterhouse markets was in a 'current' or 'flow' of interstate commerce, and was thus subject to congressional regulation. The mere fact that there may be a constant flow of commodities into a state does not mean that the flow continues after the property has arrived and has become commingled with the mass of property within the state and is there held solely for local disposition and use. So far as the poultry here in question is concerned, the flow in interstate commerce had ceased. The poultry had come to a permanent rest within the state. It was not held, used, or sold by defendants in relation to any further transactions in interstate commerce and was not destined for transportation to other states. Hence decisions which deal with a stream of interstate commerce – where goods come to rest within a state temporarily and are later to go forward in interstate commerce – and with the regulations of transactions involved in that practical continuity of movement, are not applicable here. . . .

In determining how far the federal government may go in controlling intrastate transactions upon the ground that they 'affect' interstate commerce, there is a necessary and well-established distinction between direct and indirect effects. . . . [W]here the effect of intrastate transactions upon interstate commerce is merely indirect, such transactions remain within the domain of state power. If the commerce clause were construed to reach all enterprises and transactions which could be said to have an indirect effect upon interstate commerce, the federal authority would embrace practically all the activities of the people, and the authority of the state over its domestic concerns would exist only by sufferance of the federal government. Indeed, on such a theory, even the development of the state's commercial facilities would be subject to federal control. . . .

On both the grounds we have discussed, the attempted delegation of legislative power and the attempted regulation of intrastate transactions which affect interstate commerce only indirectly, we hold the code provisions here in question to be invalid and that the judgment of conviction must be reversed.

Document 29

"Again the Covered Wagon"
Paul Taylor
July 1935

Adding to the economic distress of the 1930s was a serious drought that affected certain parts of the Great Plans for as long as eight years. Decades of overplowing, which destroyed the root systems that kept topsoil in place, combined with the dry conditions to produce an environmental disaster known as the "Dust Bowl." In 1934, and again in 1936, high winds simply blew precious soil into the sky, creating gigantic dust clouds that spread as far as New York City and Washington, DC. Oklahoma and the Texas panhandle were the hardest hit, but parts of Arkansas, New Mexico, Colorado, Iowa, Nebraska, and Kansas were affected as well. As many as 3.5 million farmers in this region, having watched as their land became effectively barren, packed up their belongings and headed to California in one of the largest migrations in U.S. history. Their arrival was noted by economist Paul Taylor, who chronicled their plight in the pages of the magazine Survey Graphic.

Source: Survey Graphic 24:7 (July 1935), p. 348.

Vast clouds of dust rise and roll across the Great Plains, obscuring the lives of people, blighting homes, hampering traffic, drifting eastward to New York and westward to California. They carry the natural riches of the plains and deposit them broadcast over the nation. Exposed by cultivation which killed the protecting grasses, and powdered by protracted drought, the rich topsoil is being stripped from tens of thousands of acres by wind erosion, leaving land and life impoverished.

Dust, drought, and protracted depression have exposed also the human resources of the plains to the bleak winds of adversity. After the drifting dust clouds drift the people; over the concrete ribbons of highway which lead out in every direction come the refugees. We are witnessing the process of social erosion and a consequent shifting of human sands in a movement which is increasing and may become great.

At Fort Yuma the bridge over the Colorado marks the southeastern portal to California. Across this bridge move shiny cars of tourists, huge trucks, an occasional horse and wagon, or a Yuma Indian on horseback. And at intervals in the other traffic appear slow-moving and conspicuous cars loaded with refugees.

The refugees travel in old automobiles and light trucks, some of them homemade, and frequently with trailers behind. All their worldly possessions are piled on the car and covered with old canvas or ragged bedding, with perhaps bedsprings atop, a small iron cook-stove on the running board, a battered trunk, lantern, and galvanized iron washtub tied on behind. Children, aunts, grandmothers and a dog are jammed into the car, stretching its capacity incredibly. A neighbor boy sprawls on top of the loaded trailer.

Most of the refugees are in obvious distress. Clothing is sometimes neat and in good condition, particularly if the emigrants left last fall, came via Arizona, and made a little money in the cotton harvest there. But sometimes it is literally in tatters. At worst, these people lack money even for a California auto license. Asked for the $3 fee, a mother with six children and only $3.40 replied, "That's food for my babies!" She was allowed to proceed without a license.

White Americans of old stock predominate among the emigrants. Long, lanky Oklahomans with small heads, blue eyes, an Abe Lincoln cut to the thighs, and surrounded by tow-headed children; bronzed Texans with a drawl, clear-cut features, and an aggressive spirit; a few Mexicans, mestizos with many children; occasionally Negroes; all are crossing over into California.

The westward movement of rural folk from Oklahoma, Texas, Arkansas and adjacent states, whence most of the refugees to California are now coming, of course is not new. The rise of cotton production in Imperial Valley[1] in 1910 started migration of cotton pickers and growers from the Southwest. The spread of cotton culture to the San Joaquin Valley[2] in 1919 accelerated the interstate movement; many came seasonally to harvest the cotton and returned, while others remained as a permanent accretion. The present migration, therefore, follows channels cut historically. But it moves, with the tremendous added impulses of drought and depression behind it, which increase its westward volume, and which may be expected to reduce the usual backflow.

---

[1] Imperial Valley is in southeastern California.
[2] The San Joaquin Valley comprises the southern half of the Central Valley of California and is the most intensively cultivated region in the state.

The immediate factors dislodging people are several. Clearly, although piecemeal and in some bewilderment, the emigrants tell the story: "We got blowed out in Oklahoma." – "Yes sir, born and raised in the state of Texas; farmed all my natural life. Ain't nothin' there to stay for – nothin' to eat. Somethin's radical wrong," said an ex-cotton farmer encamped shelterless under eucalyptus trees in Imperial Valley. A mother with seven children whose husband died in Arizona en route explained: "The drought come and burned it up. We'd have gone back to Oklahoma from Arizona, but there wasn't anything to go to." – "Lots left ahead of us – no work of no kind." – "It seems like God has forsaken us back there in Arkansas."

Curiously, not only drought and depression but also flood and the very measures which mitigate the severity of depression for some people have unloosed others. A large party of Negroes from Mississippi entering California at Fort Yuma in March reported that they had "just beat the water out by a quarter of a mile." A destitute share-crop farmer, stopping tentless by the highway near Bakersfield, with only green onions as food for his wife and children, had striven to buy a farm in Oklahoma and lost it. But he announced proudly that he had left Wagner County "clear," owing no one. In his story were echoes of crop-restriction, naturally only of its sadder side, and of conflict between cotton share-croppers on one hand and "first tenants" and landlords on the other. "It knocks thousands of fellows like me out of a crop. The ground is laying there, growing up in weeds. The landowner got the benefit and the first tenant [who finances the crop and provides teams and tools, feed and seed] says 'I can't furnish [subsistence during the growing season] any more,' so the share-crop tenant 'on halves' goes on FERA;[3] he's out. It's putting 'em down, down, down. It looks to me like overproduction is better than not having it." Another refugee who had been farm laborer and oil worker in Oklahoma, said, "Since the oil-quota, I've had no work."[4]

It is hope that draws the refugees to California, hope of finding work, of keeping off or getting off federal relief, of maintaining morale, of finding surcease of trouble. "We haven't had to have no help yet. Lots of 'em have, but we haven't," said Oklahoma pea-pickers on El Camino Real at Mission San Jose. "All I want is a chance to make an honest living." – "When a person's able

---

[3] Federal Emergency Relief Administration
[4] This paragraph refers to several New Deal programs, intended to boost agricultural product prices by controlling economic activity, that the refugees believed made their situation more difficult. See the introduction to Document 25.

to work, what's the use of begging? We ain't that kind of people," said elderly pea-pickers near Calipatria.[5]

To some few migrants without responsibility, there is hardly more in it all than adventure. A group of young hillbillies, living in a brush hut evacuated by Filipinos, can take a day off from the carrot fields of Imperial Valley, lie about barefoot at a game of cards, and blithely play Home Sweet Home on a harmonica.

Of course, many refugees do not shun relief. A California border official reports that refugees say, "People are better cared for here than in the cotton states," correctly implying one motive for emigration. Yet many who do not receive relief and are desperately in need of it for themselves and their children, avoid seeking it as long as possible. Many who would leave cannot, for lack of resources. These, like the tenants who write hopefully from Oklahoma that "If we can make a crop this year, we'll come to California," await only a good harvest to emigrate.

But there is agony in tearing up roots, even when these have been loosened by adversity. "God only knows why we left Texas, 'cept he's in a movin' mood," said a wife who accepted reluctantly the decision of her husband to leave.

Many families comfort themselves with the thought of return home when drought and depression are over. Many will return, but many others will not; they have burned their bridges without realizing it. Now the movement is west. A pregnant Oklahoma mother living without shelter in Imperial Valley while the menfolk bunched carrots for money to enable them to move on, made poignant request for directions. "Where is Tranquility, California?" To most of the refugees hope is greater than obstacles. With bedding drenched by rain while he slept in the open, with topless car and a tire gone flat, an Oklahoman with the usual numerous dependents could say, "Pretty hard on us now. Sun'll come out pretty soon and we'll be all right."

Unfortunately "tranquility" is not generally reached by those seeking refuge on the coast. Land is not readily available for new farmers nor is the local reception altogether friendly. Oregonians are already becoming concerned over the influx of settlers in their midst. California agricultural workers are restive at the increase of competitors. And the legislature of that state is presented with a bill to exclude all "indigent persons or persons liable to become public charges," and to deport all who enter in violation of the prohibition. In the spirit of the legislature which sought unconstitutionally to

---

[5] Calipatria is a city in Imperial County, California.

debar Chinese immigrants from California in the 50's, the present session is asked to exclude American "immigrants" without money.[6] "The state," said one of the sponsors of the bill, "has the power to protect itself from economic disaster. This is the justification. . . . It transcends legalistic argument." In the *Los Angeles Times* "the Lancer" cries in alarm: "That 5000 indigents are coming into Southern California. . . leaves one appalled. This is the gravest problem before the United States. . . these tattered migrations." Lamenting good roads he adds: "The Chinese, wiser than we, have delayed building a great system of highways for that very reason – to head off these dangerous migrations – indigent people stampeding from the farms into cities to live on charity. Incidentally, that was one of the reasons why Rome crashed."

The drought emigrants, however, have moved into rural California rather than to the cities. For in agriculture the labor market is highly fluid, and almost anyone is free to try his hand when work is to be done; although skill is essential to good earnings, anyone can get the opportunity to bunch some carrots. So they gravitate naturally into a labor population which moves incessantly from harvest to harvest, which lives in poverty under generally unsanitary and inadequate conditions and which competes for work in a market so glutted that even the farmers cry for protection because strikes are readily kindled when great underemployed "surpluses" collect.

Thus the refugees seeking individual protection in the traditional spirit of the American frontier by westward migration are unknowingly arrivals at another frontier, one of social conflict. In this conflict they are found on both sides. An ex-tenant farmer picking peas in Imperial Valley complains there of the great landowners who are also the bane of his class in Oklahoma whence he came, "The monied men got all the land gobbled up." In the sheds of El Centro the lettuce packers were on strike this spring. A family of refugees in dire distress naturally helped to break strike. With the earnings, they purchased an automobile needed badly for family support. They had learned what other laborers learn quickly in the highly seasonal agriculture of the coast, "A person can't get by without a car in California, like in Oklahoma."

---

[6] Concern about Chinese immigration rose in California in the 1850s, as Chinese immigrants competed for jobs. The state legislature passed legislation in the 1850s intended to limit this competition and discourage Chinese immigrants. It is unclear why the author referred to these laws as unconstitutional. He may have had in mind the 14th amendment, not ratified until 1868, or federal laws, or Supreme Court decisions which also came about after the 1850s.

Participation in more labor conflict doubtless lies ahead of the refugees coming to California, for tension in that state is not abating. The bitter criminal syndicalist trials in Sacramento[7] were hailed by extremists as a test of power; half the defendants were acquitted, half were convicted. Among the latter were the chief leaders of the agricultural strikes of 1933. Farmers and their spokesmen have exhibited great confidence in repression of agitators and pickets as a means of maintaining peace in agriculture. But still they are uneasy as the successive harvests of 1935 advance. Expending as much as $35 or $50 an acre to bring a crop to maturity, they see their entire year's return staked upon a few days of uninterrupted harvest. The fifty-odd farm strikes since December 1932 naturally have made them fearful of more interruptions, and they have organized for self-defense. "The Associated Farmers,"[8] said their spokesman before the Commonwealth Club, "intend to get laws passed that will protect them against Communists, and to see that these laws are rigidly enforced. We are not trying to beat down wages; we are not advocating illegal force or terrorism. But we will not willingly submit to having twenty or thirty automobile loads of so-called peaceful picketers parading up and down in front of our homes, threatening and intimidating, and even blockading the highways." Unions under conservative labels are almost equally opposed. "If the American Federation of Labor[9] should form farm unions, the chances are that foreign or native-born radicals would sooner or later get control of them, just as they did with the longshoremen's union." Commenting on this attitude a State Federation official said bitterly, "If we had a strike, the farmers would conveniently find one or two Communists around."

The future of the refugees, then, is hardly likely to be tranquil. They will be caught in whatever rural labor struggles arise. Like their predecessors of recent years some will find a degree of economic and physical stability in California, but others will mill incessantly through the harvests and live in squatters' camps and rural slums, unless a protecting government intervenes. The refugees are conscious of their present destitution and enforced mobility, and grope for help: "Poor folks has poor ways, you know." – "There's more or less humiliation living this way, but we can't help it. Our tent's wore out." – "Can't

---

[7] Eighteen labor leaders were tried in Sacramento for "criminal syndicalism," advocating the overthrow of the U.S. government.

[8] The Associated Farmers was an organization of farm owners and their supporters in the 1930s who sought to counter efforts to organize farm workers.

[9] The American Federation of Labor, as its name suggests, was a federation of unions, the largest such organization in the United States in the first half of the 20th century.

we have better houses?" – "What bothers us travellin' people most is we can't get no place to stay still." But the struggle against unsanitary conditions, flies, and bad water is too much for many people and they give up. "I hate to boil the water, because then it has so much scum on it," said a pea-picker who drew his water from the irrigating ditch in the usual manner.

The refugees discuss the Townsend plan.[10] They sense demoralization and the futility of continual relief: "This giving people something don't do no good." – "This relief business is all a fake anyway. When they get on it they don't want to work any more." Grasping the idea of rehabilitation, a refugee recipient of relief said, "If they'd a' give it to me in one chunk I could a' gone back and bought me a little piece o' land." But the problem is bewildering to most of them. "We was out here nine years ago; then we could get a steady job. Now it seems we can't stay in one place. We got to follow these little jobs to live." – "I'm not smart enough to know what ought to be done; it sure doesn't suit me."

Across the border at Fort Yuma the refugees are straggling west. They are not newly shod and clad, moved under government direction by train and a trim army transport, nor met by mayors and brass bands, like the drought sufferers from Minnesota bound for the colonization of Alaska.[11] But they constitute already a far greater, if unplanned and almost unnoticed redistribution of the nation's population. To the Alaskan colonists the Matanuska Valley "looks like Heaven." To an Oklahoman who crossed the Tehachapi and viewed the wild flowers of the southern San Joaquin Valley, California "looks like Paradise compared to what it was there."

But questions of the future, both immediate and remote, arise. Will California continue to look like Paradise as the harvests wear on, and the refugees realize that they are definitely a part of the under-employed labor army – white Americans, Mexicans, Negroes, and Filipinos – mobile and restless, which has engaged in strike after strike? Is it conceivable that the grandchildren of the emigrants of 1935 will take pride in placing grandmother's cook-stove and trunk in museums beside the gold-seeker's pan

---

[10] Proposed by Francis Townsend in 1933, the Townsend plan was a pension plan for the retired over 60 to be funded by a 2% national sales tax. It was a forerunner of social security. See Documents 23 and 26.

[11] As part of its efforts to deal with the economic crisis, the Federal Emergency Relief Administration set up several colonies to which distressed people could move. One of these was in Alaska, to which 203 families from the upper mid-west moved.

or the table which came 'round the Horn in '51?[12] Or will these children of distress who creep west unheralded have no share in California history and tradition? The lure of gold in the past, and of land, has been superseded by the expelling forces of drought and depression in the present.

What of the future, when mechanical cotton pickers invade the Old South, making human hands unnecessary? What of the Southern tenants and laborers under the ominous cloud of invention? What will they do? Where will they go? Are the refugees of today the last Western emigrants, or are they but forerunners of greater migrations of hope and despair to come?

---

[12] Some of those traveling to California during the 1850s gold rush came by boat, around the tip of South America, Cape Horn.

Document 30

Annual Message to Congress
President Franklin D. Roosevelt
January 3, 1936

Nineteen thirty-six was an election year. President Roosevelt was eager to fight the campaign, and saw it as a referendum on all that he and the New Deal had done. He was optimistic that he would win re-election. The economy had grown since his election in 1932; income was up, as were stock prices by more than 80 percent. Six million new jobs had opened up, bringing unemployment down by a third. Most of those unemployed had at least some work through various New Deal programs. Roosevelt began his campaign with his Annual Message to Congress, delivered to a special evening session, the first one a President had addressed. He opened his speech by discussing the rising danger of autocratic and aggressive powers overseas. He then launched into a blistering attack on his domestic political opponents, accusing them of being aggressive autocrats ganging up against the people's liberties like the autocrats overseas. Against these domestic autocrats, whom Roosevelt described as greedy and selfish, he held up the new "economic constitutional order" that his administration had put in place since 1932. Roosevelt concluded his message to Congress by quoting an inspirational passage that spoke of the present "generation whose lips are touched by fire," an allusion to Isaiah 6:6-7.

Source: Franklin D. Roosevelt, "Annual Message to Congress," January 3, 1936. Online by Gerhard Peters and John T. Woolley, The American Presidency Project. http://www.presidency.ucsb.edu/ws/?pid=15095.

. . . I realize that I have emphasized to you the gravity of the situation which confronts the people of the world. This emphasis is justified because of its importance to civilization and therefore to the United States. Peace is jeopardized by the few and not by the many. Peace is threatened by those who seek selfish power. The world has witnessed similar eras – as in the days when petty kings and feudal barons were changing the map of Europe every fortnight, or when great emperors and great kings were engaged in a mad scramble for colonial empire. We hope that we are not again at the threshold of such an era. But if face it we must, then the United States and the rest of the Americas can play but one role: through a well-ordered neutrality to do naught to encourage the contest, through adequate defense to save ourselves from embroilment and attack, and through example and all legitimate encouragement and assistance to persuade other Nations to return to the ways of peace and good-will.

The evidence before us clearly proves that autocracy in world affairs endangers peace and that such threats do not spring from those Nations devoted to the democratic ideal. If this be true in world affairs, it should have the greatest weight in the determination of domestic policies.

Within democratic Nations the chief concern of the people is to prevent the continuance or the rise of autocratic institutions that beget slavery at home and aggression abroad. Within our borders, as in the world at large, popular opinion is at war with a power-seeking minority.

That is no new thing. It was fought out in the Constitutional Convention of 1787. From time to time since then, the battle has been continued, under Thomas Jefferson, Andrew Jackson, Theodore Roosevelt and Woodrow Wilson.

In these latter years we have witnessed the domination of government by financial and industrial groups, numerically small but politically dominant in the twelve years that succeeded the World War. The present group of which I speak is indeed numerically small and, while it exercises a large influence and has much to say in the world of business, it does not, I am confident, speak the true sentiments of the less articulate but more important elements that constitute real American business.

In March, 1933, I appealed to the Congress of the United States and to the people of the United States in a new effort to restore power to those to whom it rightfully belonged. The response to that appeal resulted in the writing of a new chapter in the history of popular government. You, the members of the Legislative branch, and I, the Executive, contended for and established a new relationship between Government and people.

What were the terms of that new relationship? They were an appeal from the clamor of many private and selfish interests, yes, an appeal from the clamor of partisan interest, to the ideal of the public interest. Government became the representative and the trustee of the public interest. Our aim was to build upon essentially democratic institutions, seeking all the while the adjustment of burdens, the help of the needy, the protection of the weak, the liberation of the exploited and the genuine protection of the people's property.

It goes without saying that to create such an economic constitutional order, more than a single legislative enactment was called for. We, you in the Congress and I as the Executive, had to build upon a broad base. Now, after thirty-four months of work, we contemplate a fairly rounded whole. We have returned the control of the Federal Government to the City of Washington.

To be sure, in so doing, we have invited battle. We have earned the hatred of entrenched greed. The very nature of the problem that we faced made it necessary to drive some people from power and strictly to regulate others. I made that plain when I took the oath of office in March, 1933. I spoke of the practices of the unscrupulous money-changers who stood indicted in the court of public opinion. I spoke of the rulers of the exchanges of mankind's goods, who failed through their own stubbornness and their own incompetence. I said that they had admitted their failure and had abdicated.

Abdicated? Yes, in 1933, but now with the passing of danger they forget their damaging admissions and withdraw their abdication.

They seek the restoration of their selfish power. They offer to lead us back round the same old corner into the same old dreary street.

Yes, there are still determined groups that are intent upon that very thing. Rigorously held up to popular examination, their true character presents itself. They steal the livery of great national constitutional ideals to serve discredited special interests. As guardians and trustees for great groups of individual stockholders they wrongfully seek to carry the property and the interests entrusted to them into the arena of partisan politics. They seek – this minority in business and industry – to control and often do control and use for their own purposes legitimate and highly honored business associations; they engage in vast propaganda to spread fear and discord among the people – they would "gang up" against the people's liberties.

The principle that they would instill into government if they succeed in seizing power is well shown by the principles which many of them have instilled into their own affairs: autocracy toward labor, toward stockholders, toward consumers, toward public sentiment. Autocrats in smaller things, they seek autocracy in bigger things. "By their fruits ye shall know them."

If these gentlemen believe, as they say they believe, that the measures adopted by this Congress and its predecessor, and carried out by this Administration, have hindered rather than promoted recovery, let them be consistent. Let them propose to this Congress the complete repeal of these measures. The way is open to such a proposal.

Let action be positive and not negative. The way is open in the Congress of the United States for an expression of opinion by yeas and nays. Shall we say that values are restored and that the Congress will, therefore, repeal the laws under which we have been bringing them back? Shall we say that because national income has grown with rising prosperity, we shall repeal existing taxes and thereby put off the day of approaching a balanced budget and of starting to reduce the national debt? Shall we abandon the reasonable support and regulation of banking? Shall we restore the dollar to its former gold content?

...

Members of the Congress, let these challenges be met. If this is what these gentlemen want, let them say so to the Congress of the United States. Let them no longer hide their dissent in a cowardly cloak of generality. Let them define the issue. We have been specific in our affirmative action. Let them be specific in their negative attack.

But the challenge faced by this Congress is more menacing than merely a return to the past – bad as that would be. Our resplendent economic autocracy does not want to return to that individualism of which they prate, even though the advantages under that system went to the ruthless and the strong. They realize that in thirty-four months we have built up new instruments of public power. In the hands of a people's Government this power is wholesome and proper. But in the hands of political puppets of an economic autocracy such power would provide shackles for the liberties of the people. Give them their way and they will take the course of every autocracy of the past – power for themselves, enslavement for the public.

Their weapon is the weapon of fear. I have said, "The only thing we have to fear is fear itself." That is as true today as it was in 1933. But such fear as they instill today is not a natural fear, a normal fear; it is a synthetic, manufactured, poisonous fear that is being spread subtly, expensively and cleverly by the same people who cried in those other days, "Save us, save us, lest we perish."

I am confident that the Congress of the United States well understands the facts and is ready to wage unceasing warfare against those who seek a continuation of that spirit of fear. The carrying out of the laws of the land as enacted by the Congress requires protection until final adjudication by the highest tribunal of the land. The Congress has the right and can find the means to protect its own prerogatives.

We are justified in our present confidence. Restoration of national income, which shows continuing gains for the third successive year, supports the normal and logical policies under which agriculture and industry are returning to full activity. Under these policies we approach a balance of the national budget. National income increases; tax receipts, based on that income, increase without the levying of new taxes. That is why I am able to say to this, the Second Session of the 74th Congress, that it is my belief based on existing laws that no new taxes, over and above the present taxes, are either advisable or necessary.

National income increases; employment increases. Therefore, we can look forward to a reduction in the number of those citizens who are in need. Therefore, also, we can anticipate a reduction in our appropriations for relief.

In the light of our substantial material progress, in the light of the increasing effectiveness of the restoration of popular rule, I recommend to the Congress that we advance; that we do not retreat. I have confidence that you will not fail the people of the Nation whose mandate you have already so faithfully fulfilled.

I repeat, with the same faith and the same determination, my words of March 4, 1933: "We face the arduous days that lie before us in the warm courage of national unity; with a clear consciousness of seeking old and precious moral values; with a clean satisfaction that comes from the stern performance of duty by old and young alike. We aim at the assurance of a rounded and permanent national life. We do not distrust the future of essential democracy."

I cannot better end this message on the state of the Union than by repeating the words of a wise philosopher at whose feet I sat many, many years ago.

"What great crises teach all men whom the example and counsel of the brave inspire is the lesson: Fear not, view all the tasks of life as sacred, have faith in the triumph of the ideal, give daily all that you have to give, be loyal and rejoice whenever you find yourselves part of a great ideal enterprise. You, at this moment, have the honor to belong to a generation whose lips are touched by fire. You live in a land that now enjoys the blessings of peace. But let nothing human be wholly alien to you. The human race now passes through one of its great crises. New ideas, new issues – a new call for men to carry on the work of righteousness, of charity, of courage, of patience, and of loyalty. . . . However memory bring back this moment to your minds, let it be able to say to you: That was a great moment. It was the beginning of a new era. . . . This world in its crisis called for volunteers, for men of faith in life, of patience in service, of charity and of insight. I responded to the call however I could. I volunteered to give myself to my Master – the cause of humane and brave living. I studied, I loved, I labored, unsparingly and hopefully, to be worthy of my generation."[1]

---

[1] Josiah Royce, "A Word for the Times," *Harvard Graduates' Magazine* 23, 9 (December 1914), 208–09. Roosevelt omitted without ellipses a few phrases specific to recent graduates. A longer passage he omitted with ellipses was a call to the graduates to be "wise men and true, men fitted by life to sit in judgment or to give counsel regarding questions that the world has never faced before." In addition to being a professor at Harvard, from which Roosevelt graduated in 1903, Royce (1855–1916) was a prominent American philosopher. One of Roosevelt's many biographers, Jean Edward Smith, reports that it is unlikely that Roosevelt studied with Royce, *FDR* (New York: Random House, 2007), 30.

Document 31

United States v. Butler
Associate Justice Owen J. Roberts
January 6, 1936

In Schechter v. United States, *the Supreme Court invalidated the National Industrial Recovery Act (Documents 19 and 28). Eight months later, in the* Butler *case, it did the same with the Agricultural Adjustment Act (AAA). Under this law, farmers could enter into voluntary contracts with the federal government in which they would receive subsidies in return for their agreement to grow less of certain agricultural products. The subsidies would be paid for from revenues generated by a special tax on processors such as cotton gin operators and mill owners. By mid-1935, thanks in part to the AAA, farm income had increased by about fifty percent since 1932. However, William Butler and others involved in the Hoosac Mills, which processed cotton, brought suit against the United States to challenge the constitutionality of the AAA, when they were taxed under its provisions.*

The Schechter *case had focused on the compulsory nature of the industrial codes, so the administration believed that, because the AAA was based on voluntary contracts, it would be more acceptable to the court. They were wrong. In a 6 – 3 decision written by Associate Justice Owen J. Roberts, the court took aim at the tax on processors. The Constitution, the justices pointed out, granted the power to tax for the purpose of the "general welfare," not to bestow particular benefits on those who have agreed to adhere to special government regulations. The tax, therefore, was unconstitutional.*

Because the Butler *decision focused on the tax, and not on the principal of the subsidy, much of the AAA was salvageable. In February 1938, therefore, Congress approved – and the president quickly signed – a second Agricultural Adjustment Act that maintained the subsidies, while asserting that they would be funded from the general revenues of the federal government, and not from a special tax. Nevertheless, the* Butler *case represented a significant rebuke to the administration's use of the taxing power to pursue its New Deal agenda.*

Source: *Online from "FDR and the Supreme Court,"* The New Deal Network *(Columbia University: Institute for Learning Technologies),*
http://newdeal.feri.org/court/297US1.htm

There should be no misunderstanding as to the function of this court in such a case. It is sometimes said that the court assumes a power to overrule or control the action of the people's representatives. This is a misconception. The Constitution is the supreme law of the land ordained and established by the people. All legislation must conform to the principles it lays down. When an act of Congress is appropriately challenged in the courts as not conforming to the constitutional mandate, the judicial branch of the government has only one duty; to lay the article of the Constitution which is invoked beside the statute which is challenged and to decide whether the latter squares with the former. All the court does, or can do, is to announce its considered judgment upon the question. The only power it has, if such it may be called, is the power of judgment. This court neither approves nor condemns any legislative policy. Its delicate and difficult office is to ascertain and declare whether the legislation is in accordance with, or in contravention of, the provisions of the Constitution; and, having done that, its duty ends.

The question is not what power the federal government ought to have, but what powers in fact have been given by the people. It hardly seems necessary to reiterate that ours is a dual form of government; that in every state there are two governments; the state and the United States. Each state has all governmental powers save such as the people, by their Constitution, have conferred upon the United States, denied to the states, or reserved to themselves. The federal union is a government of delegated powers. It has only such as are expressly conferred upon it and such as are reasonably to be implied from those granted. In this respect we differ radically from nations where all legislative power, without restriction or limitation, is vested in a parliament or other legislative body subject to no restrictions except the discretion of its members.

Article 1, § 8, of the Constitution, vests sundry powers in the Congress. But[1] two of its clauses have any bearing upon the validity of the statute under review.

The third clause endows the Congress with power "to regulate Commerce ... among the several States." Despite a reference in its first section to a burden upon, and an obstruction of the normal currents of, commerce, the act under review does not purport to regulate transactions in interstate or foreign

---

[1] "But" is used here in its meaning of "only."

commerce. Its stated purpose is the control of agricultural production, a purely local activity, in an effort to raise the prices paid the farmer. Indeed, the government does not attempt to uphold the validity of the act on the basis of the commerce clause, which, for the purpose of the present case, may be put aside as irrelevant.

The clause thought to authorize the legislation, the first, confers upon the Congress power "to lay and collect Taxes, Duties, Imposts and Excises, to pay the Debts and provide for the common Defence and general Welfare of the United States. . . ." It is not contended that this provision grants power to regulate agricultural production upon the theory that such legislation would promote the general welfare. The government concedes that the phrase "to provide for the general welfare" qualifies the power "to lay and collect taxes." The view that the clause grants power to provide for the general welfare, independently of the taxing power, has never been authoritatively accepted. Mr. Justice Story[2] points out that, if it were adopted, "it is obvious that under color of the generality of the words, to 'provide for the common defense and general welfare', the government of the United States is, in reality, a government of general and unlimited powers, notwithstanding the subsequent enumeration of specific powers." The true construction undoubtedly is that the only thing granted is the power to tax for the purpose of providing funds for payment of the nation's debts and making provision for the general welfare.

Nevertheless, the government asserts that warrant is found in this clause for the adoption of the Agricultural Adjustment Act. The argument is that Congress may appropriate and authorize the spending of moneys for the "general welfare"; that the phrase should be liberally construed to cover anything conducive to national welfare; that decision as to what will promote such welfare rests with Congress alone, and the courts may not review its determination; and, finally, that the appropriation under attack was in fact for the general welfare of the United States.

The Congress is expressly empowered to lay taxes to provide for the general welfare. Funds in the Treasury as a result of taxation may be expended only through appropriation. They can never accomplish the objects for which they were collected, unless the power to appropriate is as broad as the power to tax. The necessary implication from the terms of the grant is that the public funds may be appropriated "to provide for the general welfare of the United States." These words cannot be meaningless, else they would not have been

---

[2] Joseph Story served on the Supreme Court from 1812 to 1845. His *Commentaries on the Constitution of the United States* appeared 1833.

used. The conclusion must be that they were intended to limit and define the granted power to raise and to expend money. How shall they be construed to effectuate the intent of the instrument?

Since the foundation of the nation, sharp differences of opinion have persisted as to the true interpretation of the phrase. Madison asserted it amounted to no more than a reference to the other powers enumerated in the subsequent clauses of the same section; that, as the United States is a government of limited and enumerated powers, the grant of power to tax and spend for the general national welfare must be confined to the enumerated legislative fields committed to the Congress. In this view the phrase is mere tautology, for taxation and appropriation are or may be necessary incidents of the exercise of any of the enumerated legislative powers. Hamilton, on the other hand, maintained the clause confers a power separate and distinct from those later enumerated, is not restricted in meaning by the grant of them, and Congress consequently has a substantive power to tax and to appropriate, limited only by the requirement that it shall be exercised to provide for the general welfare of the United States. Each contention has had the support of those whose views are entitled to weight. This court has noticed the question, but has never found it necessary to decide which is the true construction. Mr. Justice Story, in his Commentaries, espouses the Hamiltonian position. . . . While, therefore, the power to tax is not unlimited, its confines are set in the clause which confers it, and not in those of section 8 which bestow and define the legislative powers of the Congress. It results that the power of Congress to authorize expenditure of public moneys for public purposes is not limited by the direct grants of legislative power found in the Constitution.

But the adoption of the broader construction leaves the power to spend subject to limitations.

As Story says: "The Constitution was, from its very origin, contemplated to be the frame of a national government, of special and enumerated powers, and not of general and unlimited powers."

Again he says: "A power to lay taxes for the common defense and general welfare of the United States is not in common sense a general power. It is limited to those objects. It cannot constitutionally transcend them."

. . . We are not now required to ascertain the scope of the phrase "general welfare of the United States" or to determine whether an appropriation in aid of agriculture falls within it. Wholly apart from that question, another principle embedded in our Constitution prohibits the enforcement of the Agricultural Adjustment Act. The act invades the reserved rights of the states. It is a statutory plan to regulate and control agricultural production, a matter beyond the powers delegated to the federal government. The tax, the appropriation of the funds raised, and the direction for their disbursement, are but parts of the plan. They are but means to an unconstitutional end.

From the accepted doctrine that the United States is a government of delegated powers, it follows that those not expressly granted, or reasonably to be implied from such as are conferred, are reserved to the states or to the people. To forestall any suggestion to the contrary, the Tenth Amendment was adopted. The same proposition, otherwise stated, is that powers not granted are prohibited. None to regulate agricultural production is given, and therefore legislation by Congress for that purpose is forbidden.

It is an established principle that the attainment of a prohibited end may not be accomplished under the pretext of the exertion of powers which are granted....

The power of taxation, which is expressly granted, may, of course, be adopted as a means to carry into operation another power also expressly granted. But resort to the taxing power to effectuate an end which is not legitimate, not within the scope of the Constitution, is obviously inadmissible. ...

... If the taxing power may not be used as the instrument to enforce a regulation of matters of state concern with respect to which the Congress has no authority to interfere, may it, as in the present case, be employed to raise the money necessary to purchase a compliance which the Congress is powerless to command? The government asserts that whatever might be said against the validity of the plan, if compulsory, it is constitutionally sound because the end is accomplished by voluntary co-operation. There are two sufficient answers to the contention. The regulation is not in fact voluntary. The farmer, of course, may refuse to comply, but the price of such refusal is the loss of benefits. The amount offered is intended to be sufficient to exert pressure on him to agree to the proposed regulation. The power to confer or withhold unlimited benefits is the power to coerce or destroy. If the cotton grower elects not to accept the benefits, he will receive less for his crops; those who receive payments will be able to undersell him. The result may well be financial ruin. The coercive purpose and intent of the statute is not obscured by the fact that it has not been perfectly successful. It is pointed out that, because there still remained a minority whom the rental and benefit payments were insufficient to induce to surrender their independence of action, the

Congress has gone further, and, in the Bankhead Cotton Act,[3] used the taxing power in a more directly minatory fashion to compel submission. This progression only serves more fully to expose the coercive purpose of the so-called tax imposed by the present act. It is clear that the Department of Agriculture has properly described the plan as one to keep a non-co-operating minority in line. This is coercion by economic pressure. The asserted power of choice is illusory. . . .

But if the plan were one for purely voluntary co-operation it would stand no better so far as federal power is concerned. At best, it is a scheme for purchasing with federal funds submission to federal regulation of a subject reserved to the states.

It is said that Congress has the undoubted right to appropriate money to executive officers for expenditure under contracts between the government and individuals; that much of the total expenditures is so made. But appropriations and expenditures under contracts for proper governmental purposes cannot justify contracts which are not within federal power. And contracts for the reduction of acreage and the control of production are outside the range of that power. An appropriation to be expended by the United States under contracts calling for violation of a state law clearly would offend the Constitution. Is a statute less objectionable which authorizes expenditure of federal moneys to induce action in a field in which the United States has no power to intermeddle? The Congress cannot invade state jurisdiction to compel individual action; no more can it purchase such action. . . .

We are not here concerned with a conditional appropriation of money, nor with a provision that if certain conditions are not complied with the appropriation shall no longer be available. By the Agricultural Adjustment Act the amount of the tax is appropriated to be expended only in payment under contracts whereby the parties bind themselves to regulation by the federal government. There is an obvious difference between a statute stating the conditions upon which moneys shall be expended and one effective only upon assumption of a contractual obligation to submit to a regulation which otherwise could not be enforced. Many examples pointing the distinction might be cited. We are referred to appropriations in aid of education, and it is said that no one has doubted the power of Congress to stipulate the sort of education for which money shall be expended. But an appropriation to an

---

[3] The Bankhead Cotton Act of 1934 was intended to clarify the cotton production provision of the Agricultural Adjustment Act of 1933.

educational institution which by its terms is to become available only if the beneficiary enters into a contract to teach doctrines subversive of the Constitution is clearly bad. An affirmance of the authority of Congress so to condition the expenditure of an appropriation would tend to nullify all constitutional limitations upon legislative power.

But it is said that there is a wide difference in another respect, between compulsory regulation of the local affairs of a state's citizens and the mere making of a contract relating to their conduct; that, if any state objects, it may declare the contract void and thus prevent those under the state's jurisdiction from complying with its terms. The argument is plainly fallacious. The United States can make the contract only if the federal power to tax and to appropriate reaches the subject-matter of the contract. If this does reach the subject-matter, its exertion cannot be displaced by state action. To say otherwise is to deny the supremacy of the laws of the United States; to make them subordinate to those of a state. This would reverse the cardinal principle embodied in the Constitution and substitute one which declares that Congress may only effectively legislate as to matters within federal competence when the states do not dissent.

Congress has no power to enforce its commands on the farmer to the ends sought by the Agricultural Adjustment Act. It must follow that it may not indirectly accomplish those ends by taxing and spending to purchase compliance. The Constitution and the entire plan of our government negative any such use of the power to tax and to spend as the act undertakes to authorize. It does not help to declare that local conditions throughout the nation have created a situation of national concern; for this is but to say that whenever there is a widespread similarity of local conditions, Congress may ignore constitutional limitations upon its own powers and usurp those reserved to the states. If, in lieu of compulsory regulation of subjects within the states' reserved jurisdiction, which is prohibited, the Congress could invoke the taxing and spending power as a means to accomplish the same end, clause 1 of section 8 of article 1[4] would become the instrument for total subversion of the governmental powers reserved to the individual states.

If the act before us is a proper exercise of the federal taxing power, evidently the regulation of all industry throughout the United States may be accomplished by similar exercises of the same power. It would be possible to

---

[4] "The Congress shall have power to lay and collect taxes, duties, imposts, and excises, to pay the debts and provide for the common defence and general welfare of the United States."

exact money from one branch of an industry and pay it to another branch in every field of activity which lies within the province of the states. The mere threat of such a procedure might well induce the surrender of rights and the compliance with federal regulation as the price of continuance in business. A few instances will illustrate the thought.

Let us suppose Congress should determine that the farmer, the miner, or some other producer of raw materials is receiving too much for his products, with consequent depression of the processing industry and idleness of its employees. Though, by confession, there is no power vested in Congress to compel by statute a lowering of the prices of the raw material, the same result might be accomplished, if the questioned act be valid, by taxing the producer upon his output and appropriating the proceeds to the processors, either with or without conditions imposed as the consideration for payment of the subsidy.

We have held in *A. L. A. Schechter Poultry Corp. v. United States*. . .that Congress has no power to regulate wages and hours of labor in a local business. If the petitioner is right, this very end may be accomplished by appropriating money to be paid to employers from the federal treasury under contracts whereby they agree to comply with certain standards fixed by federal law or by contract.

Should Congress ascertain that sugar refiners are not receiving a fair profit, and that this is detrimental to the entire industry, and in turn has its repercussions in trade and commerce generally, it might, in analogy to the present law, impose an excise of 2 cents a pound on every sale of the commodity and pass the funds collected to such refiners, and such only, as will agree to maintain a certain price.

Assume that too many shoes are being manufactured throughout the nation; that the market is saturated, the price depressed, the factories running half time, the employees suffering. Upon the principle of the statute in question, Congress might authorize the Secretary of Commerce to enter into contracts with shoe manufacturers providing that each shall reduce his output, and that the United States will pay him a fixed sum proportioned to such reduction, the money to make the payments to be raised by a tax on all retail shoe dealers on their customers.

Suppose that there are too many garment workers in the large cities; that this results in dislocation of the economic balance. Upon the principle contended for, an excise might be laid on the manufacture of all garments manufactured and the proceeds paid to those manufacturers who agree to remove their plants to cities having not more than a hundred thousand population. Thus, through the asserted power of taxation, the federal government, against the will of individual states, might completely redistribute the industrial population.

A possible result of sustaining the claimed federal power would be that every business group which thought itself underprivileged might demand that a tax be laid on its vendors or vendees, the proceeds to be appropriated to the redress of its deficiency of income.

These illustrations are given, not to suggest that any of the purposes mentioned are unworthy, but to demonstrate the scope of the principle for which the government contends; to test the principle by its applications; to point out that, by the exercise of the asserted power, Congress would, in effect, under the pretext of exercising the taxing power, in reality accomplish prohibited ends. It cannot be said that they envisage improbable legislation. The supposed cases are no more improbable than would the present act have been deemed a few years ago.

Until recently no suggestion of the existence of any such power in the federal government has been advanced. The expressions of the framers of the Constitution, the decisions of this court interpreting that instrument and the writings of great commentators will be searched in vain for any suggestion that there exists in the clause under discussion or elsewhere in the Constitution, the authority whereby every provision and every fair implication from that instrument may be subverted, the independence of the individual states obliterated, and the United States converted into a central government exercising uncontrolled police power in every state of the Union, superseding all local control or regulation of the affairs or concerns of the states.

Hamilton himself, the leading advocate of broad interpretation of the power to tax and to appropriate for the general welfare, never suggested that any power granted by the Constitution could be used for the destruction of local self-government in the states. Story countenances no such doctrine. It seems never to have occurred to them, or to those who have agreed with them, that the general welfare of the United States (which has aptly been termed "an indestructible Union, composed of indestructible States,") might be served by obliterating the constituent members of the Union. But to this fatal conclusion the doctrine contended for would inevitably lead. And its sole premise is that, though the makers of the Constitution, in erecting the federal government, intended sedulously to limit and define its powers, so as to reserve to the states and the people sovereign power, to be wielded by the states and their citizens and not to be invaded by the United States, they nevertheless by a single clause gave power to the Congress to tear down the barriers, to invade the states' jurisdiction, and to become a parliament of the whole people, subject to no restrictions save such as are self-imposed. The argument, when seen in its true character and in the light of its inevitable results, must be rejected....

Document 32

"Betrayal of the Democratic Party"
Al Smith
January 25, 1936

The unprecedented nature of the New Deal guaranteed that it would generate a great deal of opposition among conservatives, including those within the Democratic Party. It is worth remembering that there was little ideological cohesion in either of the major parties – both had members ranging from the very conservative to the very liberal. In August 1934, a bipartisan group of businessmen and political leaders formed an organization called the American Liberty League, dedicated to fighting what it believed to be the radicalism of the New Deal. It was never a particularly large group – at its height in mid-1936 it had approximately 125,000 members nationwide – but because so many of its leading figures were wealthy it had little problem getting its message out.

One of the most prominent members of the American Liberty League was Al Smith (1873–1944), formerly governor of New York and the Democratic Party's candidate for president in 1928. In January 1936, he gave the following address at a meeting of the organization at the Mayflower Hotel in Washington, DC. In it he accused President Roosevelt of ignoring the party platform of 1932 and flirting with a dangerous, un-American ideology.

Source: "The Facts in the Case," Speech of Alfred E. Smith at the American Liberty League Dinner, Washington, D.C., January 25, 1936, Jouett Shouse Collection, (American Liberty League Pamphlets), Kentucky Digital Library, University of Kentucky.
http://kdl.kyvl.org/catalog/xt7wwp9t2q46_94_2?

At the outset of my remarks let me make one thing perfectly clear. I am not a candidate for any nomination by any party at any time, and what is more I do not intend to even lift my right hand to secure any nomination from any party at any time.

Further than that I have no axe to grind. There is nothing personal in this whole performance so far as I am concerned. I have no feeling against any man, woman or child in the United States....

I was born in the Democratic Party and I expect to die in it. I was attracted to it in my youth because I was led to believe that no man owned it, and furthermore that no group of men owned it, but, on the other hand, that it belonged to all the plain people in the United States.

I must make a confession. It is not easy for me to stand up here tonight and talk to the American people against the Democratic Administration. This is not easy. It hurts me. But I can call upon innumerable witnesses to testify to the fact that during my whole public life I put patriotism above partisanship. And when I see danger – I say "danger," that is, the "Stop, look, and listen" to the fundamental principles upon which this Government of ours was organized – it is difficult for me to refrain from speaking up.

Now, what are these dangers that I see? The first is the arraignment of class against class. It has been freely predicted that if we were ever to have civil strife again in this country, it would come from the appeal to passion and prejudices that comes from the demagogues that would incite one class of our people against the other.

In my time I have met some good and bad industrialists. I have met some good and bad financiers, but I have also met some good and bad laborers, and this I know, that permanent prosperity is dependent upon both capital and labor alike.

And I also know that there can be no permanent prosperity in this country until industry is able to employ labor, and there certainly can be no permanent recovery upon any governmental theory of soak the rich or soak the poor.

The next thing that I view as being dangerous to our national well-being is government by bureaucracy instead of what we have been taught to look for, government by law.

Just let me quote something from the President's message to Congress: "In thirty-four months we have built up new instruments of public power. In the hands of a people's government this power is wholesome and proper. But in the hands of political puppets of an economic autocracy such power would provide shackles for the liberties of the people."[1]

Now, I interpret that to mean: If you are going to have an autocrat, take me, but be very careful about the other fellow. There is a complete answer to that, and it rises in the minds of the great rank and file, and that answer is just this: We will never in this country tolerate any law that provides shackles for

---

[1] Smith quotes from Roosevelt's Annual Message to Congress, January 3, 1936 (Document 30; see also Document 34, in which Herbert Hoover also quotes this passage).

our people. We don't want autocrats, either in or out of office; we wouldn't even take a good one.

The next danger apparent to me is the vast building up of new bureaus of government, draining the resources of our people into a common pool and redistributing them, not by any process of law, but by the whim of a bureaucratic autocracy.

Well now, what am I here for? I am here not to find fault. Anybody can do that. I am here to make suggestions. What would I have my party do? I would have them reestablish and redeclare the principles that they put forth in that 1932 platform....

.... [N]o Administration in the history of the country came into power with a more simple, a more clear, or a more inescapable mandate than did the party that was inaugurated on the Fourth of March in 1933.

And listen, no candidate in the history of the country ever pledged himself more unequivocally to his party platform than did the President who was inaugurated on that day.

Well, here we are. Millions and millions of Democrats just like myself, all over the country, still believe in that platform. And what we want to know is why it wasn't carried out.

And listen, there is only one man in the United States of America that can answer that question....

.... [L]et's take a look at that platform, and let's see what happened to it. Here is how it started out:

"We believe that a party platform is a covenant with the people, to be faithfully kept by the party when entrusted with power, and that the people are entitled to know in plain words the terms of contract to which they are asked to subscribe. The Democratic Party solemnly promises by appropriate action to put into effect the principles, policies and reforms herein advocated and to eradicate the political methods and practices herein condemned."

My friends, these are what we call fighting words. At the time that the platform went through the air and over the wire, the people of the United States were in the lowest possible depths of despair, and the Democratic platform looked to them like the star of hope; it looked like the rising sun in the East to the mariner on the bridge of a ship after a terrible night. But what happened to it?

First plank: "We advocate immediate and drastic reduction of governmental expenditures by abolishing useless commissions and offices, consolidating departments and bureaus, and eliminating extravagance to accomplish a saving of not less than 25 per cent in the cost of the Federal Government."

Well, now, what is the fact? No offices were consolidated, no bureaus were eliminated, but on the other hand, the alphabet was exhausted in the creation of new departments. And – this is sad news for the taxpayer – the cost, the ordinary cost, what we refer to as housekeeping cost, over and above all emergencies – that ordinary housekeeping cost of government is greater today than it has ever been in any time in the history of the republic.

Another plank: "We favor maintenance of the national credit by a Federal budget annually balanced on the basis of accurate Executive estimates within revenue."

How can you balance a budget if you insist upon spending more money than you take in? Even the increased revenue won't go to balance the budget, because it is hocked before you receive it. What is worse than that[?] ... [W]e have borrowed so that we have reached a new high peak of Federal indebtedness for all time.... [T]he sin of it is that we have the indebtedness and at the end of three years we are just where we started. Unemployment and the farm problem we still have with us.

Now here is something that I want to say to the rank and file. There are three classes of people in this country; there are the poor and the rich, and in between the two is what has often been referred to as the great backbone of America, that is the plain fellow. That is the fellow that makes from one hundred dollars a month up to the man that draws down five or six thousand dollars a year. They are the great army. Forget the rich; they can't pay this debt. If you took everything they have away from them, they couldn't pay it; there ain't enough of them, and furthermore they ain't got enough.

There is no use talking about the poor; they will never pay it, because they have nothing. This debt is going to be paid by that great big middle class that we refer to as the backbone and the rank and file, and the sin of it is they ain't going to know that they are paying it. It is going to come to them in the form of indirect and hidden taxation. It will come to them in the cost of living, in the cost of clothing, in the cost of every activity that they enter into, and because it is not a direct tax, they won't think they're paying, but, take it from me, they are going to pay it.

Another plank: "We advocate the extension of Federal credit to the States to provide unemployment relief where the diminishing resources of the State make it impossible for them to provide for their needs."

That was pretty plain. That was a recognition in the national convention of the rights of the States. But how is it interpreted?

The Federal Government took over most of the relief problems, some of them useful and most of them useless. They started out to prime the pump for industry in order to absorb the ranks of the unemployed, and at the end of three years their affirmative policy is absolutely nothing better than the negative policy of the Administration that preceded them.

"We favor unemployment and old age insurance under State laws."

Now let me make myself perfectly clear so that no demagogue or no crackpot in the next week or so will be able to say anything about my attitude on this kind of legislation. I am in favor of it. And I take my hat off to no man in the United States on the question of legislation beneficial to the poor, the weak, the sick, or the afflicted, or women and children.

Because why? I started out a quarter of a century ago when I had very few followers in my State, and during that period I advocated, fought for, introduced as a legislator, and finally as Governor for eight long years, signed more progressive legislation in the interest of the men, women and children than any man in the State of New York. And the sin of this whole thing, and the part of it that worries me and gives me concern, is that this haphazard, hurry-up passage of legislation is never going to accomplish the purposes for which it was designed. And bear this in mind, follow the platform – "under state laws!"

...

... Another one: "We promise the removal of Government from all fields of private enterprise except where necessary to develop public works and national resources in the common interest."

NRA,[2] a vast octopus set up by government, that wound its arms around all the business of the country, paralyzed big business, and choked little business to death.

Did you read in the papers a short time ago where somebody said that business was going to get a breathing spell? What is the meaning of that? And where did that expression arise? I'll tell you where it comes from. It comes from the prize ring. When the aggressor is punching the head off the other fellow he suddenly takes compassion on him and he gives him a breathing spell before he delivers the knockout wallop.

---

[2] Established by the National Industrial Recovery Act (Document 19) in 1933, the National Recovery Administration sought to coordinate the activities of labor, industry and government through voluntary codes to reduce what the Roosevelt administration thought was inefficient competition. The Supreme Court ruled the NRA unconstitutional in 1935 (Document 28).

Here is another one: "We condemn the open and covert resistance of administrative officials to every effort made by congressional committees to curtail the extravagant expenditures of Government and improvident subsidies granted to private interests."

... [A]s to subsidies, why, never at any time in the history of this or any other country were there so many subsidies granted to private groups, and on such a huge scale.

The fact of the matter is that most of the cases now pending before the United States Supreme Court revolve around the point whether or not it is proper for Congress to tax all the people to pay subsidies to a particular group.[3]

Here is another one: "We condemn the extravagance of the Farm Board, its disastrous action which made the Government a speculator of farm products, and the unsound policy of restricting agricultural products to the demand of domestic markets."

What about the restriction of our agricultural products and the demands of the market? Why, the fact about that is that we shut out entirely the farm market, and by plowing under corn and wheat and the destruction of foodstuffs, food from foreign countries has been pouring into our American markets – food that should have been purchased by us from our own farmers.

In other words, while some of the countries of the Old World were attempting to drive the wolf of hunger from the doormat, the United States flew in the face of God's bounty and destroyed its own foodstuffs. There can be no question about that.

Now I could go on indefinitely with some of the other planks. They are unimportant, and the radio time will not permit it. But just let me sum up this way:

Regulation of the Stock Exchange and the repeal of the Eighteenth Amendment,[4] plus one or two minor planks of the platform that in no way touch the daily life of our people, have been carried out, but the balance of the platform was thrown in the wastebasket. About that there can be no question.

Let's see how it was carried out. Make a test for yourself. Just get the platform of the Democratic Party, and get the platform of the Socialist Party, and lay them down on your dining room table, side by side, and get a heavy

---

[3] See Document 31.
[4] The 18th amendment, ratified January 16, 1919, banned "the manufacture, sale, or transportation of intoxicating liquors within, the importation thereof into, or the exportation thereof from the United States . . . for beverage purposes." The amendment was repealed by the 21st amendment, ratified December 5, 1933.

lead pencil and scratch out the word "Democrat," and scratch out the word "Socialist," and let the two platforms lay there.

Then study the record of the present Administration up to date. After you have done that, make your mind up to pick up the platform that more nearly squares with the record, and you will put your hand on the Socialist platform. You couldn't touch the Democratic. And, incidentally, let me say, that it is not the first time in recorded history, that a group of men have stolen the livery of the church to do the work of the devil.

If you study this whole situation, you will find that that is at the bottom of all our troubles. This country was organized on the principles of representative democracy, and you can't mix Socialism or Communism with that. They are like oil and water; they refuse to mix. And incidentally, let me say to you, that is the reason why the United States Supreme Court is working overtime throwing the alphabet out of the window three letters at a time.[5]

Now I am going to let you in on something else. How do you suppose all this happened? Here is the way it happened: The young Brain Trusters[6] caught the Socialists in swimming and they ran away with their clothes.

It is all right with me. It is all right with me if they want to disguise themselves as Norman Thomas[7] or Karl Marx, or Lenin, or any of the rest of that bunch, but what I won't stand for is to let them march under the banner of Jefferson, Jackson, or Cleveland.[8]

What is worrying me is where does that leave us millions of Democrats? My mind is now fixed upon the Convention in June, in Philadelphia. The committee on resolutions is about to report, and the preamble to the platform is: "We, the representatives of the Democratic Party in Convention assembled, heartily endorse the Democratic Administration."

What happens to the disciples of Jefferson and Jackson and Cleveland when that resolution is read out? Why, for us it is a washout. There is only one of two things we can do. We can either take on the mantle of hypocrisy or we can take a walk, and we will probably do the latter.

---

[5] Smith alludes to the acronyms by which the new agencies created by the Roosevelt administration are known.

[6] The "Brains Trust" was the name commonly given to Franklin Roosevelt's closest advisers during the 1932 campaign and the early years of the New Deal.

[7] Norman Thomas (1884–1968) was a Presbyterian minister who was the Socialist Party of America candidate for President six times beginning in 1928.

[8] Grover Cleveland (1837–1908) was a leading Democratic politician and the 22nd and 24th President of the United States.

Now leave the platform alone for a little while. What about this attack that has been made upon the fundamental institutions of this country? Who threatens them, and did we have any warning of this threat?

Why, you don't have to study party platforms. You don't have to read books. You don't have to listen to professors of economics. You will find the whole thing incorporated in the greatest declaration of political principles that ever came from the hands of man, the Declaration of Independence and the Constitution of the United States.

Always have in your minds that the Constitution and the first ten amendments to it were drafted by refugees and by sons of refugees, by men with bitter memories of European oppression and hardship, by men who brought to this country and handed down to their descendants an abiding fear of arbitrary centralized government and autocracy.

And, listen, all the bitterness and all the hatred of the Old World was distilled in our Constitution into the purest democracy that the world has ever known.

There are just three principles, and in the interest of brevity, I will read them. I can read them quicker than talk them.

"First, a Federal Government, strictly limited in its power, with all other powers except those expressly mentioned reserved to the States and to the people, so as to insure state's rights, guarantee home rule, and preserve freedom of individual initiative and local control."

That is simple enough. The difference between the state constitutions and the Federal Constitution is that in the state you can do anything you want to do provided it is not prohibited by the Constitution. But in the Federal Government, according to that document, you can do only that which that Constitution tells you that you can do.

What is the trouble? Congress has overstepped its powers. It went beyond that constitutional limitation, and it has enacted laws that not only violate that, but violate the home rule and the State's rights principle.

And who says that? Do I say it? Not at all. That was said by the United States Supreme Court in the last ten or twelve days.[9]

Secondly, a government, with three independent branches; Congress to make the laws, the Executive to execute them, the Supreme Court, and so forth. You know that.

In the name of Heaven, where is the independence of Congress? Why, they just laid right down. They are flatter on the Congressional floor than the

---

[9] Smith refers to the *Butler* decision (Document 31).

rug on the table here. They surrendered all of their powers to the Executive, and that is the reason why you read in the newspapers references to Congress as the rubber-stamp Congress.

We all know that the most important bills were drafted by the brain trusters, and sent over to Congress and passed by Congress without consideration, without debate and without meaning any offense at all to my Democratic brethren in Congress, I think I can safely say, without ninety per cent of them knowing what was in the bills, what was the meaning of the list that came over. And beside certain bills was "must." What does that mean? Speaking for the rank and file of American people, we don't want any executive to tell Congress what it must do, and we don't want any Congress or the Executive jointly or severally to tell the United States Supreme Court what it must do. And, on the other hand, we don't want the United States Supreme Court to tell either of them what they must do. What we want, and what we insist upon, and what we are going to have, is the absolute preservation of this balance of power which is the keystone, the arch upon which the whole theory of democratic government has got to rest, and when you rattle it, you rattle the whole structure.

The third one is methods of amending the Constitution. Of course, when our forefathers wrote the Constitution of the United States it couldn't be possible that they had it in their minds that it was going to be all right for all time to come. So they said, "Now, we will provide a manner and method of amending it." That is set forth in the document itself, and during our national life we amended it many times. We amended it once by mistake, and we corrected it.[10] What did we do? We took the amendment out. Fine! That is the way we want to do it, by recourse to the people. But we don't want an Administration that takes a shot at it in the dark, and that ducks away from it and dodges away from it and tries to put something over in contradiction of it upon any theory that there is going to be a great public howl in favor of it, and it is possible that the United States Supreme Court may be intimidated into a friendly opinion with respect to it. But I have held all during my public life that Almighty God is with this country and He didn't give us that kind of Supreme Court.

Now this is pretty tough on me to have to go at my own party this way, but I submit that there is a limit to blind loyalty.

---

[10] A reference to the 18th amendment

As a young man in the Democratic Party, I witnessed the rise and fall of Bryan and Bryanism,[11] and I know exactly what Bryan did to our party. I knew how long it took to build it after he got finished with it. But let me say this to the everlasting credit of Bryan and the men that followed him, they had the nerve and the courage and honesty to put into the platform just what their leaders stood for. And they further put the American people into a position of making an intelligent choice when they went to the polls.

Why, the fact of this whole thing is (I speak now not only of the executive but of the legislature at the same time) that they promised one set of things, they repudiated that promise, and they launched off on a program of action totally different. Well, in 25 years of experience I have known both parties to fail to carry out some of the planks in their platform, but this is the first time that I have known a party, upon such a huge scale, not only not to carry out the planks, but to do the directly opposite thing to what they promised.

Now, suggestions – and I make these as a Democrat anxious for the success of my party, and I make them in good faith. Here are my suggestions.

No. 1: I suggest to the members of my party on Capitol Hill here in Washington that they take their minds off the Tuesday that follows the first Monday in November.[12] Just take your minds off it to the end that you may do the right thing and not the expedient thing.

Next, I suggest to them that they dig up the 1932 platform from the grave that they buried it in, read it over, and study it, breathe life into it, and follow it in legislative and executive action, to the end that they make good their promises to the American people when they put forth that platform, and the candidate that stood upon it, one hundred per cent. In short, make good.

Third, I would suggest to them that they stop compromising with the fundamental principles laid down by Jackson and Jefferson and Cleveland.

Fourth, stop attempting to alter the form and structure of our Government without recourse to the people themselves as provided in their own constitution. This country belongs to the people, and it doesn't belong to any Administration.

Next, I suggest that they read their Oath of Office to support the Constitution of the United States. And I ask them to remember that they took

---

[11] William Jennings Bryan, a Democratic congressman from Nebraska, unsuccessfully ran for president in 1896, 1900, and 1908. He and his supporters fought for the monetization of silver, leading him to be regarded by many, even in his own party, as a dangerous radical.

[12] election day

that oath with their hands on the Holy Bible, thereby calling upon God Almighty Himself to witness their solemn promise. It is bad enough to disappoint us.

Sixth, I suggest that from this moment they resolve to make the Constitution again the civil bible of the United States and pay it the same civil respect and reverence that they would religiously pay the Holy Scripture, and I ask them to read from the Holy Scripture the Parable of the Prodigal Son and to follow his example. "Stop! Stop wasting your substance in a foreign land, and come back to your Father's house."

Now, in conclusion let me give this solemn warning. There can be only one Capitol – Washington or Moscow. There can be only one atmosphere of government, the clear, pure, fresh air of free America, or the foul breath of Communistic Russia. There can be only one flag, the Stars and Stripes, or the Red Flag of the godless union of the Soviet. There can be only one National Anthem. The Star Spangled Banner or the Internationale.[13]

There can be only one victor. If the Constitution wins, we win. But if the Constitution – Stop! Stop there! The Constitution can't lose. The fact is, it has already won, but the news has not reached certain ears.

---

[13] An celebrated hymn of the socialist movement since the late 19th century, the Internationale became the first national anthem of the Soviet Union.

Document 33

Acceptance Speech at the Democratic National Convention
President Franklin D. Roosevelt
June 27, 1936

President Roosevelt won renomination easily at the Democratic convention in Philadelphia. So strong politically was Roosevelt that he was able to get the convention to overturn the rule requiring a candidate to get two-thirds of the delegates' votes to win nomination. In place since 1832, the rule had increased the power of southern delegations at the convention. In the long term, the change began the decline of southern Democratic power and helped Roosevelt win another nomination in 1940.

Roosevelt's acceptance speech, delivered outside to a nighttime crowd of more than 100,000 people, drew an extended analogy between the patriots of 1776 fighting for political freedom from their aristocratic oppressors and Americans of Roosevelt's day fighting for economic freedom from the "privilege princes of . . . new economic dynasties." Roosevelt brought his speech to a close by highlighting the importance of moral principle – faith, hope, and charity – and by declaring, in one of his most famous phrases, that "this generation of Americans has a rendezvous with destiny."

Source: Franklin D. Roosevelt: "Acceptance Speech for the Renomination for the Presidency, Philadelphia, Pa.," June 27, 1936. Online by Gerhard Peters and John T. Woolley, The American Presidency Project. http://www.presidency.ucsb.edu/ws/?pid=15314.

. . . [F]reedom, in itself and of necessity, suggests freedom from some restraining power. In 1776 we sought freedom from the tyranny of a political autocracy – from the eighteenth century royalists who held special privileges from the crown. It was to perpetuate their privilege that they governed without the consent of the governed; that they denied the right of free assembly and free speech; that they restricted the worship of God; that they put the average man's property and the average man's life in pawn to the mercenaries of dynastic power; that they regimented the people.

And so it was to win freedom from the tyranny of political autocracy that the American Revolution was fought. That victory gave the business of governing into the hands of the average man, who won the right with his neighbors to make and order his own destiny through his own Government. Political tyranny was wiped out at Philadelphia on July 4, 1776.

Since that struggle, however, man's inventive genius released new forces in our land which reordered the lives of our people. The age of machinery, of railroads; of steam and electricity; the telegraph and the radio; mass production, mass distribution – all of these combined to bring forward a new civilization and with it a new problem for those who sought to remain free.

For out of this modern civilization economic royalists carved new dynasties. New kingdoms were built upon concentration of control over material things. Through new uses of corporations, banks and securities, new machinery of industry and agriculture, of labor and capital – all undreamed of by the fathers – the whole structure of modern life was impressed into this royal service.

There was no place among this royalty for our many thousands of small business men and merchants who sought to make a worthy use of the American system of initiative and profit. They were no more free than the worker or the farmer. Even honest and progressive-minded men of wealth, aware of their obligation to their generation, could never know just where they fitted into this dynastic scheme of things.

It was natural and perhaps human that the privileged princes of these new economic dynasties, thirsting for power, reached out for control over Government itself. They created a new despotism and wrapped it in the robes of legal sanction. In its service new mercenaries sought to regiment the people, their labor, and their property. And as a result the average man once more confronts the problem that faced the Minute Man.

The hours men and women worked, the wages they received, the conditions of their labor – these had passed beyond the control of the people, and were imposed by this new industrial dictatorship. The savings of the average family, the capital of the small business man, the investments set aside for old age – other people's money – these were tools which the new economic royalty used to dig itself in.

Those who tilled the soil no longer reaped the rewards which were their right. The small measure of their gains was decreed by men in distant cities.

Throughout the Nation, opportunity was limited by monopoly. Individual initiative was crushed in the cogs of a great machine. The field open for free business was more and more restricted. Private enterprise, indeed, became too private. It became privileged enterprise, not free enterprise.

An old English judge[1] once said: "Necessitous men are not free men." Liberty requires opportunity to make a living – a living decent according to the standard of the time, a living which gives man not only enough to live by, but something to live for.

For too many of us the political equality we once had won was meaningless in the face of economic inequality. A small group had concentrated into their own hands an almost complete control over other people's property, other people's money, other people's labor – other people's lives. For too many of us life was no longer free; liberty no longer real; men could no longer follow the pursuit of happiness.

Against economic tyranny such as this, the American citizen could appeal only to the organized power of Government. The collapse of 1929 showed up the despotism for what it was. The election of 1932 was the people's mandate to end it. Under that mandate it is being ended.

The royalists of the economic order have conceded that political freedom was the business of the Government, but they have maintained that economic slavery was nobody's business. They granted that the Government could protect the citizen in his right to vote, but they denied that the Government could do anything to protect the citizen in his right to work and his right to live.

Today we stand committed to the proposition that freedom is no half-and-half affair. If the average citizen is guaranteed equal opportunity in the polling place, he must have equal opportunity in the market place.

These economic royalists complain that we seek to overthrow the institutions of America. What they really complain of is that we seek to take away their power. Our allegiance to American institutions requires the overthrow of this kind of power. In vain they seek to hide behind the Flag and the Constitution. In their blindness they forget what the Flag and the Constitution stand for. Now, as always, they stand for democracy, not tyranny; for freedom, not subjection; and against a dictatorship by mob rule and the over-privileged alike.

The brave and clear platform adopted by this Convention, to which I heartily subscribe, sets forth that Government in a modern civilization has

---

[1] Lord Robert Henley, in his ruling on a 1762 property law case

certain inescapable obligations to its citizens, among which are protection of the family and the home, the establishment of a democracy of opportunity, and aid to those overtaken by disaster.

But the resolute enemy within our gates is ever ready to beat down our words unless in greater courage we will fight for them.

For more than three years we have fought for them. This Convention, in every word and deed, has pledged that that fight will go on.

The defeats and victories of these years have given to us as a people a new understanding of our Government and of ourselves. Never since the early days of the New England town meeting have the affairs of Government been so widely discussed and so clearly appreciated. It has been brought home to us that the only effective guide for the safety of this most worldly of worlds, the greatest guide of all, is moral principle.

We do not see faith, hope and charity as unattainable ideals, but we use them as stout supports of a Nation fighting the fight for freedom in a modern civilization.

Faith – in the soundness of democracy in the midst of dictatorships.

Hope – renewed because we know so well the progress we have made.

Charity – in the true spirit of that grand old word. For charity literally translated from the original means love, the love that understands, that does not merely share the wealth of the giver, but in true sympathy and wisdom helps men to help themselves.

We seek not merely to make Government a mechanical implement, but to give it the vibrant personal character that is the very embodiment of human charity....

In the place of the palace of privilege we seek to build a temple out of faith and hope and charity....

Governments can err, Presidents do make mistakes, but the immortal Dante tells us that divine justice weighs the sins of the cold-blooded and the sins of the warm-hearted in different scales.

Better the occasional faults of a Government that lives in a spirit of charity than the consistent omissions of a Government frozen in the ice of its own indifference.

There is a mysterious cycle in human events. To some generations much is given. Of other generations much is expected. This generation of Americans has a rendezvous with destiny.

In this world of ours in other lands, there are some people, who, in times past, have lived and fought for freedom, and seem to have grown too weary to carry on the fight. They have sold their heritage of freedom for the illusion of a living. They have yielded their democracy.

I believe in my heart that only our success can stir their ancient hope. They begin to know that here in America we are waging a great and successful war. It is not alone a war against want and destitution and economic demoralization. It is more than that; it is a war for the survival of democracy. We are fighting to save a great and precious form of government for ourselves and for the world.

I accept the commission you have tendered me. I join with you. I am enlisted for the duration of the war.

Document 34

"A Third Party"
Father Charles Coughlin
July 1, 1936

Father Charles Coughlin (1891–1979), a Catholic priest in Royal Oak, Michigan, won a national following through his weekly radio broadcast, the "Golden Hour of the Little Flower," which boasted some 30 million listeners. In 1932 he enthusiastically supported Roosevelt, calling the New Deal "Christ's deal." However, he quickly became disillusioned with the president's policies, accusing Roosevelt of being too friendly to bankers. He formed a new organization in 1934 called the National Union for Social Justice, which called for the monetization of silver and the nationalization of major banks and industries. He became a supporter of Huey Long (Document 27), but after Long's assassination in 1935 he embraced the third-party candidacy of Rep. William Lemke of North Dakota. During the second half of the decade he grew increasingly sympathetic to fascism, and blamed Jews for the country's economic woes. In the following speech, broadcast on July 1, 1936, Coughlin denounced the Roosevelt administration for failing to live up to the promises of his inaugural address.

Source: Vital Speeches of the Day, *Vol. II, No. 20 (July 1, 1936), pp. 613.*

.... In the autumn of 1932, it was my privilege to address the American people on the causes of the so-called depression and upon the obvious remedies required to bring about a permanent recovery.

Those were days which witnessed a complete breakdown of the financial system under which our Western civilization had been developed. It was also evident that under this financial system there resulted a concentration of wealth and a multiplication of impoverished families. Unjust wages and unreasonable idleness were universally recognized as contradictions in an age of plenty. To my mind it was inconceivable that irrational and needless want should exist in an age of plenty.

Were there not plenty of raw materials in America? Were not our citizens and our countryside inhabited by plenty of skilled inventors, engineers, executives, workmen and farmers? At no time in the history of civilization was it possible for man to produce such an abundant supply, thanks to the benedictions of mass production machinery. At no time within the last two centuries was there such a demand on the part of our population for the thousands of good things capable of being produced in our fields and in our factories.

What was the basic cause which closed factories, which created idleness, which permitted weeds to overrun our golden fields and plowshares to rust? There was and is but one answer. Some call it lack of purchasing power. Others, viewing the problem in a more philosophic light, recognize that the financial system which was able to function in an age of scarcity was totally inadequate to operate successfully in an age of plenty.

Let me explain this statement briefly: Before the nineteenth century, the ox-cart, the spade and the crude instruments of production were handicaps to the rapid creation of real wealth.

By 1932, a new era of production had come into full bloom. It was represented by the motor car, the tractor and the power lathe, which enabled the laborer to produce wealth ten times more rapidly than was possible for his ancestors. Within the short expanse of 150 years, the problem of production had been solved, due to the ingenuity of men like Arkwright[1] and his loom, Fulton[2] and his steam engine, and Edison[3] and his dynamo. These and a thousand other benefactors of mankind made it possible for the teeming millions of people throughout the world to transfer speedily the raw materials into the thousand necessities and conveniences which fall under the common name of wealth.

Thus, with the advent of our scientific era, with its far-flung fields, its spacious factories, its humming motors, its thundering locomotives, its highly trained mechanics, it is inconceivable how such a thing as a so-called depression should blight the lives of an entire nation when there was a plentitude of everything surrounding us, only to be withheld from us because the so-called leaders of high finance persisted in clinging to an outworn theory of privately issued money, the medium through which wealth is distributed. . . .

---

[1] Richard Arkwright (1732–1792) invented some of the first textile machinery of the industrial revolution.
[2] Robert Fulton (1765–1815) is credited with developing the first commercial steamboat.
[3] Among many other inventions and projects, Thomas Edison (1847–1931) developed a system of electric power generation and distribution.

... Before the year 1932, very few persons fully realized the existence of this financial bondage.

Millions of citizens began asking the obvious questions: "Why should the farmer be forced to follow his plow at a loss?" "Why should the citizens – at least 90 percent of them – be imprisoned behind the cruel bars of want when, within their grasp, there are plenty of shoes, of clothing, of motor cars, of refrigerators, to which they are entitled?" ...

At last, when the most brilliant minds amongst the industrialists, bankers and their kept politicians had failed to solve the cause of the needless depression, there appeared upon the scene of our national life a new champion of the people, Franklin Delano Roosevelt! He spoke golden words of hope. He intimated to the American people that the system of permitting a group of private citizens to create money, then to issue it to the government as if it were real money, then to exact payment from the entire nation through a system of taxation earned by real labor and service, was immoral. With the whip of his scorn he castigated these usurers who exploited the poor. With his eloquent tongue he lashed their financial system which devoured the homes of widows and orphans.

No man in modern times received such plaudits from the poor as did Franklin Roosevelt when he promised to drive the money-changers from the temple – the money-changers[4] who had clipped the coins of wages, who had manufactured spurious money, and who had brought proud America to her knees.

March 4, 1933! I shall never forget the inaugural address, which seemed to re-echo the very words employed by Christ Himself as he actually drove the moneychangers from the temple.

The thrill that was mine was yours. Through dim clouds of the depression, this man Roosevelt was, as it were, a new savior of his people!

Oh, just a little longer shall there be needless poverty! Just another year shall there be naked backs! Just another moment shall there be dark thoughts of revolution! Never again will the chains of economic poverty bite into the hearts of simple folks, as they did in the past days of the Old Deal!

Such were our hopes in the springtime of 1933. ...

It is not pleasant for me who coined the phrase "Roosevelt or ruin" – a phrase fashioned upon promises – to voice such passionate words. But I am

---

[4] Coughlin is alluding to the story of Jesus throwing the money changers out of the temple in Jerusalem. The story is in Matthew 21:12-17, Mark 11:15-19, Luke 19: 45:48, and John 2:13-16.

constrained to admit that "Roosevelt and ruin" is the order of the day, because the moneychangers have not been driven from the temple.

My friends, I come before you tonight not to ask you to return to the Landons,[5] to the Hoovers, to the Old Deal exploiters who honestly defended the dishonest system of gold standardism and rugged individualism.[6] Their sun has set never to rise again.

America has turned its back definitely upon the platitudinous platforms of "rugged individualism." ... These Punch and Judy Republicans, whose actions and words were dominated by the ventriloquists of Wall Street, are so blind that they do not recognize, even in this perilous hour, that their gold basis and their private coinage of money have bred more radicals than did Karl Marx or Lenin. To their system ... we must never return! ...

On the other hand, the Democratic platform is discredited before it is published. Was there not a 1932 platform? By Mr. Roosevelt and his colleagues, was it not regarded as a solemn pledge to the people? Certainly it was! ... [But] it was plowed under like the cotton, slaughtered like the pigs.[7] ...

Therefore, the veracity of the future upstage pledges must be judged by the echoings of the golden voice of a lost leader.

Said he, when the flag of hope was proudly unfurled on March 4, 1933:[8] "Plenty is at our doorsteps, but the generous use of it languished in the very sight of the supply. ... Primarily, this is because the rulers of the exchange of mankind's goods have failed through their own stubbornness and their own incompetence – have admitted to their failure and abdicated. Practices of the unscrupulous money-changers stand indicted in the court of public opinion, rejected by the hearts and minds of men."[9] ...

These words, my friends, are not mine. These are the caustic, devastating words uttered by Franklin Delano Roosevelt on March 4, 1933, condemning Franklin Delano Roosevelt in November of 1936.

---

[5] Alf Landon (1887–1987) was the Republican party candidate for President in 1936.
[6] See Document 1.
[7] Coughlin refers to measures taken by the Agricultural Adjustment Administration to stabilize dropping agricultural products by reducing supply: paying farmers to take land out of cultivation and even, in some cases, destroying crops and livestock.
[8] March 4 1933 was the date of Roosevelt's inauguration as President.
[9] quoted from Roosevelt's First Inaugural Address (Document 17)

Alas! The temple still remains the private property of the moneychangers. The golden key has been handed over to them for safekeeping – the key which now is fashioned in the shape of a double cross!...

Document 35

"This Challenge to Liberty"
Herbert Hoover
October 30, 1936

Republicans took heart from the Supreme Court's invalidation of the National Industrial Recovery Act, Agricultural Adjustment Act (Documents 28 and 31), and several other New Deal measures, and looked to the 1936 election for the final repudiation of President Roosevelt's agenda. However, they faced an uphill fight, as the economy was visibly improving. Gross domestic product was fifty percent higher in 1936 than it had been when Roosevelt took office, and although unemployment remained high at 16.8 percent, it was considerably lower than it had been in 1933, when it stood at 24.75 percent. Moreover, the Republican nominee – Kansas Governor Alf Landon – was a poor campaigner who rarely traveled outside his home state. Nevertheless, leading Republicans jumped into the fight with gusto, and chief among them was former president Herbert Hoover. In the following speech, which he delivered during the final days of the campaign, he called the New Deal a "repudiation of Democracy."

Source: Herbert Hoover, Addresses Upon the American Road, 1933-1938 *(New York: Charles Scribner's Sons, 1938), p. 216 - 227. Available online from Herbert Hoover Presidential Library.*
https://hoover.archives.gov/research/ebooks/B3V1_Full.pdf

. . . . Through four years of experience this New Deal attack upon free institutions has emerged as the transcendent issue in America.

All the men who are seeking for mastery in the world today are using the same weapons. They sing the same songs. They all promise the joys of Elysium[1] without effort. But their philosophy is founded on the coercion and compulsory organization of men. True liberal government is founded on the emancipation of men. This is the issue upon which men are imprisoned and dying in Europe right now.

---

[1] A place of paradise described in Homer's *Odyssey*.

The rise of this issue has dissolved our old party lines. The New Deal repudiation of Democracy has left the Republican Party alone the guardian of the Ark of the Covenant[2] with its charter of freedom. The tremendous import of this issue, the peril to our country has brought the support of the ablest leaders of the Democratic Party. It is no passing matter which enlists side by side the fighting men who have opposed each other over many years. It is the unity demanded by a grave danger to the Republic. . . .

I realize that this danger of centralized personal government disturbs only thinking men and women. But surely the NRA[3] and the AAA[4] alone, should prove what the New Deal philosophy of government means even to those who don't think.

In these instances the Supreme Court, true to their oaths to support the Constitution, saved us temporarily. But Congress in obedience to their oaths should never have passed these acts. The President should never have signed them. But far more important than that, if these men were devoted to the American system of liberty they never would have proposed acts based on the coercion and compulsory organization of men.

Freedom does not die from frontal attack. It dies because men in power no longer believe in a system based upon Liberty.

Mr. Roosevelt on this eve of election has started using the phrases of freedom. He talks sweetly of personal liberty, of individualism, of the American system, of the profit system. He says now that he thinks well of capitalism, and individual enterprise. His devotion to private property seems to be increasing. He has suddenly found some good economic royalists.[5] And he is a staunch

---

[2] Hoover likens the "charter of freedom" – the American founding documents – to the tablets inscribed with the Ten Commandments that God gave Moses for the Israelites, instructing him to make a chest, or ark, to house them (Exodus 25:10–22).

[3] Established by the National Industrial Recovery Act (Document 19) in 1933, the National Recovery Administration sought to coordinate the activities of labor, industry and government through voluntary codes to reduce what the Roosevelt administration thought was inefficient competition. The Supreme Court ruled the NRA unconstitutional in 1935 (Document 28).

[4] The Agricultural Adjustment Administration, created by the Agricultural Adjustment Act (1933), paid subsidies to farmers to not grow crops in order to reduce the supply of these crops and raise prices for them. The Supreme Court ruled unconstitutional the use of taxes on farm product processors to pay the subsidies. A second Agricultural Adjustment Act (1938) provided for the subsidies to come from general government revenues. See Document 31.

[5] See Document 33, where Roosevelt uses the phrase "economic royalists."

supporter of the Constitution. Two days ago he rededicated the Statue of Liberty in New York. She has been the forgotten woman.

Four years ago we also heard many phrases which turned out not to mean what they were thought to have meant. In order that we may be sure this time, will Mr. Roosevelt reply in plain words:

Does he propose to revive the nine acts which the Supreme Court has rejected as invasions of the safeguards of free men?

Has he abandoned his implied determination to change the Constitution? Why not tell the American people before election what change he proposes? Does he intend to stuff the Court itself? Why does the New Deal not really lay its cards on the table?

But their illegal invasions of the Constitution are but the minor artillery with which this New Deal philosophy of government is being forced upon us. They are now using a more subtle and far more effective method of substituting personal power and centralized government for the institutions of free men. It is not by violation of the Constitution that they are making headway today. It is through taking vast sums of the people's money and then manipulating its spending to build up personal power. By this route relief has been centralized in their hands. By this route government has entered into business in competition with the citizen. In this way a score of new instruments of public power have been created. By this route the ordinary functions of government have been uselessly expanded with a double bookkeeping to conceal it. Public funds are used right and left to subsidize special groups of our citizens and special regions of the country. At public expense there is a steady drip of propaganda to poison the public mind.

Through this spending there grows a huge number of citizens with a selfish vested interest in continuing this centralization of power. It has also made millions of citizens dependent upon the government.

Thus also have been built huge political bureaucracies hungry for more power. This use of money has enabled the independence of Congress to be sapped by the pork barrel. It has subtly undermined the rights and the responsibility of States and local governments. Out of all this we see government daily by executive orders instead of by open laws openly arrived at.

The New Deal taxes are in forms which stifle the growth of small business and discourage new enterprise. By stifling private enterprise the field is tilled for further extension of government enterprise. Intricate taxes are interpreted by political bureaucrats who coerce and threaten our business men. By politically managed currency the President has seized the power to alter all wages, all prices, all debts, all savings at will. But that is not the worst. They are creating personal power over votes. That crushes the first safeguard of liberty.

Does Mr. Roosevelt not admit all this in his last report on the state of the Union: "We have built up new instruments of public power" which he admits could "provide shackles for the liberties of the people."[6] Does freedom permit any man or any government any such power? Have the people ever voted for these shackles?

Has he abandoned this "new order," this "planned economy" that he has so often talked about? Will he discharge these associates of his who daily preached the "new order" but whom he does not now allow to appear in this campaign?

Is Mr. Roosevelt not asking for a vote of confidence on these very breaches of liberty?

Is not this very increase in personal power the suicide road upon which every democratic government has died from the time of Greece and Rome down to the dozen liberal governments that have perished in Europe during this past twenty years?

. . . Rejecting these ideas we Republicans had erected agencies of government which did start our country to prosperity without the loss of a single atom of American freedom.

All the ardent peddlers of these Trojan horses[7] received sympathetic hearings from Mr. Roosevelt and joined vociferously in his election. Men are to be judged by the company they keep.

Our people did not recognize the gravity of the issue when I stated it four years ago. That is no wonder, for the day Mr. Roosevelt was elected Recovery was in progress, the Constitution was untrampled, the integrity of the government and the institutions of freedom were intact. It was not until after the election that the people began to awake. Then the realization of intended tinkering with the currency drove bank depositors into the panic that greeted Mr. Roosevelt's inauguration. Recovery was set back for two years, and hysteria was used as the bridge to reach the goal of personal government.

---

[6] Hoover quotes from Roosevelt's Annual Message to Congress, January 3, 1936 (Document 30. See as well Document 32, in which Al Smith also quotes this passage).

[7] Hoover refers to New Deal programs that were supposed to address economic difficulties but contained within them what he saw as threats to freedom. The image comes from the Aeneid and the Odyssey. To finally overcome Troy, the Greek warriors hid inside a wooden horse that the Trojans brought into their city as a trophy.

I am proud to have carried the banner of free men to the last hour of the term my countrymen entrusted it to me. It matters nothing in the history of a race what happens to those who in their time have carried the banner of free men. What matters is that the battle shall go on.

The people know now the aims of this New Deal philosophy of government. We propose instead leadership and authority in government within the moral and economic framework of the American System.

We propose to hold to the Constitutional safeguards of free men.

We propose to relieve men from fear, coercion and spite that are inevitable in personal government.

We propose to demobilize and decentralize all this spending upon which vast personal power is being built. We propose to amend the tax laws so as not to defeat free men and free enterprise.

We propose to turn the whole direction of this country toward liberty, not away from it.

The New Dealers say that all this that we propose is a worn-out System; that this machine age requires new measures for which we must sacrifice some part of the freedom of men. Men have lost their way with a confused idea that governments should run machines. Man-made machines cannot be of more worth than men themselves. Free men made these machines. Only free spirits can master them to their proper use.

The relation of our government with all these questions is complicated and difficult. They rise into the very highest ranges of economics, statesmanship, and morals.

And do not mistake. Free government is the most difficult of all government. But it is everlastingly true that the plain people will make fewer mistakes than any other group of men no matter how powerful. But free government implies vigilant thinking and courageous living and self-reliance in a people.

Let me say to you that any measure which breaks our dykes of freedom will flood the land with misery.

In the field which is more largely social our first American objective should be the protection of the health, the assurance of the education and training of every child in our land. We want children kept out of our factories. We want them kept in school. We want every character-building agency to surround them, including good homes. Freedom can march only upon the feet of educated, healthy and happy children.

We want a land of health, and greater recreation for everybody. We want more opportunity for the creation and care of beauty and those things which satisfy the spirit.

In the field which is more largely economic our first objective must be to provide security from poverty and want. We want security in living for every home. We want to see a nation built of home-owners and farm-owners.

We want to see their savings protected. We want to see them in steady jobs.

These are the first economic securities of human beings.

We want to see more and more of them insured against death and accident, unemployment and old age. We want them all secure.

The American system of liberty has driven toward these ideals for a century and a half. We realize that one-quarter of our people are not able today to have the standards we desire. But we are proud of a system that has given security and comfort to three-quarters of our families and in which even the under quarter ranks higher than that of any nation in the world.

National wisdom and national ideals require that we constantly develop the economic forces which will lift this one-quarter of our people. It requires that we at the same time attain greater stability to employment and to agriculture in the other three-quarters.

This is no occasion to elaborate the details of a program. But surely we must dump the whole New Deal theory of restriction of production, of code monopolies, of constantly higher prices for manufactured goods. We must reject their currency and credit policies, which will repeat our calamities of booms and depressions with greater heights and depths. We must reduce spending and amend the forms of taxation which now destroy enterprise and employment. We hold over-swollen fortunes must be distributed through pressure of taxes.

We hold the first essential is to improve constantly our machines and methods. That will create plenty and make it cheaper.... We hold that this can be done only by private industry and not by government. We hold it can be done only by rewarding men for skill and merit. We hold it can be done only through the energizing force of competition....

It may be that some super mind can tell us what to do each day for our own good or can even force us to do it. But we haven't seen any indication of such mind among the New Dealers. This country moves forward because each individual of all these millions, each thinking for himself, using his own best judgment, using his own skill and experience, becomes expert in bettering his family and his community. To do that they must captain their own souls. No man will be the captain of his own soul if a Tugwell[8] manages it for him.

Doubtless some one will at once arise and shout wicked capitalism, laissez-faire, special privilege, or wolfish individualism. These are the illuminated pumpkins of tomorrow night's New Deal Hallowe'en.

We hold a rule of free men which overrides all such nonsense. That is, free men must have equal rights and equal opportunities. For that the government must be the vigorous umpire. But we want a Judge Landis,[9] we do not want a Simon Legree.[10]

You might think that reform and change to meet new conditions of life are discoveries of the New Deal. Free men have always applied reform. We have been reforming and changing ever since George Washington. Democracy is not static. It is a living force. Every new idea, every new invention offers opportunity for both good and evil.

We are in need of reform every day in the week as long as men are greedy for money or power. We need a whole list of reforms right now, including the reform of these people who have created a gigantic spoils system as a method of seizing political power.

Many of the problems discussed in this campaign concern our material welfare. That is right. But there are things far more important to a nation than material welfare. It is possible to have a prosperous country under a dictatorship. It is not possible to have a free country. No great question will ever be settled in dollars and cents. Great questions must be settled on moral grounds and the tests of what makes free men. What is the nation profited if it shall gain the whole world and lose its own soul?

We want recovery. Not alone economic recovery. We must have moral recovery. And there are many elements in this.

We must re-establish truth and morals in public life. No people will long remain a moral people under a government that repudiates its obligations, that uses public funds to corrupt the people, that conceals its actions by double bookkeeping.

---

[8] Rexford Tugwell (1891–1979) was an economist and a part of Franklin D. Roosevelt's Brain Trust.

[9] Kenesaw Mountain Landis (1866–1944) was a federal judge from 1905-1922. In some of his cases, he showed a fairness and restraint that even those on trial recognized.

[10] a cruel slave owner in Harriet Beecher Stowe's novel, *Uncle Tom's Cabin*

We must have government that builds stamina into communities and men. That makes men instead of mendicants. We must stop this softening of thrift, self-reliance and self-respect through dependence on government. We must stop telling youth that the country is going to the devil and they haven't a chance. We must stop this dissipating the initiative and aspirations of our people. We must revive the courage of men and women and their faith in American liberty. We must recover these spiritual heritages of America.

All this clatter of class and class hate should end. Thieves will get into high places as well as low places and they should both be given economic security – in jail. But they are not a class. This is a classless country. If we hold to our unique American ideal of equal opportunity there can never be classes or masses in our country. To preach these class ideas from the White House is new in American life. There is no employing class, no working class, no farming class. You may pigeonhole a man or woman as a farmer or a worker or a professional man or an employer or even a banker. But the son of the farmer will be a doctor or a worker or even a banker, and his daughter a teacher. The son of a worker will be an employer – or maybe President. And certainly the sons of even economic royalists have a bad time holding the title of nobility.

The glory of our country has been that every mother could look at the babe in her arms with confidence that the highest position in the world was open to it.

The transcendent issue before us today is free men and women. How do we test freedom? It is not a catalogue of political rights. It is a thing of the spirit. Men must be free to worship, to think, to hold opinions, to speak without fear. They must be free to challenge wrong and oppression with surety of justice. Freedom conceives that the mind and spirit of man can be free only if he be free to pattern his own life, to develop his own talents, free to earn, to spend, to save, to acquire property as the security of his old age and his family.

Freedom demands that these rights and ideals shall be protected from infringement by others, whether men or groups, corporations or governments.

The conviction of our fathers was that all these freedoms come from the Creator and that they can be denied by no man or no government or no New Deal. They were spiritual rights of men. The prime purpose of liberal government is to enlarge and not to destroy these freedoms. It was for that purpose that the Constitution of the United States was enacted. For that reason we demand that the safeguards of freedom shall be upheld. It is for this reason that we demand that this country should turn its direction from a system of personal centralized government to the ideals of liberty.

And again I repeat that statement of four years ago – "This campaign is more than a contest between two men. It is a contest between two philosophies of government."

Whatever the outcome of this election that issue is set. We shall battle it out until the soul of America is saved.

Document 36

"Detroit Digs In"
Edward Levinson
January 16, 1937

The United Automobile Workers' union formed in 1935 as part of the Congress of Industrial Organizations (CIO), and after some initial success in organizing workers at small factories, decided to take on the industry's largest employer, General Motors. When GM refused to recognize the union, workers went on strike at a GM plant in Flint, Michigan, on December 30, 1936. This was unlike ordinary strikes, however, in which workers picketed outside and tried to prevent replacement workers from entering; instead they engaged in a "sit-down" strike, physically occupying the facility and refusing to allow anyone else inside. When judges issued injunctions ordering the workers to vacate the premises, they were simply ignored. When police tried to force their way in the strikers hurled metal objects on them, forcing them to withdraw. The strike quickly spread to a number of other GM plants, bringing production to a virtual halt. The left-wing journal The Nation published this highly sympathetic account of the strike's opening days.

The "sit-down" strike posed a political problem for the Roosevelt administration. A Gallup poll showed that a solid majority of Americans opposed the tactic, and even to many in the labor movement (particularly the more conservative "craft unions" of the American Federation of Labor) it appeared dangerously radical. However, the president understood how important support from the CIO had been to his recent successful reelection bid. Therefore, even though Vice President John Nance Garner urged Roosevelt to use federal troops to break the strike, the president instead called upon General Motors to recognize the UAW. GM finally did so on February 11, 1937. Practically overnight the United Automobile Workers became one of the most powerful labor organizations in the country.

Source: The Nation 144:3 (January 16, 1937), pp. 64-66. Available online from The Social Welfare History Project (*Virginia Commonwealth University Libraries*). http://socialwelfare.library.vcu.edu/eras/great-depression/detroit-digs-1937/

The future of the Committee for Industrial Organization, [the] most hopeful development in the history of the American labor movement, lies in the hands of the sitdown strikers who have occupied Fisher Body Plant No. 1 at Flint, Michigan.

The sitdowners tell the story in the simple verses of their homespun "Song of the Fisher Body Strike." The dies,[1] key to most of General Motors production, had been loaded on a railroad car in the plant yard. They were to be shipped to some less strong union center, possibly Pontiac. "When the dies they started moving, the union men they had a meeting to decide right then and there what must be done," says the song, chanted in nasal tones to the tune of "The Martins and the Coys."[2] And, "When they loaded up a box-car full of dies, the union boys they stopped them, and the railroad workers backed them. . . ."

> Now they really started out to strike in earnest,
>
> They took possession of the gates and buildings too.
>
> They placed a guard in either clockhouse,
>
> Just to keep the non-union men out,
>
> And they took the keys and locked the gates up, too.

The attempt to move the dies was regarded by the International union, the United Automobile Workers of America, as a breach of faith. The plant was occupied on December 30. On the previous Tuesday a union committee had submitted demands and asked for a reply by the following Monday. The management's answer was to load the dies on the box-car. Although strikes were already in effect in Atlanta, Kansas City, and Cleveland, the International union had not intended as yet to force the issue on a national scale. But General Motors in Fisher Body No. 1 at Flint provided the spark. Fisher Body No. 2 at Flint followed No. 1 on strike, and walkouts, sitdowns, or both followed in Norwood (Ohio), Anderson (Indiana), Janesville (Wisconsin), Kansas City, Toledo, and Detroit. Helpless, General Motors was forced to shut down additional plants in Anderson, Atlanta, Bay City, Dayton, Flint, Kansas City, Muncie, Saginaw, and Detroit. Today 88,000 General Motors employees are out.

---

[1] molds for forming metal
[2] The "Martins and the Coys" was a novelty song popular in 1936 that imitated traditional country music, referred to later in the document as "hill-billy songs."

Attention has been shifted from the scattered front-line trenches to union and corporation general headquarters in Detroit. The first week of the strike has been marked by the total failure of peace efforts; the negotiations have served chiefly to clarify the issues in the conflict and to reveal the determination of both sides. The union is ready now to sit down and bargain for an agreement. The corporation insists, however, that the five occupied plants – in Flint, Cleveland, Detroit, and Anderson – must first be evacuated. In other words, they are asking the union to surrender its arms and then resume the war.

The union does not take time to make any theoretical defense of its right to hold the factories. They say they will not surrender to the corporation the dies and sixty-day supply of glass now in Fisher Body No. 1 at Flint, and that they will not march out of the plants so that professional strike-breakers and thug guards may walk in. Homer Martin, president of the union, declares the sitdowners have found a heavy supply of tear gas and other equipment of war in the plants. Under the circumstances the union feels that law and peace are in its keeping. It is taking scrupulous care of the machinery.

That General Motors wants evacuation of the plants only to gain an advantage in a resumption of the war is obvious. The corporation insists it will grant none of the union demands. It says it will "recognize" the union – along with company unions – for collective-bargaining purposes, but will not grant recognition of the union as the sole bargaining agency. For the sake of getting down to peace talks, the union has agreed to waive its demand for exclusive recognition before a conference, but it is asking for other guaranties before it will withdraw the sitdowners. The workers ask that no dies be moved, that vigilante movements and circulation of synthetic employee "loyalty" pledges be ended, that the Flint injunction – obtained from a judge who had 1,000 shares of General Motors stock tucked away in his judicial robes – be vacated, and that negotiations be started on a national basis. To this, William S. Knudsen, executive vice-president of General Motors, has given a flat no. According to its memorandum to Governor Frank Murphy, dogged but unsuccessful seeker of peace, the corporation will not even agree to bargain for a national agreement.

General Motors must have known it was making an offer which the union could not consider without inviting a repetition of the collapse of the 1934 strike.[3] While talking peace to Governor Murphy it has thrown up breastworks for a fight to the end.

First-line attacks of the corporation have taken the form of sponsoring vigilante movements. These have come to the surface in both Flint and Saginaw. In Flint an "Alliance for Security of Our Jobs, Our Homes, and Our Community" has come into existence. It is headed by a former paymaster at the Buick plant and a former mayor of Flint, George E. Boysen. This gentleman insists he is financing the "alliance" from his own pocket. Its strategy has been to enroll as members automobile workers who wish to return to work. Mr. Boysen has variously estimated the membership of the "alliance" at 2,000, 5,000, and 12,000, but he called off a parade planned for Saturday night rather than display the weakness of the movement. The headquarters of the alliance on the main Flint thoroughfare were dark and closed early Saturday evening, while hundreds of citizens patrolled the street. The reporters who have flocked to Flint find Mr. Boysen something of a crackpot.

But all this does not mean that the Flint Alliance has folded up. The technique of these "spontaneous" movements of loyal home folk has always been to depend on outside thugs as ringleaders. The strategy has been outlined by the ebullient Pearl L. Bergoff,[4] who planned it to combat the Akron rubber strike that threatened in 1935. "It was going to be a new idea," said the Red Demon. "No more imported strike-breakers, just local people doing the job." But the nucleus of the "local people," he added, was to be four or five hundred imported mercenaries. To meet the threat of the Flint Alliance, several hundred automobile strikers from other cities are camped in Flint, and hundreds more are available on a few hours' call. The discipline of the strikers is remarkable. Company agents tried to incite a riot Thursday night, when they smashed a strikers' loud-speaker and a meeting near union headquarters, but the riots they hoped to stage did not develop. The sitdown strike leaders tell of other provocation. They have a strict rule that no liquor is to be brought into the occupied plant, and the only time the rule was violated, they say, was on New Years Eve when they permitted some company foremen to enter the plant. Since then there has been no drinking and no foreman has been allowed "to snoop around" among the men.

---

[3] Passage of the National Industrial Recovery Act (1933; see Document 19) spurred labor organizing, which led to numerous strikes in 1934, including in the automobile industry, several of which were violent.

[4] Bergoff (1876–1947) was a professional strikebreaker. "Red Demon" was a nickname for Bergoff, indicating that he frightened "reds" (communists), that is, strikebreakers.

The other leading practice of the corporation has been to stir up resentment against the union and intimidate its employees by circulation of "loyalty" pledges. Many of these are distributed by mail with return post cards enclosed. The entire method is devised to frighten strikers with threats of a black list. Some workers who have refused to sign have been discharged outright. By now the petitions have become worthless, except to provide headlines for the kept press. Union leaders have told the workers to go ahead and sign them and then forget about them.

To buttress these pressures, the *Flint Journal*, which is virtually a company organ, displays on its first page a three-column picture of police armed with clubs, tears-gas guns, gas masks, bullet-proof vests, ammunition, and clubs. The papers of the smaller cities, such as the *Flint Journal* and the *Saginaw News*, are abject in their crawling before the corporation. The metropolitan press is less crude. Detroit's papers pathetically feature unsubstantiated peace reports, hoping against hope that there will not be a long conflict in which they may be forced to take sides. The *Detroit News* did not print the impeachment demand filed against Judge Black of Flint or the union's revelations of his ownership of General Motors stock until these things were no longer news. The *Detroit Free Press* refers to the alleged imminent return to work of employees as "hopeful news." The *Cleveland Press* headlines Wyndham Mortimer, vice-president of the union and resident of Cleveland for twenty-six years, as an "outside agitator." On the whole, the fault is not with the correspondents on the scene. There are distinctive examples of impartiality and an understanding of the forces at work on both sides. One of these, it is pleasant to report, is the *Chicago Daily News*. Another fine piece of reporting was the account of the Flint Fisher Body No. 1 sitdown published in New York's *Daily News*.

Passing from the lofty stability of the General Motors building in Detroit to the tense but calm offices of the baby union which has tied up the giant corporation, one thinks constantly of the men in Flint's Fisher Body Plant No. 1. Police and kitchen committees, runners to the union headquarters, strike and executive committees, and a general assembly every afternoon at four have placed the destiny of the strike in the hands of the rank and file. Leaders are verbally slow but mentally clear. Rank-and-file cooperation has made the "chief of police" the best loved man in the plant. There is no grumbling, although the men have been in the plant for eleven days and nights. Wives come to the windows to pass in laundry and food, which goes immediately into the general commissary. Women may not enter, but children may be passed through the windows for brief visits with their fathers. Every night at eight the strikers' band of three guitars, a violin, a mouth organ, and a squeeze box broadcast over a loud-speaker for the strikers and the women and children outside. Spirituals and hill-billy songs fill out the program, which closes with "Solidarity Forever."[5]

P. S. I forgot to mention the American Federation of Labor, an easy thing to do these days. It has no members to speak of in the automobile plants, although John P. Frey[6] undertook to order his followers back to work. The craft unions have no contracts with General Motors. Their leaders' telegrams supporting the corporation against the strikers was a piece of work worthy of a feeble-minded Judas. The move has turned out to be a boomerang. The strikers are comforted by the fact that the A. F. of L. is openly against them and not among their supposed friends, where it would be in a position to attempt a more damaging betrayal, as in 1934.[7]

---

[5] perhaps the best known union anthem, sung to the tune of "The Battle Hymn of the Republic"

[6] Frey (1871–1957) was the head of the metal trades department in the American Federation of Labor.

[7] The American Federation of Labor did not support the 1934 strikes.

Document 37

Second Inaugural Address
President Franklin D. Roosevelt
January 20, 1937

On November 3, 1936, Franklin D. Roosevelt won reelection in the most lopsided presidential race in U.S. history. The popular vote went for Roosevelt by a margin of 27,747,636 to 16,679,543, and the president carried 46 of the 48 states; only Maine and Vermont went for the Republican candidate, Kansas Governor Alf Landon. Meanwhile, Democrats strengthened their hold on Congress, with the Republican contingent reduced to a mere 88 in the House of Representatives (out of a total of 435) and 16 in the Senate (out of a total of 96). The party had secured victory thanks to support from industrial workers, big-city political machines, farmers, white southerners, and African-Americans – a grouping that came to be known as the "New Deal coalition."

Roosevelt's second inaugural was the first to be held on January 20, rather than the traditional March 4. The Twentieth Amendment, which had been ratified by the states in 1932 and 1933, was designed to reduce the period during which a "lame-duck" president and Congress remained in office after the election. Emboldened by his overwhelming electoral success, President Roosevelt insisted in his second inaugural address that the New Deal remained far from finished. Although he offered little in the way of specifics, he promised to devote his second term to helping the poor – the "one-third of a nation ill-housed, ill-clad, ill-nourished."

Source: Franklin D. Roosevelt, "Inaugural Address," January 20, 1937. Online by Gerhard Peters and John T. Woolley, The American Presidency Project. http://www.presidency.ucsb.edu/ws/?pid=15349.

My fellow countrymen. When four years ago we met to inaugurate a President, the Republic, single-minded in anxiety, stood in spirit here. We dedicated ourselves to the fulfillment of a vision – to speed the time when there would be for all the people that security and peace essential to the pursuit of happiness. We of the Republic pledged ourselves to drive from the temple of our ancient faith those who had profaned it; to end by action, tireless and unafraid, the stagnation and despair of that day. We did those first things first.

Our covenant with ourselves did not stop there. Instinctively we recognized a deeper need – the need to find through government the instrument of our united purpose to solve for the individual the ever-rising problems of a complex civilization. Repeated attempts at their solution without the aid of government had left us baffled and bewildered. For, without that aid, we had been unable to create those moral controls over the services of science which are necessary to make science a useful servant instead of a ruthless master of mankind. To do this we knew that we must find practical controls over blind economic forces and blindly selfish men.

We of the Republic sensed the truth that democratic government has innate capacity to protect its people against disasters once considered inevitable, to solve problems once considered unsolvable. We would not admit that we could not find a way to master economic epidemics just as, after centuries of fatalistic suffering, we had found a way to master epidemics of disease. We refused to leave the problems of our common welfare to be solved by the winds of chance and the hurricanes of disaster.

In this we Americans were discovering no wholly new truth; we were writing a new chapter in our book of self-government.

This year marks the one hundred and fiftieth anniversary of the Constitutional Convention which made us a nation. At that Convention our forefathers found the way out of the chaos which followed the Revolutionary War; they created a strong government with powers of united action sufficient then and now to solve problems utterly beyond individual or local solution. A century and a half ago they established the Federal Government in order to promote the general welfare and secure the blessings of liberty to the American people.

Today we invoke those same powers of government to achieve the same objectives.

Four years of new experience have not belied our historic instinct. They hold out the clear hope that government within communities, government within the separate States, and government of the United States can do the things the times require, without yielding its democracy. Our tasks in the last four years did not force democracy to take a holiday.

Nearly all of us recognize that as intricacies of human relationships increase, so power to govern them also must increase – power to stop evil; power to do good. The essential democracy of our nation and the safety of our people depend not upon the absence of power, but upon lodging it with those whom the people can change or continue at stated intervals through an honest and free system of elections. The Constitution of 1787 did not make our democracy impotent.

In fact, in these last four years, we have made the exercise of all power more democratic; for we have begun to bring private autocratic powers into their proper subordination to the public's government. The legend that they were invincible – above and beyond the processes of a democracy – has been shattered. They have been challenged and beaten.

Our progress out of the depression is obvious. But that is not all that you and I mean by the new order of things. Our pledge was not merely to do a patchwork job with secondhand materials. By using the new materials of social justice we have undertaken to erect on the old foundations a more enduring structure for the better use of future generations.

In that purpose we have been helped by achievements of mind and spirit. Old truths have been relearned; untruths have been unlearned. We have always known that heedless self-interest was bad morals; we know now that it is bad economics. Out of the collapse of a prosperity whose builders boasted their practicality has come the conviction that in the long run economic morality pays. We are beginning to wipe out the line that divides the practical from the ideal; and in so doing we are fashioning an instrument of unimagined power for the establishment of a morally better world.

This new understanding undermines the old admiration of worldly success as such. We are beginning to abandon our tolerance of the abuse of power by those who betray for profit the elementary decencies of life.

In this process evil things formerly accepted will not be so easily condoned. Hard-headedness will not so easily excuse hardheartedness. We are moving toward an era of good feeling. But we realize that there can be no era of good feeling save among men of good will.

For these reasons I am justified in believing that the greatest change we have witnessed has been the change in the moral climate of America.

Among men of good will, science and democracy together offer an ever-richer life and ever-larger satisfaction to the individual. With this change in our moral climate and our rediscovered ability to improve our economic order, we have set our feet upon the road of enduring progress.

Shall we pause now and turn our back upon the road that lies ahead? Shall we call this the promised land? Or, shall we continue on our way? For "each age is a dream that is dying, or one that is coming to birth."[1]

Many voices are heard as we face a great decision. Comfort says, "Tarry a while." Opportunism says, "This is a good spot." Timidity asks, "How difficult is the road ahead?"

True, we have come far from the days of stagnation and despair. Vitality has been preserved. Courage and confidence have been restored. Mental and moral horizons have been extended.

But our present gains were won under the pressure of more than ordinary circumstances. Advance became imperative under the goad of fear and suffering. The times were on the side of progress.

To hold to progress today, however, is more difficult. Dulled conscience, irresponsibility, and ruthless self-interest already reappear. Such symptoms of prosperity may become portents of disaster! Prosperity already tests the persistence of our progressive purpose.

Let us ask again: Have we reached the goal of our vision of that fourth day of March 1933? Have we found our happy valley?

I see a great nation, upon a great continent, blessed with a great wealth of natural resources. Its hundred and thirty million people are at peace among themselves; they are making their country a good neighbor among the nations. I see a United States which can demonstrate that, under democratic methods of government, national wealth can be translated into a spreading volume of human comforts hitherto unknown, and the lowest standard of living can be raised far above the level of mere subsistence.

But here is the challenge to our democracy: In this nation I see tens of millions of its citizens – a substantial part of its whole population – who at this very moment are denied the greater part of what the very lowest standards of today call the necessities of life.

I see millions of families trying to live on incomes so meager that the pall of family disaster hangs over them day by day.

I see millions whose daily lives in city and on farm continue under conditions labeled indecent by a so-called polite society half a century ago.

I see millions denied education, recreation, and the opportunity to better their lot and the lot of their children.

---

[1] Roosevelt quotes the last two lines of "Ode," written by Arthur O'Shaughnessy (1844–1881).

I see millions lacking the means to buy the products of farm and factory and by their poverty denying work and productiveness to many other millions.

I see one-third of a nation ill-housed, ill-clad, ill-nourished.

But it is not in despair that I paint you that picture. I paint it for you in hope – because the nation, seeing and understanding the injustice in it, proposes to paint it out. We are determined to make every American citizen the subject of his country's interest and concern; and we will never regard any faithful law-abiding group within our borders as superfluous. The test of our progress is not whether we add more to the abundance of those who have much; it is whether we provide enough for those who have too little.

If I know aught of the spirit and purpose of our Nation, we will not listen to comfort, opportunism, and timidity. We will carry on.

Overwhelmingly, we of the Republic are men and women of good will; men and women who have more than warm hearts of dedication; men and women who have cool heads and willing hands of practical purpose as well. They will insist that every agency of popular government use effective instruments to carry out their will.

Government is competent when all who compose it work as trustees for the whole people. It can make constant progress when it keeps abreast of all the facts. It can obtain justified support and legitimate criticism when the people receive true information of all that government does.

If I know aught of the will of our people, they will demand that these conditions of effective government shall be created and maintained. They will demand a nation uncorrupted by cancers of injustice and, therefore, strong among the nations in its example of the will to peace.

Today we reconsecrate our country to long-cherished ideals in a suddenly changed civilization. In every land there are always at work forces that drive men apart and forces that draw men together. In our personal ambitions we are individualists. But in our seeking for economic and political progress as a nation, we all go up, or else we all go down, as one people.

To maintain a democracy of effort requires a vast amount of patience in dealing with differing methods, a vast amount of humility. But out of the confusion of many voices rises an understanding of dominant public need. Then political leadership can voice common ideals, and aid in their realization.

In taking again the oath of office as President of the United States, I assume the solemn obligation of leading the American people forward along the road over which they have chosen to advance.

While this duty rests upon me I shall do my utmost to speak their purpose and to do their will, seeking Divine guidance to help us each and every one to give light to them that sit in darkness and to guide our feet into the way of peace.

Document 38

"Fireside Chat" on the Plan for Reorganization of the Judiciary
President Franklin D. Roosevelt
March 9, 1937

President Roosevelt was outraged when the Supreme Court invalidated two of the most important New Deal initiatives – the National Industrial Recovery Act and the Agricultural Adjustment Act (Documents 19, 28, 31) – on what he regarded as an outmoded interpretation of the Constitution. Like many liberals, he believed that much of the problem stemmed from a bloc of four conservative Supreme Court justices – the so-called "Four Horsemen" – who seemed to oppose any federal intrusion into economic affairs. Given that there was a total of nine justices on the Court, all the Horsemen needed to do to block any New Deal measure was to convince one more justice that their interpretation was correct.

Emboldened by his overwhelming reelection victory in 1936, the president in February called congressional leaders and members of his cabinet to a meeting at the White House, and informed them that the Judicial Procedures Reform Act was being put before Congress that same day. Many of the justices on the Supreme Court were elderly, the president explained, and needed more assistance in working through the Court's heavy caseload. The act, therefore, proposed to add a new justice for every member above seventy years of age. Given the makeup of the current Court, this would allow Roosevelt to name no fewer than six new justices. There was nothing unconstitutional about Roosevelt's plan, since the Constitution does not specify how many judges the Supreme Court should have. When some in Congress balked at Roosevelt's plan – accusing the president of trying to "pack" the Court – he took to the airwaves in one of his famous "Fireside Chats."

Source: Franklin D. Roosevelt, "Fireside Chat," March 9, 1937. Online by Gerhard Peters and John T. Woolley, The American Presidency Project. http://www.presidency.ucsb.edu/ws/?pid=15381.

. . . . The American people have learned from the depression. For in the last three national elections an overwhelming majority of them voted a mandate that the Congress and the President begin the task of providing that protection – not after long years of debate, but now.

The Courts, however, have cast doubts on the ability of the elected Congress to protect us against catastrophe by meeting squarely our modern social and economic conditions. *paints the court as enemy*

We are at a crisis in our ability to proceed with that protection. It is a quiet crisis. There are no lines of depositors outside closed banks. But to the far-sighted it is far-reaching in its possibilities of injury to America.

I want to talk with you very simply about the need for present action in this crisis – the need to meet the unanswered challenge of one-third of a Nation ill-nourished, ill-clad, ill-housed.

Last Thursday I described the American form of Government as a three-horse team provided by the Constitution to the American people so that their field might be plowed. The three horses are, of course, the three branches of government – the Congress, the Executive and the Courts. Two of the horses are pulling in unison today; the third is not. Those who have intimated that the President of the United States is trying to drive that team, overlook the simple fact that the President, as Chief Executive, is himself one of the three horses.

It is the American people themselves who are in the driver's seat.

It is the American people themselves who want the furrow plowed.

It is the American people themselves who expect the third horse to pull in unison with the other two.

I hope that you have re-read the Constitution of the United States in these past few weeks. Like the Bible, it ought to be read again and again.

It is an easy document to understand when you remember that it was called into being because the Articles of Confederation under which the original thirteen States tried to operate after the Revolution showed the need of a National Government with power enough to handle national problems. In its Preamble, the Constitution states that it was intended to form a more perfect Union and promote the general welfare; and the powers given to the Congress to carry out those purposes can be best described by saying that they were all the powers needed to meet each and every problem which then had a national character and which could not be met by merely local action.

But the framers went further. Having in mind that in succeeding generations many other problems then undreamed of would become national problems, they gave to the Congress the ample broad powers "to levy taxes . . . and provide for the common defense and general welfare of the United States."

That, my friends, is what I honestly believe to have been the clear and underlying purpose of the patriots who wrote a Federal Constitution to create a National Government with national power, intended as they said, "to form a more perfect union ... for ourselves and our posterity."

For nearly twenty years there was no conflict between the Congress and the Court. Then Congress passed a statute which, in 1803, the Court said violated an express provision of the Constitution. The Court claimed the power to declare it unconstitutional and did so declare it. But a little later the Court itself admitted that it was an extraordinary power to exercise and through Mr. Justice Washington laid down this limitation upon it: "It is but a decent respect due to the wisdom, the integrity and the patriotism of the legislative body, by which any law is passed, to presume in favor of its validity until its violation of the Constitution is proved beyond all reasonable doubt."

But since the rise of the modern movement for social and economic progress through legislation, the Court has more and more often and more and more boldly asserted a power to veto laws passed by the Congress and State Legislatures in complete disregard of this original limitation.

In the last four years the sound rule of giving statutes the benefit of all reasonable doubt has been cast aside. The Court has been acting not as a judicial body, but as a policy-making body.

When the Congress has sought to stabilize national agriculture, to improve the conditions of labor, to safeguard business against unfair competition, to protect our national resources, and in many other ways, to serve our clearly national needs, the majority of the Court has been assuming the power to pass on the wisdom of these Acts of the Congress – and to approve or disapprove the public policy written into these laws. . . .

We have, therefore, reached the point as a Nation where we must take action to save the Constitution from the Court and the Court from itself. We must find a way to take an appeal from the Supreme Court to the Constitution itself. We want a Supreme Court which will do justice under the Constitution – not over it. In our Courts we want a government of laws and not of men.

I want – as all Americans want – an independent judiciary as proposed by the framers of the Constitution. That means a Supreme Court that will enforce the Constitution as written – that will refuse to amend the Constitution by the arbitrary exercise of judicial power – amendment by judicial say-so. It does not mean a judiciary so independent that it can deny the existence of facts universally recognized.

How then could we proceed to perform the mandate given us? It was said in last year's Democratic platform, "If these problems cannot be effectively solved within the Constitution, we shall seek such clarifying amendment as will assure the power to enact those laws, adequately to regulate commerce, protect public health and safety, and safeguard economic security." In other words, we said we would seek an amendment only if every other possible means by legislation were to fail.

When I commenced to review the situation with the problem squarely before me, I came by a process of elimination to the conclusion that, short of amendments, the only method which was clearly constitutional, and would at the same time carry out other much needed reforms, was to infuse new blood into all our Courts. We must have men worthy and equipped to carry out impartial justice. But, at the same time, we must have Judges who will bring to the Courts a present-day sense of the Constitution – Judges who will retain in the Courts the judicial functions of a court, and reject the legislative powers which the courts have today assumed....

What is my proposal? It is simply this: whenever a Judge or Justice of any Federal Court has reached the age of seventy and does not avail himself of the opportunity to retire on a pension, a new member shall be appointed by the President then in office, with the approval, as required by the Constitution, of the Senate of the United States.

That plan has two chief purposes. By bringing into the judicial system a steady and continuing stream of new and younger blood, I hope, first, to make the administration of all Federal justice speedier and, therefore, less costly; secondly, to bring to the decision of social and economic problems younger men who have had personal experience and contact with modern facts and circumstances under which average men have to live and work. This plan will save our national Constitution from hardening of the judicial arteries.

The number of Judges to be appointed would depend wholly on the decision of present Judges now over seventy, or those who would subsequently reach the age of seventy.

If, for instance, any one of the six Justices of the Supreme Court now over the age of seventy should retire as provided under the plan, no additional place would be created. Consequently, although there never can be more than fifteen, there may be only fourteen, or thirteen, or twelve. And there may be only nine....

Those opposing this plan have sought to arouse prejudice and fear by crying that I am seeking to "pack" the Supreme Court and that a baneful precedent will be established.

What do they mean by the words "packing the Court"?

Let me answer this question with a bluntness that will end all honest misunderstanding of my purposes.

If by that phrase "packing the Court" it is charged that I wish to place on the bench spineless puppets who would disregard the law and would decide specific cases as I wished them to be decided, I make this answer: that no President fit for his office would appoint, and no Senate of honorable men fit for their office would confirm, that kind of appointees to the Supreme Court.

But if by that phrase the charge is made that I would appoint and the Senate would confirm Justices worthy to sit beside present members of the Court who understand those modern conditions, that I will appoint Justices who will not undertake to over-ride the judgment of the Congress on legislative policy, that I will appoint Justices who will act as Justices and not as legislators – if the appointment of such Justices can be called "packing the Courts," then I say that I and with me the vast majority of the American people favor doing just that thing – now....

It is the clear intention of our public policy to provide for a constant flow of new and younger blood into the Judiciary. Normally every President appoints a large number of District and Circuit Judges and a few members of the Supreme Court. Until my first term practically every President of the United States had appointed at least one member of the Supreme Court. President Taft appointed five members and named a Chief Justice; President Wilson, three; President Harding, four, including a Chief Justice; President Coolidge, one; President Hoover, three, including a Chief Justice.

Such a succession of appointments should have provided a Court well-balanced as to age. But chance and the disinclination of individuals to leave the Supreme bench have now given us a Court in which five Justices will be over seventy-five years of age before next June and one over seventy. Thus a sound public policy has been defeated....

Like all lawyers, like all Americans, I regret the necessity of this controversy. But the welfare of the United States, and indeed of the Constitution itself, is what we all must think about first. Our difficulty with the Court today rises not from the Court as an institution but from human beings within it. But we cannot yield our constitutional destiny to the personal judgment of a few men who, being fearful of the future, would deny us the necessary means of dealing with the present.

This plan of mine is no attack on the Court; it seeks to restore the Court to its rightful and historic place in our system of Constitutional Government and to have it resume its high task of building anew on the Constitution "a system of living law." The Court itself can best undo what the Court has done....

During the past half century the balance of power between the three great branches of the Federal Government, has been tipped out of balance by the

Courts in direct contradiction of the high purposes of the framers of the Constitution. It is my purpose to restore that balance. You who know me will accept my solemn assurance that in a world in which democracy is under attack, I seek to make American democracy succeed. You and I will do our part.

[Handwritten note: S court is essential to the vitality of the New Deal → it should not be political — but this consists of politics]

Document 39

Radio Address on Judicial Reorganization
Senator Carter Glass
March 29, 1937

Given that Congress had given him just about everything he had asked for during his first term, President Roosevelt did not expect the furor that resulted from his judicial reorganization plan. There was token resistance from the Republicans, but there were so few of them left in Congress that they hardly mattered. He was shocked, then, when members of his own party lined up to attack what they called the "court-packing" plan. Although Roosevelt had defended the reorganization on the grounds that it would make the Court more efficient, everyone understood what the president's real motives were. Moreover, he had taken the congressional leadership for granted, failing to involve them in the drafting of the bill. To many, the whole affair had the appearance of a royal proclamation, placed before Congress for a rubber stamp of approval. The following radio address by Sen. Carter Glass (D-VA) was typical in suggesting that the president was behaving like a dictator.

The Judicial Procedures Reform Act was defeated in the Senate by a vote of 70 to 20. It was Roosevelt's first major legislative defeat. However, he was happy to learn in late March and early April that the Supreme Court had reversed two of its previous rulings against the New Deal. Some claimed that the "court-packing" plan had frightened some of the justices into changing their positions, but this proved to be untrue – the decisions had been made before the plan had been announced. In May one of the conservative "Four Horsemen" announced his retirement, giving the president the opportunity to nominate a more liberal justice and thereby alter the makeup of the Court. However, the fight over judicial reorganization marked the end of the happy relationship between Roosevelt and Congress.

Source: Vital Speeches of the Day 3:11 (March 15, 1937), p. 386.

Never in my career until now have I ventured to debate before the public a measure pending in the Senate and awaiting decision there; but the proponents of the problem to which I shall address myself tonight have seemed fearful of a deliberate consideration of the proposal to pack the

Supreme Court of the United States; they have defiantly avowed their purpose to take the discussion into every forum, with the unconcealed intention of bringing pressure to bear on members of Congress to submit obediently to the frightful suggestion which has come to them from the White House.

The challenge has been accepted by those who oppose the repugnant scheme to disrupt representative government in the nation, and the battle is on to the end. . . .

There has been some talk about "organized propaganda" against this unabashed proposition to pack the Supreme Court for a specified purpose! Propaganda was first organized in behalf of the scheme right here in Washington and has proceeded with unabated fury from the White House fireside to nearly every rostrum in the country. . . .

This entire nation is aroused over the many definite proposals to reverse the deliberate judgments of an independent court and to substitute for them the previously pledged opinions of judicial subalterns. With men of this undisguised radical type campaigning the country freely applying their wretched opprobriums to the Supreme Court, those who resist the shocking movement are impertinently reproached with "organizing propaganda"!

I challenge any proponent of this packing contrivance to examine the thousands upon thousands of personal letters and telegrams sent to me and find in them anything but individual indignation at the proposal to make an executive puppet of our supreme judicial tribunal.

For myself, I think we should right now have "organized propaganda" – in the sense that the men and women of America who value the liberties they have enjoyed for 150 years should, with unexampled spontaneity, exercise their constitutional right of petition and, with all the earnestness of their souls, protest to Congress against this attempt to replace representative government with an autocracy. . . .

What does this court-packing scheme signify if it does not reflect the fury of its proponents against the Supreme Court of the United States for certain of its recent decisions asserting the rights of the States and individuals and private business under the law and prohibiting the proposed invasion of these by ill-digested Congressional legislation, largely devised by inexperienced and incompetent academicians? That is precisely what it is all about.

Had the judicial decisions sanctioned these rankly unconstitutional measures, who believes there would have been this unrestrained abuse of the court and this unprecedented attempt to flank the Constitution by putting on the bench six judicial wet-nurses to suckle the substance out of the opinions of jurists whose spirit of independence, thank God, keeps pace with their profound knowledge of the law?. . . .

What other and how many peculiar schemes of government are to be presented for submissive legislative action in confident expectation that they will meet with the favor of the "biased" half dozen who are to adorn the bench, is left to our imagination, because not exactly specified in the proclaimed program. We are simply given to understand that the President has a "mandate from the people" to so reconstitute the Supreme Court as to have it sanction whatever the White House proposes to an agreeing Congress, particularly if it involves no "check upon unauthorized freedom," to quote Grover Cleveland again, or "restraint on dangerous liberty."[1]

But we know there has been no such mandate from the people to rape the Supreme Court or to tamper with the Constitution. The Constitution belongs to the people. It was written by great representatives of the people, chosen for the purpose, and was ratified by the people as the supreme charter of their government, to be respected and maintained with the help of God.

With the consent and by mandate of the people, their Constitution provides how it may be amended to meet the requirements of the ages. It has always been so, and no administration in the history of the Republic has attempted to flank the Constitution by a legislative short-cut so vividly denounced by Woodrow Wilson as "an outrage upon constitutional morality."[2]

The people were not asked for any such mandate. They were kept in ignorance of any such purpose. They were told that the liberal aims of the President could very likely be achieved within the limitations of the Constitution; and if not, we would suggest to the people amendments that would authorize such certain things to be done. When once it was intimated by political adversaries that the Supreme Court might be tampered with, the insinuation was branded as a splenetic libel. . . .

---

[1] Grover Cleveland, "Address at the Celebration of the Organization of the Supreme Court," February 4, 1890

[2] In *Constitutional Government in the United States* (1907), Woodrow Wilson noted that Congress could "overcome a hostile majority in any court" by appointing more judges to the court, since the Constitution gives Congress the power to "ordain and establish" courts inferior to the Supreme Court (Article III, section 1). The Constitution also does not specify the size of the Supreme Court. Still, Wilson had made the same point about "packing the court" in 1886 in an article in the *Atlantic*, "Responsible Government Under the Constitution." In both the article and the later book, he dismissed the possibility of court packing as unthinkable. In the *Atlantic* article he referred to it as an "outrage on constitutional morality."

Convicted by his own official reports of inaccurate assertions about congestion of the Supreme Court calendar, and now flatly contradicted on this and other points by the Chief Justice and associates, there is nothing left of his bitter assault on the court more notable than the brutal contention that six eminent members "get out" and give place to six others of a compliant type, in the selection of whom the Department of Justice would probably have a cunning hand.

Of course the proposal being discussed will not contribute to the efficiency of the court. It will do in this case particularly what Thomas Jefferson pungently deplored when he declared, "The multiplication of judges only enables the weak to outvote the wise." The fact is their proposed bill will cure none of the alleged evils which offend their ideas of judicial reform.

Why should we not proceed, as in honor we are bound to do, by first contriving legislation for social and economic security, painstakingly drafted by competent lawyers with a clear conception of the constitutional prohibitions against invading the rights of business and individuals by a species of confiscation and by utter indifference for reserved powers of the States?

Why should we not quit legislating by pious preambles and conform our enactments to the requirements of the Constitution and thus put upon notice the cabal of amateur experimenters that we will have no more of their trash. . . .

The predominant question is whether the practice of a century under an independent judiciary is to be abruptly terminated by authorizing the President to seize the court by the process of packing, in order to compel agreement with the Executive views.

Should this be done without "a mandate from the people?"

Should the people be ignored and, without asking their consent in the usual way, submit helplessly to having their Constitution tortured into meanings which have been declared in contravention of the fundamental law?

If Andrew Jackson was right in asserting that "Eternal vigilance by the people is the price of liberty," God knows that never before since the establishment of the Republic could the people better be warned to preserve their priceless heritage. The talk about "party loyalty" being involved in the opposition to this extraordinary scheme is a familiar species of coercion. It is sheer poppycock. No political party since the establishment of the government ever dared make an issue of packing the Supreme Court. . . .

Should the iniquitous scheme go through, the intelligence and character of the nation will be interested to know what lawyer of notable attainments or independent spirit would be willing to go on the Supreme Court bench in such circumstances or could regard such an appointment as an honor.

Doubtless there are practitioners eager for such recognition; but are they men whom the nation would prefer or who could feel comfortable in association with those now constituting the court?

I am but an unlearned layman, untrained in the ethics of the legal profession; nevertheless, I cannot escape the conclusion that any man of approved sensibility who should accept such a distinction would experience trouble in outliving the mistake. Moreover, I have a distinct premonition that the people of America would not confidently trust to the supreme decision of such a court the life, liberty and pursuit of happiness guaranteed by the Constitution.

I am far from intimating that the President of the United States is incapable of selecting suitable men for the Supreme Court. I am simply accepting his own word and that of his spokesmen to the effect that he wants men "biased" in behalf of his legislative and administrative projects, who may be counted on to reverse the Supreme Court decisions already rendered and give such other decisions of policy as may be desired.

This is not my view alone; it is the conclusion of millions of alarmed citizens throughout the nation....

Abraham Lincoln, at Gettysburg, thought the Civil War was a test of whether a "government of the people, by the people, for the people" should perish from the face of the earth.

Just as profoundly are some of us convinced that no threat to representative democracy since the foundation of the Republic has exceeded in its evil portents this attempt to pack the Supreme Court of the United States and thus destroy the purity and independence of this tribunal of last resort.

Document 40

Message to Congress on Establishing Minimum Wages and Maximum Hours

President Franklin D. Roosevelt
May 24, 1937

The Fair Labor Standards Act of 1938 was a direct consequence of the 1935 Schechter decision, in which the Supreme Court declared the National Industrial Recovery Act to be unconstitutional (Document 28). The Court had done this on two grounds: Congress had no jurisdiction over economic activity that was not clearly part of interstate commerce; and Congress could not surrender its legislative authority to an agency of the executive branch. Two years later, however, in National Labor Relations Board v. Jones, the Court reversed itself on the question of interstate commerce, effectively broadening its interpretation of the "Commerce Clause" (Article 1, Section 8, Clause 3 of the Constitution) so as to include virtually any economic activity. This opened the door to new legislation regulating the conditions of labor, so long as it clearly came from Congress, and not any executive agency. President Roosevelt formally asked Congress to pass such a law in the following speech, which he delivered in late May 1937.

The Fair Labor Standards Act set a minimum wage of twenty-five cents per hour, with a series of scheduled increases to raise it to forty cents by 1945. It also established a maximum work week of forty-four hours, to be reduced gradually to forty hours by 1940; employers who wanted their employees to work beyond that were forced to pay 50 percent more ("time and a half for overtime"). Finally, the law prohibited the employment of children under sixteen years of age.

Source: Franklin D. Roosevelt, "Message to Congress on Establishing Minimum Wages and Maximum Hours." Online by Gerhard Peters and John T. Woolley, The American Presidency Project.
http://www.presidency.ucsb.edu/ws/?pid=15405.

The time has arrived for us to take further action to extend the frontiers of social progress. Such further action initiated by the legislative branch of the government, administered by the executive, and sustained by the judicial, is within the common sense framework and purpose of our Constitution and receives beyond doubt the approval of our electorate.

The overwhelming majority of our population earns its daily bread either in agriculture or in industry. One-third of our population, the overwhelming majority of which is in agriculture or industry, is ill-nourished, ill-clad and ill-housed.

The overwhelming majority of this Nation has little patience with that small minority which vociferates today that prosperity has returned, that wages are good, that crop prices are high and that government should take a holiday.

The truth of the matter, of course, is that the exponents of the theory of private initiative as the cure for deep-seated national ills want in most cases to improve the lot of mankind. But, well intentioned as they may be, they fail for four evident reasons – first, they see the problem from the point of view of their own business; second, they see the problem from the point of view of their own locality or region; third, they cannot act unanimously because they have no machinery for agreeing among themselves; and, finally, they have no power to bind the inevitable minority of chiselers within their own ranks.

Though we may go far in admitting the innate decency of this small minority, the whole story of our Nation proves that social progress has too often been fought by them. In actual practice it has been effectively advanced only by the passage of laws by state legislatures or the National Congress.

Today, you and I are pledged to take further steps to reduce the lag in the purchasing power of industrial workers and to strengthen and stabilize the markets for the farmers' products. The two go hand in hand. Each depends for its effectiveness upon the other. Both working simultaneously will open new outlets for productive capital. Our Nation so richly endowed with natural resources and with a capable and industrious population should be able to devise ways and means of insuring to all our able-bodied working men and women a fair day's pay for a fair day's work. A self-supporting and self-respecting democracy can plead no justification for the existence of child labor, no economic reason for chiseling workers' wages or stretching workers' hours.

Enlightened business is learning that competition ought not to cause bad social consequences which inevitably react upon the profits of business itself. All but the hopelessly reactionary will agree that to conserve our primary resources of man power, government must have some control over maximum hours, minimum wages, the evil of child labor and the exploitation of unorganized labor....

One of the primary purposes of the formation of our federal union was to do away with the trade barriers between the states. To the Congress and not to the states was given the power to regulate commerce among the several states. Congress cannot interfere in local affairs[,] but when goods pass through the channels of commerce from one state to another they become subject to the power of the Congress, and the Congress may exercise that power to recognize and protect the fundamental interests of free labor.

And so to protect the fundamental interests of free labor and a free people we propose that only goods which have been produced under conditions which meet the minimum standards of free labor shall be admitted to interstate commerce. Goods produced under conditions which do not meet rudimentary standards of decency should be regarded as contraband and ought not to be allowed to pollute the channels of interstate trade.

These rudimentary standards will of necessity at the start fall far short of the ideal. Even in the treatment of national problems there are geographical and industrial diversities which practical statesmanship cannot wholly ignore. Backward labor conditions and relatively progressive labor conditions cannot be completely assimilated and made uniform at one fell swoop without creating economic dislocations....

Allowing for a few exceptional trades and permitting longer hours on the payment of time and a half for overtime, it should not be difficult to define a general maximum working week. Allowing for appropriate qualifications and general classifications by administrative action, it should also be possible to put some floor below which the wage ought not to fall. There should be no difficulty in ruling out the products of the labor of children from any fair market. And there should also be little dispute when it comes to ruling out of the interstate markets products of employers who deny to their workers the right of self-organization and collective bargaining, whether through the fear of labor spies, the bait of company unions, or the use of strikebreakers. The abuses disclosed by the investigations of the Senate must be promptly curbed.[1]

With the establishment of these rudimentary standards as a base we must seek to build up, through appropriate administrative machinery, minimum wage standards of fairness and reasonableness, industry by industry, having due regard to local and geographical diversities and to the effect of unfair labor conditions upon competition in interstate trade and upon the maintenance of industrial peace....

As we move resolutely to extend the frontiers of social progress, we must be guided by practical reason and not by barren formulae. We must ever bear

---

[1] Probably a reference to the investigations led by Robert M. La Follette (R-Wisconsin) into anti-union activities.

in mind that our objective is to improve and not to impair the standard of living of those who are now undernourished, poorly clad and ill-housed.

We know that over-work and under-pay do not increase the national income when a large portion of our workers remain unemployed. Reasonable and flexible use of the long established right of government to set and to change working hours can, I hope, decrease unemployment in those groups in which unemployment today principally exists.

Our problem is to work out in practice those labor standards which will permit the maximum but prudent employment of our human resources to bring within the reach of the average man and woman a maximum of goods and of services conducive to the fulfillment of the promise of American life.

Legislation can, I hope, be passed at this session of the Congress further to help those who toil in factory and on farm. We have promised it. We cannot stand still.

Document 41

"Fireside Chat" on the Recession
Franklin D. Roosevelt
April 14, 1938

The economic recovery that had been underway since 1935 continued through the first six months of Roosevelt's second term. By the middle of 1937 gross national product had finally returned to where it had been in 1930 (although it would be another four years before it would return to pre-Depression levels), and unemployment had fallen to just over 14 percent. However, that summer the situation took a serious turn for the worse. The market value of stocks traded on the New York Stock Exchange dropped by more than 40 percent, manufacturing output fell by 37 percent, and unemployment surged to nearly 19 percent.

What brought this about? There were likely multiple causes. The president, convinced that full-scale recovery was underway, had begun cutting back on spending, and in July announced his intent to submit the first balanced budget of his presidency. New banking regulations increased the size of the cash reserves that banks were required to hold, causing financial institutions to curtail lending. Finally, the first payroll taxes for Social Security were withheld in 1937. All of these led to a significant reduction in the amount of money circulating in the economy.

Whatever the cause, the "recession" (as Roosevelt called it, to distinguish it from the Depression of 1929-1933) posed a serious political problem for the president and his party. As Rep. Maury Maverick (D-TX) admitted to his colleagues in the House, "Now we Democrats have to admit that we are floundering. We have pulled all the rabbits out of the hat, and there are no more rabbits. . . . We are a confused, bewildered group of people, and we are not delivering the goods." In mid-April President Roosevelt spoke to the American people through his favorite medium – the radio – to announce a massive new spending program that he hoped would put the economy back on the road to recovery.

Source: "Fireside Chat," April 14, 1938. Online by Gerhard Peters and John T. Woolley, The American Presidency Project. http://www.presidency.ucsb.edu/ws/?pid=15628.

... Five years ago we faced a very serious problem of economic and social recovery. For four and a half years that recovery proceeded apace. It is only in the past seven months that it has received a visible setback.

And it is only within the past two months, as we have waited patiently to see whether the forces of business itself would counteract it, that it has become apparent that government itself can no longer safely fail to take aggressive government steps to meet it.

This recession has not returned us to the disasters and suffering of the beginning of 1933. Your money in the bank is safe; farmers are no longer in deep distress and have greater purchasing power; dangers of security speculation have been minimized; national income is almost 50% higher than it was in 1932; and government has an established and accepted responsibility for relief.

But I know that many of you have lost your jobs or have seen your friends or members of your families lose their jobs, and I do not propose that the Government shall pretend not to see these things. I know that the effect of our present difficulties has been uneven; that they have affected some groups and some localities seriously but that they have been scarcely felt in others. But I conceive the first duty of government is to protect the economic welfare of all the people in all sections and in all groups. I said in my Message opening the last session of the Congress that if private enterprise did not provide jobs this spring, government would take up the slack – that I would not let the people down. We have all learned the lesson that government cannot afford to wait until it has lost the power to act.

Therefore, my friends, I have sent a Message of far-reaching importance to the Congress....

I pointed out to the Congress that the national income – not the Government's income but the total of the income of all the individual citizens and families of the United States – every farmer, every worker, every banker, every professional man and every person who lived on income derived from investments – that national income had amounted, in the year 1929, to eighty-one billion dollars. By 1932 this had fallen to thirty-eight billion dollars. Gradually, and up to a few months ago, it had risen to a total, an annual total; of sixty-eight billion dollars – a pretty good come-back from the low point....

I went on to point out to the Senate and the House of Representatives that all the energies of government and business must be directed to increasing the national income, to putting more people into private jobs, to giving security and a feeling of security to all people in all walks of life.

I am constantly thinking of all our people – unemployed and employed alike – of their human problems, their human problems of food and clothing and homes and education and health and old age. You and I agree that security is our greatest need – the chance to work, the opportunity of making a reasonable profit in our business – whether it be a very small business or a larger one – the possibility of selling our farm products for enough money for our families to live on decently. I know these are the things that decide the well-being of all our people.

Therefore, I am determined to do all in my power to help you attain that security and because I know that the people themselves have a deep conviction that secure prosperity of that kind cannot be a lasting one except on a basis of business fair dealing and a basis where all from the top to the bottom share in the prosperity.... I came to the conclusion that the present-day problem calls for action both by the Government and by the people, that we suffer primarily from a failure of consumer demand because of lack of buying power. It is up to us to create an economic upturn....

I went on in my Message today to propose three groups of measures and I will summarize my recommendations.

First, I asked for certain appropriations which are intended to keep the Government expenditures for work relief and similar purposes during the coming fiscal year at the same rate of expenditure as at present. That includes additional money for the Works Progress Administration; additional funds for the Farm Security Administration; additional allotments for the National Youth Administration, and more money for the Civilian Conservation Corps, in order that it can maintain the existing number of camps now in operation.

These appropriations, made necessary by increased unemployment, will cost about a billion and a quarter dollars more than the estimates which I sent to the Congress on the third of January last.

Second, I told the Congress that the Administration proposes to make additional bank reserves available for the credit needs of the country. About one billion four hundred million dollars of gold now in the Treasury will be used to pay these additional expenses of the Government, and three-quarters of a billion dollars of additional credit will be made available to the banks by reducing the reserves now required by the Federal Reserve Board.

These two steps, taking care of relief needs and adding to bank credits, are in our best judgment insufficient by themselves to start the Nation on a sustained upward movement.

Therefore, I came to the third kind of Government action which I consider to be vital....

The third proposal is to make definite additions to the purchasing power of the Nation by providing new work over and above the continuing of the old work.

First, to enable the United States Housing Authority to undertake the immediate construction of about three hundred million dollars worth of additional slum clearance projects.

Second, to renew a public works program by starting as quickly as possible about one billion dollars worth of needed permanent public improvements in our states, and their counties and cities.

Third, to add one hundred million dollars to the estimate for Federal aid highways in excess of the amount that I recommended in January.

Fourth, to add thirty-seven million dollars over and above the former estimate of sixty-three million for flood control and reclamation.

Fifth, to add twenty-five million dollars additional for Federal buildings in various parts of the country.

In recommending this program I am thinking not only of the immediate economic needs of the people of the Nation, but also of their personal liberties – the most precious possession of all Americans. I am thinking of our democracy. I am thinking of the recent trend in other parts of the world away from the democratic ideal.

Democracy has disappeared in several other great nations – disappeared not because the people of those nations disliked democracy, but because they had grown tired of unemployment and insecurity, of seeing their children hungry while they sat helpless in the face of government confusion, government weakness, – weakness through lack of leadership in government. Finally, in desperation, they chose to sacrifice liberty in the hope of getting something to eat. We in America know that our own democratic institutions can be preserved and made to work. But in order to preserve them we need to act together, to meet the problems of the Nation boldly, and to prove that the practical operation of democratic government is equal to the task of protecting the security of the people.

Not only our future economic soundness but the very soundness of our democratic institutions depends on the determination of our Government to give employment to idle men. The people of America are in agreement in defending their liberties at any cost, and the first line of that defense lies in the protection of economic security. Your Government, seeking to protect democracy, must prove that Government is stronger than the forces of business depression.

History proves that dictatorships do not grow out of strong and successful governments but out of weak and helpless governments. If by democratic methods people get a government strong enough to protect them from fear and starvation, their democracy succeeds, but if they do not, they grow impatient. Therefore, the only sure bulwark of continuing liberty is a government strong enough to protect the interests of the people, and a people strong enough and well enough informed to maintain its sovereign control over its government.

We are a rich Nation; we can afford to pay for security and prosperity without having to sacrifice our liberties into the bargain.

In the first century of our republic we were short of capital, short of workers and short of industrial production, but we were rich, very rich in free land, and free timber and free mineral wealth. The Federal Government of those days rightly assumed the duty of promoting business and relieving depression by giving subsidies of land and other resources.

Thus, from our earliest days we have had a tradition of substantial government help to our system of private enterprise. But today the Government no longer has vast tracts of rich land to give away and we have discovered, too, that we must spend large sums of money to conserve our land from further erosion and our forests from further depletion. The situation is also very different from the old days, because now we have plenty of capital, banks and insurance companies loaded with idle money; plenty of industrial productive capacity and many millions of workers looking for jobs. It is following tradition as well as necessity, if Government strives to put idle money and idle men to work, to increase our public wealth and to build up the health and strength of the people – and to help our system of private enterprise to function again.

It is going to cost something to get out of this recession this way but the profit of getting out of it will pay for the cost several times over. Lost working time is lost money. Every day that a workman is unemployed, or a machine is unused, or a business organization is marking time, it is a loss to the Nation. Because of idle men and idle machines this Nation lost one hundred billion dollars between 1929 and the spring of 1933, in less than four years. This year you, the people of this country, are making about twelve billion dollars less than you were last year.

If you think back to the experiences of the early years of this Administration you will remember the doubts and fears expressed about the rising expenses of Government. But to the surprise of the doubters, as we proceeded to carry on the program which included Public Works and Work Relief, the country grew richer instead of poorer.

It is worthwhile to remember that the annual national people's income was thirty billion dollars more last year in 1937 than it was in 1932. It is true that the national debt increased sixteen billion dollars, but remember that in that increase must be included several billion dollars' worth of assets which eventually will reduce that debt and that many billion dollars of permanent public improvements – schools, roads, bridges, tunnels, public buildings, parks and a host of other things meet your eye in every one of the thirty-one hundred counties in the United States.

No doubt you will be told that the Government spending program of the past five years did not cause the increase in our national income. They will tell you that business revived because of private spending and investment. That is true in part, for the Government spent only a small part of the total. But that Government spending acted as a trigger, a trigger to set off private activity. That is why the total addition to our national production and national income has been so much greater than the contribution of the Government itself....

The Government contribution of land that we once made to business was the land of all the people. And the Government contribution of money which we now make to business ultimately comes out of the labor of all the people. It is, therefore, only sound morality, as well as a sound distribution of buying power, that the benefits of the prosperity coming from this use of the money of all the people ought to be distributed among all the people – the people at the bottom as well as the people at the top. Consequently, I am again expressing my hope that the Congress will enact at this session a wage and hour bill putting a floor under industrial wages and a limit on working hours – to ensure a better distribution of our prosperity, a better distribution of available work, and a sounder distribution of buying power.[1]

You may get all kinds of impressions in regard to the total cost of this new program, or in regard to the amount that will be added to the net national debt. It is a big program. Last autumn in a sincere effort to bring Government expenditures and Government income into closer balance, the Budget I worked out called for sharp decreases in Government spending during the coming year. But, in the light of present conditions, conditions of today, those estimates turned out to have been far too low. This new program adds two billion and sixty-two million dollars to direct Treasury expenditures and

---

[1] The Fair Labor Standards Act was finally passed in June 1938, to become effective on October 24, 1938. See Documents 40 and 42.

another nine hundred and fifty million dollars to Government loans – the latter sum, because they are loans, will come back to the Treasury in the future.

The net effect on the debt of the Government is this – between now and July 1, 1939 – fifteen months away – the Treasury will have to raise less than a billion and a half dollars of new money.

Such an addition to the net debt of the United States need not give concern to any citizen, for it will return to the people of the United States many times over in increased buying power and eventually in much greater Government tax receipts because of the increase in the citizen income....

Finally I should like to say a personal word to you.

I never forget that I live in a house owned by all the American people and that I have been given their trust.

I try always to remember that their deepest problems are human. I constantly talk with those who come to tell me their own points of view – with those who manage the great industries and financial institutions of the country – with those who represent the farmer and the worker – and often, very often with average citizens without high position who come to this house. And constantly I seek to look beyond the doors of the White House, beyond the officialdom of the National Capital, into the hopes and fears of men and women in their homes. I have travelled the country over many times. My friends, my enemies, my daily mail bring to me reports of what you are thinking and hoping. I want to be sure that neither battles nor burdens of office shall ever blind me to an intimate knowledge of the way the American people want to live and the simple purposes for which they put me here.

In these great problems of government I try not to forget that what really counts at the bottom of it all is that the men and women willing to work can have a decent job, – a decent job to take care of themselves and their homes and their children adequately; that the farmer, the factory worker, the storekeeper, the gas station man, the manufacturer, the merchant – big and small – the banker who takes pride in the help that he can give to the building of his community – that all of these can be sure of a reasonable profit and safety for the earnings that they make – not for today nor tomorrow alone, but as far ahead as they can see. I can hear your unspoken wonder as to where we are headed in this troubled world. I cannot expect all of the people to understand all of the people's problems; but it is my job to try to understand all of the problems.

I always try to remember that reconciling differences cannot satisfy everyone completely. Because I do not expect too much, I am not disappointed. But I know that I must never give up – that I must never let the greater interest of all the people down, merely because that might be for the moment the easiest personal way out.

I believe that we have been right in the course we have charted. To abandon our purpose of building a greater, a more stable and a more tolerant America would be to miss the tide and perhaps to miss the port. I propose to sail ahead. I feel sure that your hopes and I feel sure that your help are with me. For to reach a port, we must sail – sail, not lie at anchor, sail, not drift.

Document 42

Speech on the Fair Labor Standards Act
Representative Wade Kitchens
May 16, 1938

Although President Roosevelt first proposed the Fair Labor Standards Act in May 1937, it was subject to several delays. The "court-packing" fight occupied much of the legislature's time through the summer, and conservative Democrats managed to keep the bill from reaching the floor of the House for several months thereafter. Southerners such as Democratic Representative Wade Kitchens of Arkansas – whose speech in opposition to the bill follows – found it particularly offensive. As they pointed out, fewer than three percent of industrial workers outside the South earned below the proposed minimum wage, while in the South nearly 20 percent did. The new law, they argued, was nothing but a means of destroying southern industry. Indeed, many of the bill's most enthusiastic sponsors were northern businessmen who feared competition from lower-paying southern firms.

Ultimately the bill passed in mid-June, 1938, but not without substantial revision, as one legislator after another sought immunity for the industries in his district. As a result, the final version contained so many exemptions and loopholes that one supporter suggested that the Secretary of Labor report within ninety days "whether anyone is subject to the bill."

The Fair Labor Standards Act is widely regarded as the New Deal's final gasp. As Roosevelt affixed his signature to it, he was heard to sigh, "That's that." Although he may not have realized at the time, he had just signed the last major piece of New Deal legislation.

Source: *Congressional Record*, 75th Cong., 3rd sess., vol. 83, pt. 6 (May 16, 1938), pp. 6911-6913.

... [T]he proposed bill has the most far-reaching implications of injustice and discrimination to southern labor and industry. In fact, it is directed against southern, western, and mid-western labor and industry. We have very little interstate industry in Arkansas. We are just beginning to obtain some industry for our labor. Our great trouble is a lack of industry and jobs. There can be no jobs nor wages without industry....

Speech on the Fair Labor Standards Act

... This bill, in my opinion, will create, centralize, and sectionalize industry in the New England States, and further protect and foster monopolies. I hear Members on the floor of the House, and in the cloakrooms say that all small businesses, if unable to pay what they call a "living wage," should be destroyed. But, they lose sight of the fact that what is a living wage in one section is not in another. What is a living wage? This bill purports to define it, but I disagree with the definition. It falls far too short. They prefer that he receives no wage at all unless he receives the same wages as paid by a large million-dollar factory. By their votes and their efforts, they are against all southern, western, and mid-western labor and industry, and favor monopolies and million-dollar corporations. They are against the farmers and the consumers likewise, because any aid to the large industrial corporations ... and to their labor, will be at the expense of farmers and other laborers and consumers....

Pay rolls are met with money from bank deposits. They cannot be met without money. These pay rolls are met from demand deposits in our banks. The State of New York has about $750 demand deposits for each man, woman, and child in the state. In our State, and many other Southern, Western, and mid-Western States, we have around $50 in demand deposits per capita. In other words, in New York State there is available for labor 15 times as much money per capita as there is in Arkansas. In the State of New Jersey there is seven times as much money available for labor in demand deposits as in Arkansas. In Connecticut, where the population is 250,000 less than in Arkansas, the demand deposits are two and a half times that of Arkansas.

No Southern State has attained anywhere near as high per capita demand deposits as these New England industrial States. American wages must, of necessity, vary widely from State to State because of this great difference in available money for pay rolls. Wages are governed by the amount of money available, and by the conditions existing at the particular plant. These discriminations and inequalities cannot be put upon the same basis, and a uniform wage, if attempted, will be impractical....

I submit, if we are going to fix a minimum wage for some laborers, then fix minimum wage or price for the farmer and his products. Why not help him and his family, because his sweatshop requires as much hard work, perspiration, and longer hours than any other sweatshop in this country? If the farmer be given a fair price, the industrial laborer will prosper. If Congress, under this law, can fix minimum wage, it can fix maximum wage, and the price on all things in interstate commerce or having to do with interstate commerce. If Congress can fix minimum or maximum wage under this bill, then it can fix minimum or maximum salaries for all business in the United States. I submit that when all this great business is turned over to some bureau or secretary in Washington to manage, to define what is and what is not interstate commerce, then we have destroyed individual rights, collective rights, State rights, Constitutional rights, and substituted the dictates of man for law and the Constitution....

It is my opinion that the title of this bill should read: "A bill for an act in the interest of and to help create more monopolies, aid the financiers and controllers of large industry, . . . regiment labor and industry, take away from labor the right to contract individually or collectively, cripple, if not destroy, present southern labor and industry, prevent further industry located in the South, West, or Midwest, deprive citizens in four-fifths of the country of jobs, further deprive the children of southern, western, and Midwestern parents of educational advantages, fair share of industrial taxes and wealth, occupational opportunities, and for other discriminatory purposes."

Document 43

"Fireside Chat" on "Purging" the Democratic Party
President Franklin D. Roosevelt
June 24, 1938

Frustrated by the setbacks that his administration had encountered in its second term, President Roosevelt took the bold step of intervening in the 1938 Democratic primaries. His targets were conservative Democrats – mostly southerners – who had joined Republicans in opposing New Deal measures. In races across the country, he stumped for liberal candidates and denounced conservative incumbents as traitors to the cause of reform. He explained his efforts in the following speech, in which he defended his administration's domestic record and blamed the sagging economy on his political opponents.

The plan backfired. Critics, deliberately using a term associated with Stalin's Soviet Union, suggested that Roosevelt was trying to "purge" his party of dissenters, and he was accused of attempting to establish a dictatorship. In the end, all but one of the incumbents whom the president had campaigned against managed to hold on to their seats – and, unsurprisingly, they were more than determined to resist Roosevelt's agenda. In addition, the 1938 elections produced major gains for the Republican Party; while they had nowhere close to a majority in either house, Republicans were strong enough that they could, in combination with conservative Democrats, block any major new White House initiative. Meanwhile the president was increasingly focused on events beyond America's shores, as a new world war seemed likely. The New Deal had come to an end.

Source: Franklin D. Roosevelt, "Fireside Chat," June 24, 1938. Online by Gerhard Peters and John T. Woolley, The American Presidency Project. http://www.presidency.ucsb.edu/ws/?pid=15662.

. . . . Our Government, happily, is a democracy. As part of the democratic process, your President is again taking an opportunity to report on the progress of national affairs, to report to the real rulers of this country – the voting public.

The Seventy-Fifth Congress, elected in November, 1936, on a platform uncompromisingly liberal, has adjourned. Barring unforeseen events, there will be no session until the new Congress, to be elected in November, assembles next January.

On the one hand, the Seventy-Fifth Congress has left many things undone.

For example, it refused to provide more businesslike machinery for running the Executive Branch of the Government. The Congress also failed to meet my suggestion that it take the far-reaching steps necessary to put the railroads of the country back on their feet.

But, on the other hand, the Congress, striving to carry out the Platform on which most of them were elected, achieved more for the future good of the country than any Congress did between the end of the World War and the spring of 1933.

I mention tonight only the more important of these achievements.

1. The Congress improved still further our agricultural laws to give the farmer a fairer share of the national income, to preserve our soil, to provide an all-weather granary, to help the farm tenant towards independence, to find new uses for farm products, and to begin crop insurance.

2. After many requests on my part the Congress passed a Fair Labor Standards Act, what we call the Wages and Hours Bill.[1] That Act – applying to products in interstate commerce – ends child labor, sets a floor below wages and a ceiling over hours of labor.

Except perhaps for the Social Security Act,[2] it is the most far-reaching, the most far-sighted program for the benefit of workers ever adopted here or in any other country. Without question it starts us toward a better standard of living and increases purchasing power to buy the products of farm and factory.

Do not let any calamity-howling executive with an income of $1,000.00 a day, who has been turning his employees over to the Government relief rolls in order to preserve his company's undistributed reserves, tell you – using his stockholders' money to pay the postage for his personal opinions – tell you that a wage of $11.00 a week is going to have a disastrous effect on all American industry. Fortunately for business as a whole, and therefore for the Nation, that type of executive is a rarity with whom most business executives most heartily disagree.

3. The Congress has provided a fact-finding Commission to find a path through the jungle of contradictory theories about wise business practices – to find the necessary facts for any intelligent legislation on monopoly, on price-

---

[1] See Documents 40, 41 and 42.
[2] See Documents 23 and 26.

fixing and on the relationship between big business and medium-sized business and little business. Different from a great part of the world, we in America persist in our belief in individual enterprise and in the profit motive; but we realize we must continually seek improved practices to insure the continuance of reasonable profits, together with scientific progress, individual initiative, opportunities for the little fellow, fair prices, decent wages and continuing employment.

4. The Congress has coordinated the supervision of commercial aviation and air mail by establishing a new Civil Aeronautics Authority; and it has placed all postmasters under the civil service for the first time in our national history.

5. The Congress has set up the United States Housing Authority to help finance large-scale slum clearance and provide low rent housing for the low income groups in our cities. And by improving the Federal Housing Act, the Congress has made it easier for private capital to build modest homes and low rental dwellings.

6. The Congress has properly reduced taxes on small corporate enterprises, and has made it easier for the Reconstruction Finance Corporation[3] to make credit available to all business. I think the bankers of the country can fairly be expected to participate in loans where the Government, through the Reconstruction Finance Corporation, offers to take a fair portion of the risk.

7. So, too, the Congress has provided additional funds for the Works Progress Administration, the Public Works Administration, the Rural Electrification Administration, the Civilian Conservation Corps and other agencies,[4] in order to take care of what we hope is a temporary additional number of unemployed at this time and to encourage production of every kind by private enterprise.

All these things together I call our program for the national defense of our economic system. It is a program of balanced action – of moving on all fronts at once in intelligent recognition that all of our economic problems, of every group, and of every section of the country are essentially one problem.

---

[3] Established by the Reconstruction Finance Corporation Act, passed by Congress during the Hoover administration in 1932, the Reconstruction Finance Corporation was a government corporation that provided loans to banks and other businesses. It remained in operation until 1957. See Document 7.

[4] All of these were New Deal agencies.

8. Finally, because of increasing armaments in other nations and an international situation which is definitely disturbing to all of us, the Congress has authorized important additions to the national armed defense of our shores and our people.

On another important subject, the net result of a struggle in the Congress has been an important victory for the people of the United States –a lost battle which won a war.

You will remember that on February 5, 1937, I sent a Message to the Congress dealing with the real need of Federal Court reforms of several kinds.[5] In one way or another, during the sessions of this Congress, the ends –the real objectives – sought in that Message, have been substantially attained.

The attitude of the Supreme Court towards constitutional questions is entirely changed. Its recent decisions are eloquent testimony of a willingness to collaborate with the two other branches of Government to make democracy work. The Government has been granted the right to protect its interests in litigation between private parties involving the constitutionality of Federal statutes, and to appeal directly to the Supreme Court in all cases involving the constitutionality of Federal statutes; and no single judge is any longer empowered to suspend a Federal statute on his sole judgment as to its constitutionality. Justices of the Supreme Court may now retire at the age of seventy after ten years of service; a substantial number of additional judgeships have been created in order to expedite the trial of cases; and greater flexibility has been added to the Federal judicial system by allowing judges to be assigned to congested districts.

Another indirect accomplishment of this Congress has been its response to the devotion of the American people to a course of sane consistent liberalism. The Congress has understood that under modern conditions Government has a continuing responsibility to meet continuing problems, and that Government cannot take a holiday of a year, or a month, or even a day just because a few people are tired or frightened by the inescapable pace of this modern world in which we live.

Some of my opponents and some of my associates have considered that I have a mistakenly sentimental judgment as to the tenacity of purpose and the general level of intelligence of the American people.

I am still convinced that the American people, since 1932, continue to insist on two requisites of private enterprise, and the relationship of Government to it. The first is a complete honesty at the top in looking after the

---

[5] See Document 38.

use of other people's money, and in apportioning and paying individual and corporate taxes according to ability to pay. The second is sincere respect for the need of all at the bottom to get work – and through work to get a really fair share of the good things of life, and a chance to save and rise.

After the election of 1936 I was told, and the Congress was told, by an increasing number of politically and worldly-wise people that I should coast along, enjoy an easy Presidency for four years, and not take the Democratic platform too seriously. They told me that people were getting weary of reform through political effort and would no longer oppose that small minority which, in spite of its own disastrous leadership in 1929, is always eager to resume its control over the Government of the United States.

Never in our lifetime has such a concerted campaign of defeatism been thrown at the heads of the President and the Senators and Congressmen as in the case of this Seventy-Fifth Congress. Never before have we had so many Copperheads[6] among us – and you will remember that it was the Copperheads who, in the days of the War between the States, tried their best to make Lincoln and his Congress give up the fight, let the Nation remain split in two and return to peace – peace at any price.

This Congress has ended on the side of the people. My faith in the American people – and their faith in themselves – have been justified. I congratulate the Congress and the leadership thereof and I congratulate the American people on their own staying power.

One word about our economic situation. It makes no difference to me whether you call it a recession or a depression. In 1932 the total national income of all the people in the country had reached the low point of thirty-eight billion dollars in that year. With each succeeding year it rose. Last year, 1937, it had risen to seventy billion dollars – despite definitely worse business and agricultural prices in the last four months of last year. This year, 1938, while it is too early to do more than give an estimate, we hope that the national income will not fall below sixty billion dollars. We remember also that banking and business and farming are not falling apart like the one-hoss shay[7], as they did in the terrible winter of 1932-1933.

---

[6] The "Copperheads" were mostly Midwestern Democrats with agrarian interests and Southern roots. An editorialist likened their call for peace with the Confederacy to the behavior of a well-camouflaged snake that strikes without warning.

[7] A one-horse shay is a carriage drawn by one horse. A popular poem described one that was wonderfully constructed but then suddenly fell apart.

Last year mistakes were made by the leaders of private enterprise, by the leaders of labor and by the leaders of Government – all three.

Last year the leaders of private enterprise pleaded for a sudden curtailment of public spending, and said they would take up the slack. But they made the mistake of increasing their inventories too fast and setting many of their prices too high for their goods to sell.

Some labor leaders goaded by decades of oppression of labor made the mistake of going too far. They were not wise in using methods which frightened many well-wishing people. They asked employers not only to bargain with them but to put up with jurisdictional disputes at the same time.

Government too made mistakes – mistakes of optimism in assuming that industry and labor would themselves make no mistakes – and Government made a mistake of timing in not passing a farm bill or a wage and hour bill last year.

As a result of the lessons of all these mistakes we hope that in the future private enterprise – capital and labor alike – will operate more intelligently together, and in greater cooperation with their own Government than they have in the past. Such cooperation on the part of both of them will be very welcome to me. Certainly at this stage there should be a united stand on the part of both of them to resist wage cuts which would further reduce purchasing power....

From March 4, 1933 down, not a single week has passed without a cry from the opposition "to do something, to say something, to restore confidence." There is a very articulate group of people in this country, with plenty of ability to procure publicity for their views, who have consistently refused to cooperate with the mass of the people, whether things were going well or going badly, on the ground that they required more concessions to their point of view before they would admit having what they called "confidence."

... It is my belief that many of these people who have been crying aloud for "confidence" are beginning today to realize that that hand has been overplayed, and that they are now willing to talk cooperation instead. It is my belief that the mass of the American people do have confidence in themselves – have confidence in their ability, with the aid of Government, to solve their own problems.

It is because you are not satisfied, and I am not satisfied, with the progress that we have made in finally solving our business and agricultural and social problems that I believe the great majority of you want your own Government to keep on trying to solve them. In simple frankness and in simple honesty, I need all the help I can get – and I see signs of getting more help in the future from many who have fought against progress with tooth and nail.

And now following out this line of thought, I want to say a few words about the coming political primaries.

Fifty years ago party nominations were generally made in conventions – a system typified in the public imagination by a little group in a smoke-filled room who made out the party slates.

The direct primary[8] was invented to make the nominating process a more democratic one – to give the party voters themselves a chance to pick their party candidates.

What I am going to say to you tonight does not relate to the primaries of any particular political party, but to matters of principle in all parties – Democratic, Republican, Farmer-Labor, Progressive, Socialist or any other. Let that be clearly understood.

It is my hope that everybody affiliated with any party will vote in the primaries, and that every such voter will consider the fundamental principles for which his or her party is on record. That makes for a healthy choice between the candidates of the opposing parties on Election Day in November.

An election cannot give the country a firm sense of direction if it has two or more national parties which merely have different names but are as alike in their principles and aims as peas in the same pod.

In the coming primaries in all parties, there will be many clashes between two schools of thought, generally classified as liberal and conservative. Roughly speaking, the liberal school of thought recognizes that the new conditions throughout the world call for new remedies.

Those of us in America who hold to this school of thought, insist that these new remedies can be adopted and successfully maintained in this country under our present form of government if we use government as an instrument of cooperation to provide these remedies. We believe that we can solve our problems through continuing effort, through democratic processes instead of Fascism or Communism. We are opposed to the kind of moratorium on reform which, in effect, is reaction itself.

Be it clearly understood, however, that when I use the word "liberal," I mean the believer in progressive principles of democratic, representative government and not the wild man who, in effect, leans in the direction of Communism, for that is just as dangerous as Fascism.

---

[8] a primary in which party members vote directly for candidates

The opposing or conservative school of thought, as a general proposition, does not recognize the need for Government itself to step in and take action to meet these new problems. It believes that individual initiative and private philanthropy will solve them – that we ought to repeal many of the things we have done and go back, for instance, to the old gold standard, or stop all this business of old age pensions and unemployment insurance, or repeal the Securities and Exchange Act, or let monopolies thrive unchecked – return, in effect, to the kind of Government that we had in the nineteen twenties.

Assuming the mental capacity of all the candidates, the important question which it seems to me the primary voter must ask is this: "To which of these general schools of thought does the candidate belong?"

As President of the United States, I am not asking the voters of the country to vote for Democrats next November as opposed to Republicans or members of any other party. Nor am I, as President, taking part in Democratic primaries.

As the head of the Democratic Party, however, charged with the responsibility of carrying out the definitely liberal declaration of principles set forth in the 1936 Democratic platform, I feel that I have every right to speak in those few instances where there may be a clear-cut issue between candidates for a Democratic nomination involving these principles, or involving a clear misuse of my own name.

Do not misunderstand me. I certainly would not indicate a preference in a state primary merely because a candidate, otherwise liberal in outlook, had conscientiously differed with me on any single issue. I should be far more concerned about the general attitude of a candidate towards present day problems and his own inward desire to get practical needs attended to in a practical way. We all know that progress may be blocked by outspoken reactionaries, and also by those who say "yes" to a progressive objective, but who always find some reason to oppose any specific proposal to gain that objective. I call that type of candidate a "yes, but" fellow.

And I am concerned about the attitude of a candidate or his sponsors with respect to the rights of American citizens to assemble peaceably and to express publicly their views and opinions on important social and economic issues. There can be no constitutional democracy in any community which denies to the individual his freedom to speak and worship as he wishes. The American people will not be deceived by anyone who attempts to suppress individual liberty under the pretense of patriotism.

This being a free country with freedom of expression – especially with freedom of the press, as is entirely proper – there will be a lot of mean blows struck between now and Election Day. By "blows" I mean misrepresentation and personal attack and appeals to prejudice. It would be a lot better, of course, if campaigns everywhere could be waged with arguments instead of with blows.

I hope the liberal candidates will confine themselves to argument and not resort to blows. In nine cases out of ten the speaker or the writer who, seeking to influence public opinion, descends from calm argument to unfair blows hurts himself more than his opponent.

The Chinese have a story on this – a story based on three or four thousand years of civilization: Two Chinese coolies were arguing heatedly in the midst of a crowd. A stranger expressed surprise that no blows were being struck. His Chinese friend replied: "The man who strikes first admits that his ideas have given out."

I know that neither in the summer primaries nor in the November elections will the American voters fail to spot the candidate whose ideas have given out.

Appendices

Appendix A: Thematic Table of Contents

Hoover's Response to the Economic Crisis

2. President Herbert Hoover, Statement announcing a Series of Conferences with Representatives of Business, Industry, Agriculture, and Labor, November 15, 1929

3. President Herbert Hoover, Statement on the Signing of the Smoot-Hawley Tariff, June 16, 1930

4. Representative Jacob Milligan, Speech on the Smoot-Hawley Tariff, July 3, 1930

5. President Herbert Hoover, Press Statement on the Use of Federal Funds for Relief, February 3, 1931

6. President Herbert Hoover, Veto of the Muscle Shoals Resolution, March 3, 1931

7. President Herbert Hoover, Special Message to Congress on Economic Recovery Program, January 4, 1932

11. President Herbert Hoover, Veto of the Emergency Relief and Construction Bill, July 11, 1932

12. President Herbert Hoover, Statement on the Dispersal of the Bonus Army, July 29, 1932

13. Philo D. Burke, Letter from Bonus Army leader to President Hoover, July 29, 1932

16. President Herbert Hoover, Letter to Senator Simeon Fess, February 21, 1933

The Election of 1932

9. Franklin D. Roosevelt, Radio Address on "The Forgotten Man," April 7, 1932

10. Franklin D. Roosevelt, Acceptance Speech at the Democratic National Convention, July 2, 1932

14. Franklin D. Roosevelt, Commonwealth Club Address, September 23, 1932

15. President Herbert Hoover, Consequences of the Proposed New Deal, October 31, 1932

Roosevelt and the New Deal

17. President Franklin D. Roosevelt, First Inaugural Address, March 4, 1933
18. President Franklin D. Roosevelt, Call for Legislation to Create the Tennessee Valley Authority, April 10, 1933
19. President Franklin D. Roosevelt, "Fireside Chat" on the Purposes and Foundations of the Recovery Program, July 24, 1933
22. President Franklin D. Roosevelt, Speech to Congress on Foreign Trade, March 2, 1934
23. President Franklin D. Roosevelt, Speech to Congress on Social Security, January 17, 1935

Opposition to the New Deal

26. Representative James W. Wadsworth, Speech on Social Security, April 19, 1935
27. Senator Huey P. Long, Statement on the Share Our Wealth Society, May 23, 1935
32. Al Smith, "Betrayal of the Democratic Party," January 25, 1936
34. Father Charles Coughlin, "A Third Party," July 1, 1936
35. Herbert Hoover, "This Challenge to Liberty," October 30, 1936
42. Representative Wade Kitchens, Speech on the Fair Labor Standards Act, May 16, 1938

The Election of 1936 and the End of the New Deal

32. Al Smith, "Betrayal of the Democratic Party," January 25, 1936
33. President Franklin D. Roosevelt, Acceptance Speech at the Democratic National Convention, June 27, 1936
34. Father Charles Coughlin, "A Third Party," July 1, 1936
35. Herbert Hoover, "This Challenge to Liberty," October 30, 1936
37. President Franklin D. Roosevelt, Second Inaugural Address, January 20, 1937
40. President Franklin D. Roosevelt, Message to Congress on Establishing Minimum Wages and Maximum Hours, May 24, 1937

41. President Franklin D. Roosevelt, "Fireside Chat" on the Recession, April 14, 1938

43. President Franklin D. Roosevelt, "Fireside Chat" on "Purging" the Democratic Party, June 24, 1938

Labor and the New Deal

8. The Norris-La Guardia Act, March 23, 1932

20. "Black Labor and the Codes," Editorial, *Opportunity*, August 1933

21. Mauritz A. Hallgren, "The Right to Strike," *The Nation*, November 8, 1933

24. Senator Robert F. Wagner, Speech on the National Labor Relations Act, February 21, 1935

36. Edward Levinson, "Detroit Digs In," January 16, 1937

42. Representative Wade Kitchens, Speech on the Fair Labor Standards Act, May 16, 1938

Roosevelt and the Supreme Court

28. *Schechter Poultry Corp. v. United States*, May 27, 1935

31. *United States v. Butler*, January 6, 1936

38. President Franklin D. Roosevelt, "Fireside Chat" on the Plan for Reorganization of the Judiciary, March 9, 1937

39. Senator Carter Glass, Radio Address on Judicial Reorganization, March 29, 1937

40. President Franklin D. Roosevelt, Message to Congress on Establishing Minimum Wages and Maximum Hours, May 24, 1937

African-Americans and the New Deal

20. "Black Labor and the Codes," Editorial, *Opportunity*, August 1933

25. E.E. Lewis, "Black Cotton Farmers and the AAA," March 1935

Appendix B: Study Questions

For each of the Documents in this collection, we suggest below in section A questions relevant for that document alone and in Section B questions that require comparison between documents.

1. Herbert Hoover, Speech on the "Principles and Ideals of the United States Government," October 22, 1928

A. What does Hoover regard as the dangers of the "projection of government in business"? What is Hoover's definition of "liberalism"? What does he regard as the proper functions of government? What does Hoover mean by the "American system"?

B. How do Hoover's views on the role of government differ from those of Franklin D. Roosevelt in his Commonwealth Club Address (Document 14)? How does his definition of "liberalism" differ from that of Roosevelt in Document 10? How does this campaign speech compare with Hoover's later addresses – Documents 15 and 35? Is there any evidence that his views changed over time?

2. President Herbert Hoover, Statement announcing a Series of Conferences with Representatives of Business, Industry, Agriculture, and Labor, November 15, 1929

A. What does Hoover believe to be the cause of the economic crisis? What role does he envision the federal government playing in dealing with this problem?

B. How does Hoover's response to the economic crisis compare to that made by Roosevelt in his Second Inaugural Address (Document 37)? How does Hoover's interpretation of the causes of the crisis compare with that expressed in his letter to Senator Simeon Fess (Document 16)?

3. President Herbert Hoover, Statement on the Signing of the Smoot-Hawley Tariff, June 16, 1930

A. What reservations does Hoover seem to have about this particular bill? Why has he decided to sign it, despite his reservations?

B. How might Hoover respond to the claims made by Rep. Jacob Milligan in Document 4? How does this measure fit with Hoover's understanding of the proper role of the federal government, as expressed in Documents 1, 15, and 35? How do his views on trade compare to those of Roosevelt, as seen in Document 22?

4. Representative Jacob Milligan, Speech on the Smoot-Hawley Tariff, July 3, 1930

A. What does Milligan find so objectionable about the new tariff law? Why does he suggest that it would be more appropriately called the "Hoover-Grundy" bill?

B. How do Milligan's views on trade differ from those of his fellow Democrat Roosevelt, as laid out in Document 22?

5. President Herbert Hoover, Press Statement on the Use of Federal Funds for Relief, February 3, 1931

A. What does Hoover see as the dangers in using federal money for "charitable purposes"? How does he prefer to see relief efforts handled? How does Hoover respond to the suggestion that he lacks "human sympathy for those who suffer"? Are there any circumstances in which he would approve the use of federal funds to assist those suffering from the economic crisis?

B. How do Hoover's opinions on the use of federal funds for relief compare to those of Roosevelt, as seen in his Fireside Chats on the "forgotten man" and on the purposes of his recovery program (Document 9 and 19), and his proposed Social Security plan (Document 23)?

6. President Herbert Hoover, Veto of the Muscle Shoals Resolution, March 3, 1931

A. On what grounds does Hoover object to government operation of the Muscle Shoals facility? What does it tell us about his overall view of the role of government? What does he suggest as an alternative?

B. How do Hoover's views on this subject compare to those of Roosevelt, as put forward in Document 18?

7. President Herbert Hoover, Special Message to Congress on Economic Recovery Program, January 4, 1932

A. What steps is Hoover calling on Congress to take to address the economic crisis? What, specifically, is the purpose of the Reconstruction Finance Corporation? Why does he compare the efforts to bring about recovery to "a great war"? Why does he believe it is possible for the United States to pursue recovery "independent of the rest of the world"?

B. How do Hoover's proposals here line up with his views on the proper role of the federal government, as expressed in Document 1? Does he seem to have changed his mind in any way? How does his use of the war analogy compare to that of Roosevelt in Document 17?

8. The Norris-La Guardia Act, March 23, 1932

A. What reasoning does this document offer for why courts must not be allowed to issue injunctions against labor unions? What specific activities does the act protect against injunctions? Why do you think Hoover was willing to sign this piece of legislation?

B. Does Hoover's approval of this bill conflict with his earlier stated views on the role of the federal government (Document 1)? To what extent might the labor disputes described in Documents 21 and 36 be attributed to this bill? How does Norris-LaGuardia compare with the National Labor Relations Act (described in Document 24)?

9. Franklin D. Roosevelt, Radio Address on "The Forgotten Man," April 7, 1932

A. Who, according to Roosevelt, is "the forgotten man"? Which Hoover policies does he single out for criticism? What measures does he propose for solving the economic crisis?

B. How does this speech compare with his later campaign addresses (Documents 10 and 14)? How does it compare with his first inaugural address (Document 17)? How does his vision of the role of government compare with that of Hoover, as expressed in Documents 1 and 15?

10. Franklin D. Roosevelt, Acceptance Speech at the Democratic National Convention, July 2, 1932

A. What does Roosevelt regard as symbolic about his decision to travel to Chicago personally to accept his party's nomination? How does he distinguish his own liberalism from both radicalism and reaction? What does Roosevelt see as the cause of the Depression? On what grounds does he criticize Hoover's handling of the crisis?

B. How does Roosevelt's definition of liberalism differ from that put forward by Hoover in Document 1? How does his explanation of the causes of the Depression compare with those of Hoover in Document 16? How does his understanding of the U.S. economy differ from Hoover's, as seen in Document 15?

11. President Herbert Hoover, Veto of the Emergency Relief and Construction Bill, July 11, 1932

A. On what grounds does Hoover object to the use of the Reconstruction Finance Corporation to provide federal loans to states, and to the general public? What does he suggest as an alternative arrangement?

B. Referring to Document 7, would you say that Hoover was correct in asserting that this proposed use of the Reconstruction Finance Corporation was a radical departure from the agency's intent? How might Roosevelt, in Documents 9 and 14, have been referring to Hoover's veto of this bill?

12. President Herbert Hoover, Statement on the Dispersal of the Bonus Army, July 29, 1932

A. How does Hoover defend the use of federal troops to disperse the Bonus Army? Based on the information Hoover had at his disposal, do you think his decision was justified?

B. How does this account of the dispersal of the Bonus Army compare with that of Philo T. Burke (Document 13)? Based on Roosevelt's comments in Documents 9 and 10, do you think he would have acted differently if he had been president?

13. Philo D. Burke, Letter from Bonus Army leader to President Hoover, July 29, 1932

A. What or whom does Burke blame for the plight of the country's veterans? Why does he refer to Hoover as "Andy Mellon's President"? Why does he believe that Hoover acted as he did toward the Bonus Army?

B. How does Burke's account of the dispersal of the Bonus Army compare to that of Hoover (Document 12)?

14. Franklin D. Roosevelt, Commonwealth Club Address, September 23, 1932

A. Why, according to Roosevelt, was individualism appropriate in the late 18th and 19th centuries, but not in the 20th? What does he mean when he claims that "the day of enlightened administration has come"? Who or what does Roosevelt blame for the Depression?

B. How does Roosevelt's interpretation of the problems facing the country compare with that of Hoover, as expressed in Documents 15 and 16? How does his analysis of the recent past differ from that put forward by Hoover in Document 15? How does his view of the country's future differ from Hoover's vision?

15. President Herbert Hoover, Consequences of the Proposed New Deal, October 31, 1932

A. What does Hoover regard as the primary cause of the Depression? Why does he believe that it is more important to focus on the past thirty years, rather than the last three? Why does he believe that Roosevelt's New Deal will be dangerous for the country?

B. How does Hoover's account of the origins of the Depression compare with that of Roosevelt, as seen in Documents 9, 10, and 14? How does this campaign address compare with his campaign speech in 1928 (Document 1), or his speech on behalf of Alf Landon in 1936 (Document 35)?

16. President Herbert Hoover, Letter to Senator Simeon Fess, February 21, 1933

A. Why is Hoover addressing this letter to Senator Fess? What, according to the president, accounts for the ups and downs of the economy since 1931? Why does he blame President-elect Roosevelt for the conditions prevailing in early 1933?

B. How does Hoover's account of current economic conditions compare to the argument he makes in Document 15? How does his interpretation differ from that of Roosevelt in Documents 10 and 14?

17. President Franklin D. Roosevelt, First Inaugural Address, March 4, 1933

A. What does Roosevelt mean when he says that "the only thing we have to fear is fear itself"? What actions does he say are necessary to solve the economic crisis? How and why does he use military analogies ("great army of our people") to make his arguments?

B. How does Roosevelt's use of the analogy of war compare to Hoover's in Document 7? Does Roosevelt's logic in this speech flow naturally from the claims he made in Document 14? How does the plan Roosevelt puts forward in his First Inaugural Address compare with the plan he outlines in his Second Inaugural Address (Document 37)?

18. President Franklin D. Roosevelt, Call for Legislation to Create the Tennessee Valley Authority, April 10, 1933

A. What good does Roosevelt see coming from government development of the Tennessee Valley Authority? What does he mean when he says that the country has "just grown"?

B. How does Roosevelt's proposal compare to the Muscle Shoals bill vetoed by Hoover in 1931 (Document 6)? What does a comparison of these documents tell us about the ways in which each president regarded the role of the federal government? To what extent does this proposal reflect the goal of "enlightened administration" laid out by Roosevelt in Document 14?

19. President Franklin D. Roosevelt, "Fireside Chat" on the Purposes and Foundations of the Recovery Program, July 24, 1933

A. What accomplishments does Roosevelt seem proudest of at this point in his presidency? What distinction does he draw between those measures that he views as "foundation stones" and the "links which will build us a more lasting prosperity"? How is the National Industrial Recovery Act supposed to work?

B. How do the measures listed here fit with the overall approach to governance laid out by Roosevelt in Documents 14 and 17? How does

Roosevelt's presentation of the AAA and NIRA differ from the criticisms of these programs found in Documents 20, 25, 32 and 42?

20. "Black Labor and the Codes," Editorial, *Opportunity*, August 1933

A. What do the editors of Opportunity find objectionable about the National Industrial Recovery Act? Why do they believe that white as well black workers should be concerned about the codes that have been approved thus far?

B. Taken together with Document 25, why might African-Americans have had reason to be disappointed with the New Deal thus far? Why do you think they supported Roosevelt regardless? How does this criticism of the NIRA compare with those put forward by Al Smith (Document 32) and Father Charles Coughlin (Document 34)?

21. Mauritz Hallgren, "The Right to Strike," *The Nation*, November 8, 1933

A. Why, according to the author, is labor unrest on the rise in 1933? How does this wave of strikes differ from those of earlier eras? What challenge do they pose for the Roosevelt administration?

B. How might the Norris-La Guardia Act (Document 8) and the National Industrial Recovery Act (described in Document 19) have encouraged the rise in labor militancy? In what way would the National Labor Relations Act (described in Document 24) encourage this trend even further?

22. President Franklin D. Roosevelt, Speech to Congress on Foreign Trade, March 2, 1934

A. What did the Reciprocal Trade Agreements Act propose to do? Why does Roosevelt believe that it will be beneficial? Why does he warn Congress that "quick results are not to be expected"?

B. How does Roosevelt's understanding of international trade differ from Hoover's, as expressed in Document 3? How does it compare to that of Rep. Jacob Milligan, found in Document 4?

23. President Franklin D. Roosevelt, Speech to Congress on Social Security, January 17, 1935

A. What does Roosevelt's Social Security plan entail? How is it to be funded? Why does the president believe it is necessary?

B. How does this proposal fit in with Roosevelt's call for "enlightened administration" in Document 14? How does the president's view of Social Security compare with that of Rep. James Wadsworth, as expressed in Document 26?

24. Senator Robert F. Wagner, Speech on the National Labor Relations Act, February 21, 1935

A. Why does Wagner believe that this bill is necessary? On what grounds does he claim that the bill is "novel neither in philosophy nor in content"? What misconceptions about the bill does he attempt to clear up?

B. In what sense does Mauritz Hallgren's account of labor unrest (Document 21) help us to understand why Roosevelt was hesitant to endorse the National Labor Relations Act? How does the act build on the Norris-La Guardia Act (Document 8) and the National Industrial Recovery Act (described in Document 19)?

25. E.E. Lewis, "Black Cotton Farmers and the AAA," March 1935

A. How, according to Lewis, has the Agricultural Adjustment Administration disadvantaged black farmers? What special "handicaps" does the black farmer face that his white counterpart does not?

B. Taken together with Document 20, why might African-Americans have had reason to be disappointed with the New Deal thus far? Why do you think they supported Roosevelt regardless? How does this criticism of the AAA compare with those put forward in Document 31, United States v. Butler?

26. Representative James W. Wadsworth, Speech on Social Security, April 19, 1935

A. What misgivings does Wadsworth have regarding how Social Security is to be funded? Why does he think it poses a danger to the republic? How does he predict the program will develop? Have his predictions come true?

B. How does this speech compare with Hoover's invocation of "rugged individualism" in Document 1? Based on Documents 14 and 23, how might Roosevelt respond to Wadsworth's criticisms?

27. Senator Huey P. Long, Statement on the Share Our Wealth Society, May 23, 1935

A. What does Long regard as the fundamental cause of the Depression? In what ways does he think the New Deal has fallen short? What does he propose as a remedy? How does he seek to justify his program?

B. How does Long's critique of the New Deal compare with that of Father Coughlin in Document 34? How does it compare with the criticisms made by Al Smith in Document 32, and by Hoover in Document 35?

28. *Schechter Poultry Corp. v. United States*, Chief Justice Charles Evans Hughes, May 27, 1935

A. On what grounds does the Court find the NIRA unconstitutional? What do the justices think of the administration's claim that the law was justified on the basis of the severity of the economic crisis? On what do they base their conclusion that the poultry code was not legal under the Commerce Clause of the Constitution?

B. Based on your reading of Document 19, why do you think this decision was regarded as such a devastating blow to Roosevelt's agenda? How does the reasoning in this case compare to that used by the Court in Document 31?

29. Paul Taylor, "Again the Covered Wagon," July 1935

A. What motives led thousands of Americans to move to California in the mid-1930s? What challenges did they face when they arrived there? Why is their presence a matter of concern to more established residents of California?

B. How does the plight of the migrants compare to that of African-Americans, as seen in Documents 20 and 25?

30. President Franklin D. Roosevelt, Annual Message to Congress, January 3, 1936

A. What did Roosevelt mean when he spoke of an "economic constitutional order"? How would such an order differ from the one that existed when Roosevelt took office?

B. How does the Supreme Court's decision in Document 31 affect the new order Roosevelt was trying to build? Are Al Smith's criticisms of the New Deal (Document 32) criticisms of this new economic order? What are Smith's criticisms?

31. *United States v. Butler*, Associate Justice Owen J. Roberts, January 6, 1936

A. On what grounds does the Court find the AAA unconstitutional? Why does so much of the decision rest on the definition of the term "general welfare"? Why do the justices regard it as a dangerous precedent?

B. How does the reasoning in this case compare to that used by the Court in Document 28? Why do you think the Court was divided on this issue, whereas the decision in Schechter was unanimous? Which decision do you think was more painful to the administration, and why?

32. Al Smith, "Betrayal of the Democratic Party," January 25, 1936

A. In what ways does Smith believe that Roosevelt has not been faithful to the Democratic Party's 1932 platform? Why does he think the New Deal is an example of socialism? What does he call on his fellow Democrats to do?

B. How does Smith's critique of the New Deal compare to that of Hoover in Document 35? How does it compare to the criticisms by Huey Long in Document 27, and Father Coughlin in Document 34?

33. President Franklin D. Roosevelt, Acceptance Speech at the Democratic National Convention, June 27, 1936

A. What was Roosevelt's purpose in drawing a comparison between the Revolution in 1776 and his efforts since taking office? When Roosevelt spoke of a "rendezvous with destiny," what did he mean?

B. Compare the argument and rhetoric of this speech with Roosevelt's Commonwealth Address (Document 14). Has he changed his views or his manner of expressing them?

34. Father Charles Coughlin, "A Third Party," July 1, 1936

A. Why did Coughlin initially support Roosevelt and the New Deal? Why has he turned against them now?

B. How does Coughlin's criticism of Roosevelt compare with that of Huey Long in Document 27? Both Coughlin and Al Smith (in Document 32) cite the Democratic Party Platform of 1932. How does Coughlin's understanding of that document compare with Smith's?

35. Herbert Hoover, "This Challenge to Liberty," October 30, 1936

A. What does Hoover find so objectionable about the New Deal? Why does he believe that it is a "repudiation of democracy"? How does he defend his own tenure as president? What does Hoover mean when he says that the nation needs not only economic recovery, but "moral recovery"?

B. How does this speech compare with what Hoover told listeners in Document 15? How does it compare with the criticism made by Al Smith in Document 32? How does critique differ from those of Huey Long (Document 27) and Father Coughlin (Document 34)?

36. Edward Levinson, "Detroit Digs In," January 16, 1937

A. What was particularly controversial about the strike against General Motors? What measures did the company take to break the strike? Why did the strike ultimately succeed?

B. How does the labor activity described here compare to that described in Document 21? How might the National Labor Relations Act (described by Sen. Robert Wagner in Document 24) have paved the way for this sort of strike?

37. President Franklin D. Roosevelt, Second Inaugural Address, January 20, 1937

A. How does Roosevelt attempt to show that the New Deal is in line with established constitutional tradition? Why do you think he feels the need to do this? What does Roosevelt consider the greatest accomplishments of his first term? What goals does he set for himself for his second term?

B. How does this speech compare with Roosevelt's first inaugural address (Document 17) and his 1936 State of the Union Address (Document 30)? In what sense might it be regarded as a response to his recent critics – Huey Long (Document 27), Al Smith (Document 32), Father Coughlin (Document 34), and Herbert Hoover (Document 35)?

38. President Franklin D. Roosevelt, "Fireside Chat" on the Plan for Reorganization of the Judiciary, March 9, 1937

A. Why does Roosevelt think that the federal judiciary needs to be changed? How does he invoke the Constitution to defend this? What is his proposal, and on what grounds does he seek to justify it?

Study Questions 257

B. What examples from Documents 28 and 31 might Roosevelt cite of "outdated" legal thinking that judicial reorganization seeks to correct? How might Roosevelt respond to the accusations made by Sen. Carter Glass in Document 39?

39. Senator Carter Glass, Radio Address on Judicial Reorganization, March 29, 1937

A. On what grounds does Glass attack Roosevelt's judicial reform proposal? What does he mean when he calls it the "court-packing" plan? What sources does he cite in making his arguments, and why?

B. How does Glass's understanding of the Constitution differ from that of Roosevelt, as expressed in Documents 17, 33, and 37? How does it compare to that of Herbert Hoover in Document 33, or Al Smith in Document 32?

40. President Franklin D. Roosevelt, Message to Congress on Establishing Minimum Wages and Maximum Hours, May 24, 1937

A. Why does he reject the notion that, because the economy is improving, "government should take a holiday"? Why does he think that this legislation will improve economic conditions? What does he mean when he says that government policy must be guided by "practical reason" rather than "barren formulae"?

B. How does this speech compare with Roosevelt's address on the NIRA (Document 19)? How does the Fair Labor Standards Act differ from that earlier piece of legislation? How might Roosevelt respond to the objections to this bill raised by Rep. Wade Kitchens in Document 42?

41. President Franklin D. Roosevelt, "Fireside Chat" on the Recession, April 14, 1938

A. How, according to Roosevelt, is the current "recession" to be distinguished from the "Depression" of 1929-1932? Why does he draw such a distinction? What measures does he propose for addressing the situation? What does he fear will happen if government does not act to bring the country back on its course to recovery?

B. How does Roosevelt's message compare with his first inaugural, similarly made during a time of economic crisis (Document 17)? Based on Documents 15 and 35, how do you think Herbert Hoover would respond to the claims Roosevelt makes in this speech?

42. Representative Wade Kitchens, Speech on the Fair Labor Standards Act, May 16, 1938

A. Why does Kitchens believe that this proposal will hurt his home state? Why does he ultimately think it is dangerous for the country as a whole?

B. How does Kitchens' critique of the Fair Labor Standards Act compare with the criticisms levied against the National Industrial Recovery Act in Documents 21, 28, 31, and 32?

43. President Franklin D. Roosevelt, "Fireside Chat" on "Purging" the Democratic Party, June 24, 1938

A. What does Roosevelt cite as the most important legislative accomplishments of his second term so far? On what grounds does he suggest that the goals he sought to attain through his "court-packing" plan have largely been achieved? Why does he use the term "Copperheads" in reference to Democrats who have opposed his agenda? In what way does he intend to involve himself in the Democratic primaries, and why?

B. How do Documents 39 and 42 help us to understand why Roosevelt decided to pursue such a course? How might this speech have played into the hands of those such as Al Smith (in Document 32), Herbert Hoover (in Document 35), Carter Glass (in Document 39) and Wade Kitchens (in Document 42) who suggested that the New Deal was a menace to American liberties?

Appendix C:
Suggestions For Further Reading

Anthony J. Badger, *The New Deal: The Depression Years, 1933-1940* (Chicago: Ivan R. Dee, 2002).

Alan Brinkley, *The End of Reform: New Deal Liberalism in Recession and War* (New York: Vintage, 1996).

Albert Fried, *FDR and His Enemies* (New York: St. Martin's, 1999).

Alonzo L. Hamby, *Man of Destiny: FDR and the Making of the American Century* (New York: Basic, 2015).

Glen Jeansonne, *Herbert Hoover: A Life* (New York: Berkley, 2016).

Ira Katznelson, *Fear Itself: The New Deal and the Origins of Our Time* (New York: Liveright, 2014).

David M. Kennedy, *Freedom from Fear: The American People in Depression and War, 1929-1945* (New York: Oxford University Press, 2001).

William E. Leuchtenberg, *Franklin D. Roosevelt and the New Deal* (New York: Harper Perennial, 2009).

Robert S. McElvaine, *The Great Depression: America, 1929-1941* (New York: Times, 1993).

Kim Phillips-Fein, *Invisible Hands: The Businessmen's Crusade Against the New Deal* (New York: W.W. Norton, 2010).

Charles Rappleye, *Herbert Hoover in the White House: The Ordeal of the Presidency* (New York: Simon & Schuster, 2016).

Amity Shlaes, *The Forgotten Man: A New History of the Great Depression* (New York: Harper Perennial, 2008).

James F. Simon, *FDR and Chief Justice Hughes: The President, the Supreme Court, and the Epic Battle Over the New Deal* (New York: Simon & Schuster, 2012).

Harvard Sitkoff, *A New Deal for Blacks: The Emergence of Civil Rights as a National Issue: The Depression Decade, 30th Anniversary Edition* (New York: Oxford University Press, 2008).

G. Edward White, *The Constitution and the New Deal* (Cambridge: Harvard University Press, 2002).